Jewish Childhood in Kraków

Jewish Childhood in Kraków

A Microhistory of the Holocaust

JOANNA SLIWA

RUTGERS UNIVERSITY PRESS

NEW BRUNSWICK, CAMDEN, AND NEWARK,

NEW JERSEY, AND LONDON

Library of Congress Cataloging-in-Publication Data
Names: Sliwa, Joanna, author.
Title: Jewish childhood in Kraków: a microhistory of the Holocaust / Joanna Sliwa.
Description: New Brunswick: Rutgers University Press, [2021] | Includes bibliographical
    references and index.
Identifiers: LCCN 2020050917 | ISBN 9781978822931 (paperback) | ISBN 9781978822948
    (hardcover) | ISBN 9781978822955 (epub) | ISBN 9781978822962 (mobi) |
    ISBN 9781978822979 (pdf)
Subjects: LCSH: Jewish children—Poland—Kraków—History—20th century. |
    World War, 1939–1945—Children—Poland—Kraków. | Children and war—Poland—
    Kraków—History—20th century. | Holocaust, Jewish (1939–1945)—Poland—Kraków. |
    Jews—Poland—Kraków—History—20th century. | Jewish ghettos—Poland—
    Kraków—History—20th century. | Krakow (Poland)—Ethnic relations—20th century.
Classification: LCC DS134.6 .S58 2021 | DDC 940.53/1800830943862—dc23
LC record available at https://lccn.loc.gov/2020050917

A British Cataloging-in-Publication record for this book is available from the British Library.

♾ The paper used in this publication meets the requirements of the American National
Standard for Information Sciences—Permanence of Paper for Printed Library Materials,
ANSI Z39.48-1992.

www.rutgersuniversitypress.org

Manufactured in the United States of America

To the children for whom this history was a reality

Contents

Note on Terminology

This book employs the terms "Jew," "Pole," "German," and "Aryan" to emphasize the categories and terminology used by the historical actors themselves and which are expressed in contemporary and postwar sources. These are complex, and, I recognize, imprecise, terms. Yet they are ubiquitous in scholarship and accentuate the divisions that prevailed during the time period under consideration.

Although Poland as a country did not exist between 1939 and 1945, I use the term "Poland" to mean a geographic area that had been Polish territory before World War II.

The spelling of place-names distinguishes their status and function during the Holocaust. Thus, Płaszów (with Polish diacritics) signifies a district in the city of Kraków, and Plaszow indicates the German-created camp therein. I use the Polish spelling of Kraków throughout. This was how both Poles and Jews continued to refer to the city.

This book is about Jewish children's Holocaust experiences. Thus, I employ the names that children used during that time in the text.

Jewish Childhood in Kraków

Introduction

"The entrance to Kazimierz, the old ghetto of Cracow," reads the caption of a black-and-white photograph that shows the silhouettes of four people in a court-yard surrounded by balconied tenements in the historic Jewish quarter in Kraków. The Russian Jewish photographer Roman Vishniac captured this scene during his American Jewish Joint Distribution Committee mission to Eastern Europe between 1935 and 1938. Part of a fund-raising campaign on behalf of East European Jews, the picture appeared in Vishniac's album *A Vanished World* (1983). An iconic image, it prompted Steven Spielberg, who directed the feature film *Schindler's List* (1993), to select that particular picturesque passageway to portray a scene in the city's Holocaust-era ghetto. Kazimierz was neither a pre-war nor a wartime Jewish ghetto. Yet cinematography and photography create powerful and enduring symbols that facilitate viewers' engagement with history. The "girl in the red coat" who appears as the sole color image in an otherwise black-and-white *Schindler's List* is another case in point. She expresses the suffering of Jewish children during the Holocaust but leaves the complexities of their lives to the viewers' imagination. This book goes beyond these archetypal snapshots of Kraków's Jewish history.

At its core, this book is about people and places. Through the lens of Jewish children's experiences, it explores the events and processes that framed the Holocaust in German-occupied Poland in general, and in Kraków in particular. The decisions, attitudes, and behaviors of adults—whose identities in wartime were clearly defined as Germans, Jews, and Poles—toward Jewish children, as well as the children's own responses, affected young people's Holocaust experiences in the occupied city, the ghetto, and the camp. Jewish children's survival in Kraków required young people and adults acting on their behalf (both Jews and non-Jews) to employ a strategy of concealment, semi-illegality, and deception.

"Jewish children" denotes individuals whom the German authorities defined in racial terms as Jews, and whose age the Germans eventually capped at fourteen. Between September 1939, when the Germans occupied Kraków, and January 1945, when the Soviets liberated the city, the ways Kraków's Jewish children viewed themselves were irrelevant. Nazi policies and actions, themselves marked by inconsistencies and frictions as the Nazis negotiated their own political, military, and economic interests, shaped children's lives. Therefore, the legal category of a "Jew" in the German-created Kraków District and in the city itself evolved from anyone of Jewish faith and anyone whose parent was Jewish (November 1939) to a person descended from Jewish grandparents (August 1940), a definition that applied to all Jews in German-occupied Poland (General Government). If Nazi racial ideology vacillated, so did Nazi policy on setting the age for Jewish "adults," which, in turn, depended on a Jew's suitability for forced labor. Definitions of race and age hinged on timing and the law issuer's agenda. A decree of the German-appointed city commandant specified the cut-off age at twelve (October 1939). That outlook changed a month before the creation of the ghetto (February 1941), when the city commandant ordered all Jewish youths over fourteen to be treated as adults (workers). This demarcation remained in effect until the end of the war.

Faced with the Germans' capricious yet organized persecution, both children and their caregivers tried to adjust their survival strategies to the changing circumstances. One way to keep the Jewish community afloat for the future and the children alive in the present was to conceal young people from the direct view of the Germans and their collaborators. Children occupied an important place in the Nazi worldview on creating an "Aryan" racial community. Young people deemed as Aryan by Nazi ideology embodied the future, renewal, and health. They were an asset to the nation. All other children, such as Roma and Sinti, children with disabilities, and Jewish children, posed a threat to the unity and purity of the imagined society of Aryans. As the Germans saw children as the continuity of the "Jewish race," in time they saw Jewish children as impediments to realizing the Nazi plan of genocide. Then too, the German authorities labeled young Jews useless, as they could not work. Early in the German occupation, Kraków Jews understood they had to present themselves as economically advantageous to the Germans. They removed children from the Germans' sight to the extent possible. Children absorbed that message. Jewish children during the Holocaust in Kraków maintained a concealed presence. They were often confined to homes and institutions created specifically for them. They were physically present in the occupied city, the ghetto, and the nearby Plaszow camp. The Germans were aware of that. Still, many children were hidden or camouflaged.

To the Jews, children symbolized a visible conduit for hope and a Jewish future. Thus, young people, because they relied on external help, needed protection and care, as well as the knowledge and tools to carry on as Jews after the war. Jewish adults—parents, community leaders, welfare workers, children's activists—were invested in securing children's well-being. Efforts to support children's lives fulfilled both pragmatic and emotional goals. On the one hand, they fostered Jewish continuity; on the other hand, they lifted Jews' morale. A focus on children allows one to glean the various efforts (formal and informal) and rationale of Jewish leaders, activists, and ordinary Jews to sustain Jewish child life, as well as the consequences of their decisions and actions. But children themselves were keen observers and avid participants in the unfolding reality.

As the histories highlighted in this book demonstrate, a child's gender; age; appearance; familial, social, religious, and economic background; and prior experiences all influenced his or her trajectory between 1939 and 1945. So, too, did luck, timing, and geography. Age determined children's perceptions and behavior. Even their physical size affected how they experienced events and what they witnessed. Centering on children offers a key perspective on how the Holocaust affected different groups of Jews. Jewish children endured the same stages of Nazi anti-Jewish policy in Kraków as adults, including dispossession, resettlement, ghettoization, exploitation, deportation, incarceration, and annihilation. Looking at the ways in which young people negotiated these shifts propels key questions: How did children, as members of a subgroup of society, and as witnesses and victims, experience the Holocaust? What were Nazi policy and actions toward young people? How did Jewish leaders and community members respond to the children's plight? What were the reactions of non-Jews?

My exploration of Jewish children's experiences elucidates the wartime history of a city that the Germans called Krakau and the Poles continued to refer to as Kraków. Designated as the German command center and deemed Germanic in origin by the occupiers,[1] Kraków assumes key importance for the history of the Holocaust in Poland, the heart of prewar Jewish life in Europe and home to more than three million Jews, including nearly one million children under the age of fourteen.[2] In Poland, the Germans pursued all their mechanisms for annihilating Jews. The case of Kraków enables us to trace the stages of the Nazi anti-Jewish program, those that defined Jews' fate in general and those that differed from the policies that the Germans adopted elsewhere. This book zooms in on the history of the Kraków ghetto and on the neighboring camp in the city's Płaszów district. On a micro level, I scrutinize daily life in the city of Kraków, which served as a strategic, historical, cultural, and religious hub before the war. Kraków was always a major center in the Lesser Poland region. In the course of centuries, it acquired Prussian architectural influences and adherence to Austrian culture. But Kraków's administration, demography, size, landscape, and nomenclature changed during the German occupation. These factors affected Jewish children's chances of rescue on the "Aryan side," spaces beyond the areas the Germans restricted for Jews' presence, such as the ghetto and, later, the camp.

From the Jewish perspective, Kraków, called Kroke by Yiddish speakers, stood at the crossroads of eastern and western Jewry. It was the spiritual and cultural center for Jews—the "Jerusalem of Galicia"—in Austria-Hungary after the partitions of Poland in the eighteenth century. In 1931, Kraków had the fourth-largest Jewish population in Poland with a community of 56,515.[3] Residents who identified in religious terms as Jews represented 25.8 percent of Kraków's population, and Jews in prewar Kraków Province made up close to 6 percent of all of Poland's Jews. Jews in Kraków Province, including those in the city, were the third-largest Jewish community in Poland to use Polish as their language, and the second to last to use Yiddish. The Jews of Kraków were largely acculturated, with a strong historical and religious grounding in the city. Jewish children raised in Kraków before World War II were the first generation to live in an independent Poland; they spoke Polish and were educated in Polish or attended Polish schools. Judaism differentiated them from other Poles. The prewar role of Kraków and the self-identification of its Jewish minority largely as Jewish Poles—meaning Polish citizens of Jewish religion—framed the impact of the German occupation on Kraków Jews, and their responses to oppression.

The city served numerous roles during the Nazi era. From the Germans' perspective, Kraków was an administrative center, the model Germanic city, a German industrial base, and part of the labor (and then concentration) camp system. By contrast, Kraków was a refuge for German and Austrian Jews until the outbreak of the war. Later it acquired the role of an asylum and transit site for expellees, Jews and non-Jews, from areas annexed by Nazi Germany (1939), the Reich, and for returnees from territories occupied by the Soviet Union who continued to arrive in the city through 1940. Between 1941 and 1943, the city was the location of a Jewish ghetto. The non-Jewish side of the city became a hiding place for those Jews who managed to reach it. With a window of escape that remained slightly ajar even until mid-1944, Kraków assumed the role of a departure point for transborder rescue missions. This book explores these different functions of the city and their consequences for Jews.

In focusing on a geographic area and various spatial notions, this book capitalizes on the robust research that considers the role of site, space, place, landscape, and topography.[4] I position children's experiences in the context of Poland as occupied territory, Kraków District, the city of Kraków, and its neighborhoods. Throughout the book, I zoom in on children's experiences in particular sites, such as the ghetto and camp. Buildings and rooms became places of persecution and confinement, but also sites of residence, care, and hiding. In addition to these closed structures, Jewish children experienced the Holocaust outside (e.g., the streets). If some sites were gender specific (e.g., a hostel for boys), others were geared toward age groups (e.g., nurseries) and still others responded to particular needs (e.g., shelters for refugees). Threaded in the book are spatial concepts that defined children's lives (e.g., displacement and concentration). Mobility manifested itself through modes of transportation that some children employed in the process of leading covert lives, but also through changing hiding places and fleeing from Kraków. In the case of the latter, transborder escapes proceeded across mountains and forests.

However, this book is primarily a social history of Jewish children in Kraków during the Holocaust, and as such it deals with daily life, human relations, and ethnic tensions. A recurring theme of continuity and change peels layers of children's experiences throughout the stages of Nazi persecution of the Jews in Kraków and the phases of the Holocaust in Poland more broadly. The six chapters offer roughly both a chronological and a thematic arc.

Chapter 1 investigates how children endured the first year and a half of the German occupation, before the creation of the ghetto. Parents and Jewish community leaders devised ways to continue to support their youngest. In particular, they focused on lifting the disadvantaged population—Jewish refugees. Jewish adults began to understand that protecting children from the Germans meant creating an illusion of the children's absence.

Chapter 2 is framed in the context of Nazi ghettoization policy and what it meant for a child to be confined to the ghetto. It discusses changes in family dynamics. But primarily, it centers on the notion of Jewish (victim) responses to persecution through the lens of children's coping strategies and resilience.

Chapter 3 picks up the thread of Jewish children's agency to examine the surreptitious methods that young people, and adults acting on their behalf, employed. In extreme conditions imposed by the German occupation, Jewish children emerged as links between the Jewish and non-Jewish sections of the city, as breadwinners, but also as resisters and rescuers.

Children assumed adult roles and risked their lives, but they remained in need of adult supervision and care. Chapter 4 scrutinizes the stages and extent of relief efforts geared toward children in the Kraków ghetto. I weave in ideas on child welfare and philanthropy, and a focus on marginalized groups (refugees, orphans, the abandoned, and the poor).

Children, according to Nazi ideology, were dispensable. Yet some managed to enter the Plaszow camp and lead a furtive existence or live there semi-illegally. Through the lens of children, chapter 5 charts the role of the camp within the General Government, Kraków District, and the city of Kraków as a labor and concentration camp, prison, holding pen, transit hub, and killing site, all wrapped in one. Opportunities for survival often depended on a prisoner's status within the camp hierarchy or, in the case of children, on a relative's status. This chapter engages in this complex and uncomfortable realm of Jews' Holocaust experience.

If a small number of children were smuggled out of Plaszow onto the Aryan side, others never entered the camp. Chapter 6 analyzes individual and organized efforts to protect Jewish children, and the dangers associated with these activities.

Networks and the role Jews played in them underscore the notion of Jews as rescuers (a phenomenon that has only recently been gaining attention). Aside from these adult networks, children, too, asserted their agency to operate clandestinely on the streets, in hiding, and by passing as non-Jews.

The epilogue engages with post-Holocaust history. It highlights aspects of Jewish child life in Kraków in the immediate aftermath of the Holocaust when child survivors confronted the reality of loss and an expectation to rebuild their lives against the background of postwar violence and persistent antisemitism. The Holocaust experiences of Jewish children are key to understanding the choices and trajectories of child survivors later in life.

Interrogating these various themes requires integrating the perspectives of Jews, non-Jewish Poles, and Germans on Jewish child life in Kraków during the Holocaust. Thus, this book is grounded in a range of sources in Polish, German, Yiddish, Hebrew, and English and typically used by historians: official and unofficial records, postwar trial proceedings, correspondence, photographs, and newspapers.

In addition to the traditional canon of archival materials, I turned to personal accounts—diaries, memoirs, autobiographies, written testimonies, and oral histories of survivors and witnesses—to glean information about the past. Like other historical sources, these must be used with care. Personal histories were recorded at different times, in various places, and in certain contexts, thus shaping what was conveyed and how. Memory is selective and, as survivors and witnesses age, it is also failing. Then too, some people are reluctant to share their private thoughts and life histories. Because of their age during the Holocaust, child survivors rarely recall dates, names, or chronology. Yet they remember specific events that had an impact on them and their families. They can speak about how they internalized the changes that occurred around them, and how Nazi anti-Jewish policy affected them on a personal level. Children's accounts shed light on aspects of young people's lives during the Holocaust that cannot be culled from official German documents, or those produced by adult witnesses. A critical mass of child survivor testimonies, when examined against each other and corroborated by other sources, illuminates how stages of the Holocaust influenced daily life and relations among people.

A history of people and places, this book examines the daily life of Jews in Kraków during the Holocaust through the lens of Jewish children. In so doing, it offers a microhistory of Jewish childhood in Kraków and how the Holocaust evolved in German-occupied Poland. Ultimately, this book tells a history that few survived.

CHAPTER 1

Navigating Shifts in the City

"In 1937 I remember talk about Hitler," Rena Ferber recalled in an account told many years after the events unfolded. "My aunt and uncle from Berlin came. They were talking when they saw the children were asleep." Rena, a Jewish girl from Kraków, was about eight years old when the Ferbers' relatives came to them as refugees. Curious, children eavesdropped on adults' hushed conversations. The situation in Germany, however, was geographically, physically, and emotionally distant for Jewish children in Kraków. "Something was happening over there [in Nazi Germany], not to me. My life was still the same," Rena explained.[1]

And yet Jewish life in prewar Poland was far from idyllic. Polish nationalists sought to solve the "Jewish Question," or the idea that Jews dominated key sectors of Polish public life and were the source of problems in the Second Polish Republic, by pushing Jews out of the national, social, and economic life and pressing them to emigrate. That strategy included violent attacks against Jews throughout Poland. In Kraków, right-wing Polish youths targeted Jewish merchants in the Market Square, clashed with Jewish university students, and damaged the Jewish dormitory. Non-Jewish children often bullied their Jewish peers. For these young Jews, antisemitism was an integral part of their lives. Still, it was the onset of the war that marked a caesura.

"Life changed completely. Right away," Celina Karp recalled of the first days after the German army occupied Kraków on 6 September 1939, when she was ten years old.[2] While many families sheltered children from news about the evolving war and others were too young to comprehend the events, children like Celina experienced an abrupt rift in their lives. Many internalized the disquiet that permeated their homes. They observed uniformed men harassing passersby on the street. And they confronted tangible danger once Nazi anti-Jewish laws and actions targeted them directly and they personally suffered the consequences of exclusion.

In the period between September 1939, when the German army advanced toward and later captured Kraków, and March 1941, when the German civilian administration established a ghetto in the city, profound changes occurred in Jewish children's lives. At the onset of the war, many children experienced abrupt separation from their loved ones who either joined the Polish army or escaped to seek refuge. Children also experienced rupture from their homes and routines when some fled together with their relatives. For those who remained in or returned to Kraków, Nazi policy defined and degraded them based on their "race." Nazi interpretation of age deprived young people of their childhoods. Loss marked Jewish children's lives in the occupied city in other ways, too. The German occupiers appropriated the apartments in which Jewish children lived. They plundered ritual, sentimental, and utility items from homes. Nor did the Germans stop with expropriation. In contrast to other localities throughout German-occupied Poland, the German administration expelled Jews from Kraków to progressively make the city free of Jews. Together with their families, many children were displaced within the city, while others were resettled outside Kraków, but within the borders of German-occupied Poland.

Children old enough to recognize the shifts interpreted them based on their own age-appropriate faculties. Parents, on the other hand, tried to shield their children from the Germans' cascading anti-Jewish policies, including by concealing a child's age. Overwhelmed with both the number of local Jewish children requiring assistance and the influx of refugees to Kraków, Jewish leaders struggled to address the growing needs while faced with depleting resources. Housing, food, hygiene, and education were pressing matters. Child welfare activists drew on familiar forms of assistance to solve new problems, thus employing continuity in times of great change. As a survival strategy, adults created spaces specifically for children, aiming to make their existence less visible to the Germans.

––––––

Anti-Jewish laws and violence against Jews in the Reich, and the world powers' passive response to Hitler's territorial demands in 1933–1939, worried Kraków's Jews. Many began to prepare for another war. Some considered emigration. Ruth Salomon was eleven when her mother tried to persuade Ruth's father to escape before the Germans invaded Poland.[3] But Ruth's father dismissed his wife's trepidation, recalling the German army during the war of 1914–1918 and lauding Germany's advanced culture.[4]

Planning to emigrate or leaving was one response to the tense political situation. Like the Salomons, however, most families stayed in Kraków and prepared for war as best as they could. Many Jewish children spent the summer of 1939 outside the city in the countryside, the mountains, resorts, and camps. Before ten-year-old Abraham Englander and his siblings departed for vacation, their mother made nametags for them in case war erupted and they got lost. As it happened, Abraham arrived home three days before the Germans rolled across the border. "On the way home I saw scenarios that I couldn't understand as a child," he recalled.[5] From the window of the train, he observed Polish soldiers beating peasant recruits. He grasped that something dangerous was happening.

Children took clues by observing their environment. Younger children, in particular, felt the tension experienced by adults and sensed a difference in their situation. This shift elicited new emotions. Bernhard Kempler, who was just over three, explained, "Mostly what I remember are not specific events, but a general sense of change, that it was a frightening change."[6] Other children, sheltered by adults, were unaware of what was happening. Jerzy Hoffman was nearly six at the start of the war. "I led a fairly normal life until then," he recalled. "If my parents were expecting something, they certainly didn't let me know."[7]

Left with little, if any, information about what was happening, children tried to explain the tense situation in their own terms. A fanciful child, nine-year-old Stella Müller romanticized the war. "I imagined the war in a very colorful way, as very attractive. For me, war had almost something of a movie quality. I thought that men would go outside, carry huge beautiful sabres, and bravely fight in front of their homes."[8] She derived these ideas from songs that her father, a World War I veteran, sang to her as lullabies. As a child, Stella could not and did not fathom the violence of war. War was an abstract concept for children. "When I heard the war broke out, I was happy," Henryka Offman, a ten-year-old girl, admitted.[9] In school, she learned about the wars that had been fought, and was exalted to see one for herself. Henryka remembered that her excitement about war also translated into joy because of the unanticipated holiday from school. Nine-year-old Ruth Eisland recalled, "I came home and I said 'Oh, wonderful, the war broke out, I won't have to go to school.' And my father gave me a slap on my face. . . . He was of course aware of what that meant, while I wasn't aware at all. I only was thinking I will do nothing."[10]

Henryka and Ruth were among the approximately 6,400 Jewish students in Kraków registered in the 1938–1939 school year. Of that number, 2,100 children attended six public elementary schools in the city, 1,500 were enrolled in middle and secondary schools, and 2,800 received education in Jewish private schools.[11] Instead of attending convocation ceremonies on 1 September, the traditional beginning of the school year, Jewish children received real-life schooling about war.

The period from 1 September, when the Germans invaded Poland, to 6 September 1939, when they reached Kraków, was tumultuous. Tension turned into frenzy. "I remember people panicking. There was a general fear," Celina Karp recalled.[12] That feeling united Krakovians. Safety was the most important concern for all. Cellars and ground-floor apartments were designated as bomb shelters. Nonperishable supplies were in demand. Bernard Offen, eleven years old, recalled open warehouses with flour, bread, chocolate, and cigarettes; goods that he hauled on a cart for his family.[13] Iziek Geizhals, the same age as Bernard, observed the precautions that adults undertook, digging trenches and covering windows to protect them during air raids. "I didn't understand it at the time why they are getting prepared like this, because I had such a confidence in our army that I just wouldn't believe in it that they [the Germans] would do it [invade] that fast."[14]

Belief in the strong Polish military crumbled as German trucks, tanks, and soldiers entered the city. At first, children were excited. Bernard Offen recalled, "I was so curious, [I] walked out of the apartment house . . . to watch soldiers and trucks and guns and artillery. . . . And when I walked out a German soldier jumped off one of those trucks and took a shot at me."[15] Exhilaration turned into fear. It was a pivotal moment. Stella Müller explained, "From this moment my memory became almost photographic . . . because from that moment on tremendous changes began to occur compared to the very joyful childhood that I had had until then."[16]

———

Marking a caesura, the outbreak of war was carved into children's memories because of the separation from loved ones that it entailed. "I remember that day because my father and his brothers . . . and a lot of the neighbors who were Jewish, the Jewish men, were afraid," Rena Ferber recalled. "And they decided they would try to escape. They would go towards Lwów . . . thinking that the war would be over very soon. And then they would come back."[17] Fearing the approaching German army and its treatment of civilians, a number of Jewish men fled the city. Women and children, it was assumed, would be safe from harassment. Many remained. Others stayed because of the lack of resources for a journey. The uncertainty of finding shelter at the destination and the dangers and inconveniences associated with travel were other factors. Gendered norms designated women as caretakers for their relatives, apartments, and sometimes businesses.

While some Jewish men escaped eastward for fear of persecution, others left their homes in response to the general military call to fight for their homeland. Ewa Kleinberg was eight years old and her sister Anna three when their father left. "One day Papa set out from Kraków on a bicycle to join the army," Ewa recalled. "We never saw him again."[18] Telling their stories after the war, children emphasized the parting and hurried goodbyes as a defining moment of the war.

Jewish men were not the only ones to leave Kraków. Entire families fled. With little time to prepare, families packed a few items and either hired carts and cars or set out on foot. Some families headed to nearby towns or to the countryside. Abraham Blim, then nine years old, and his family arrived in Proszowice, a town seventeen miles from Kraków, on 3 September 1939. But the town was as restless as Kraków and the Blims returned that same night.[19] Other families escaped eastward expecting to remain until the situation stabilized. Marcel Baral was seven years old when his family came to Zgłobień, a village 124 miles east of Kraków where the Barals hoped to find safety with their relatives.[20] Like many other Jewish families, however, they understood the danger posed by the swift incursion of the German army, and they proceeded with their three children farther—toward Lwów. The roads filled with many other refugees going in the same direction. Bombardments, chaos, and suffering became routine. These journeys introduced Jewish children—en route to what their parents perceived as refuge—to war.

While Kraków Jews continued to flee in search of a safe haven in eastern Poland, the Soviet Army invaded Poland from the east on 17 September 1939 in accordance with the nonaggression pact signed on 23 August 1939 between the Soviet and German foreign ministers. The pact sanctioned the partition of Poland roughly along the Bug River, and on 13 November 1939, Germans closed the border, blocking routes in that direction. Unable to breach the frontier or reach other destinations, some Poles (Jews and gentiles) reconsidered their escape decisions and returned to Kraków. Others came back after learning about German military advances in eastern Poland. Still other Jews were deceived by rumors that the situation in German-occupied Poland had stabilized. Finally, life under the Soviets in their area of partitioned Poland disheartened many. Censure, stigmatization, prohibitions, deportations to the Far East—these actions, which the Soviets applied against perceived state enemies, instilled fear in many Jews. But it took time to become aware of the consequences of the German and Soviet occupations.

The Barals decided to retreat from Lwów, then under Soviet occupation (and renamed Lvov), shortly after their arrival. Marcel Baral's parents, Polish Jews who came of age when Kraków was part of the Austro-Hungarian Empire, considered the Germans more civilized than the Soviets. But the border was officially closed. Unflagging in their decision to return to Kraków, they had two choices: escape clandestinely or trick the Germans in the local Soviet-German population transfer commission and return "legally." The Barals seized the opportunity offered by the German-Soviet Treaty of Friendship, Cooperation, and Demarcation. This addendum to the German-Soviet nonaggression pact signed on 28 September 1939 allowed ethnic Germans to move across the German-Soviet border and into German-controlled areas. Marcel Baral's mother took advantage of her fluency in German to request her family's relocation. The Barals returned to Kraków, passing as German nationals.[21]

Much had changed in the city since the Barals' and other Jews' departure, especially regarding the population and civil administration. A considerable number of Jewish and non-Jewish Krakovians had fled from Kraków, and a wave of Jewish and non-Jewish refugees of all ages from areas annexed to Germany had swept through the city. Their numbers reached about fourteen thousand. Some stayed; others continued their journeys. Those who remained needed assistance: lodging, food, and clothing. Help for refugees in Kraków unfolded in three stages. In the first stage, in September 1939, refugees passed through Kraków, staying there only temporarily. While in the first part of September activists aided refugees mostly from western Poland, in the second half of that month, the help shifted to returnees from the east. The second stage of help occurred in October and November when expellees looked for permanent shelter in Kraków. The third wave of refugees arrived in December after Germany delineated its new eastern border.

The Polish authorities responded as constructively as they could under the circumstances, with the Polish government establishing the National Social Self-Help Committee (Ogólnopolski Komitet Samopomocy Społecznej) the first day of the war. In Kraków, the city's president, Stanisław Klimecki, and metropolitan archbishop, Prince Adam Sapieha, created the Citizens' Help Committee (Obywatelski Komitet Pomocy) on 5 September 1939, which assisted some ninety-four thousand people. Jewish and non-Jewish social workers, activists, and clergy members operated shelters and soup kitchens and organized necessities for refugees. Kraków's Jewish Community offered sixty asylums. The smallest housed twenty to thirty people, and the largest had a capacity of nine hundred.[22] Most of the buildings (synagogues, factory buildings, offices), however, were ill suited for habitation. The flow of newcomers and the threat of epidemics triggered divisions in a community already overwhelmed with population fluctuations and diminishing resources. For example, the Jewish Community observed that some homeowners in the Podgórze section of the city treated refugees as intruders and refused to allow them to use common water pumps.

The situation of locals and refugees, whose fates became intertwined, was complicated by the installation of a new regime in the city. At first, the German military took control of Kraków. The Germans replaced (23 September 1939) the Polish president of Kraków with a German, Ernst Zörner, who became the city commissar (Der Stadtkommissar der Stadt Krakau). Once Poland officially surrendered on 27 September 1939, the military handed control of Kraków to a German civilian administration. With it, the city's demography changed abruptly. German civilians, military, and police arrived en masse. That ruling elite envisioned a particular role for the city within the broader German strategy for all of occupied Poland.

Describing the city as inherently Germanic, the Nazi regime designated Kraków as the administrative center and the capital of the General Government for the Occupied Polish Territories on 26 October 1939. Hitler shortened it to "the General Government" on 8 July 1940 to mark the area as an integral part of Nazi Germany. Later, on 15 August 1941, the governor general, Hans Frank, Germanized the city's name to Krakau, but its residents continued to call the city by its

Polish name. Frank appropriated the historic Wawel Castle as his headquarters. A major municipal center in the region, Kraków was named the seat of Kraków District (Distrikt Krakau), one of four districts in the General Government, including Lublin, Radom, and Warsaw. (In August 1941, Galicia became the fifth district.) Dr. Otto Wächter assumed the position of its chief (*Der Chef des Distrikts Krakau*). As one of the twelve counties (*Kreise*) in the district, Kraków became the base for the city commandant (*Stadthauptmann*).[23] Both the district chief and the city commandant promulgated and implemented policies that affected all Krakovians. The governor general issued decrees that concerned the entire General Government. The Nazi secret police, Gestapo, and specifically its Jewish Affairs cell, was responsible for controlling Kraków's Jewish population.[24]

Most significantly, the Germans reorganized Kraków Jews' communal life. The Gestapo chief ordered Marek Bieberstein, a local social activist and educator, to form a twenty-four-member Jewish Council (Judenrat) and approved it on 12 September 1939. The Jewish Council, known in Kraków as the Jewish Community (Gmina Żydowska), represented all Jews in Kraków.[25] Its chairman received orders from the local German administration (first from the Gestapo, and from January 1940 from the city commandant) and was responsible for instituting those decrees and ensuring Jews' compliance. The council's tasks ranged from organizing forced labor, collecting taxes and contributions, and registering the population to enforcing sanitary regulations and providing welfare and medical services for Kraków's Jews.

The activities of Jewish welfare agencies also changed radically. Activists recognized the need for a centralized system to streamline aid distribution. The Germans were interested in creating an umbrella for all charitable and welfare efforts so that they could better control them. As of 29 May 1940, the Head Welfare Council (Naczelna Rada Opiekuńcza) oversaw the activities of three distinct agencies that catered to separate national groups: the Poles through the Main Welfare Council (Rada Główna Opiekuńcza), the Ukrainians through the Ukrainian Main Council (Ukraińska Rada Główna), and the Jews through the Jewish Social Self-Help (Żydowska Samopomoc Społeczna). Headquartered in Kraków and chaired by Michał Weichert, the Jewish Social Self-Help operated locally through Jewish municipal welfare committees. It became the official Jewish branch of the Head Welfare Council and the only Jewish association recognized by the Germans, and thus the main source of relief efforts for Jews in Kraków (and in the General Government).

Eager to assess Kraków's Jewish population, the Germans ordered the Jewish Council to conduct a census from 8 to 24 November 1939. Meanwhile, the district chief defined anyone who fell under the category of "Jew" in his geographic realm of influence. This was anyone of the Jewish faith, and anyone whose mother or father was of Jewish background. This decree was based on a racial law that ruled in Nazi Germany.[26] The census itself was connected to the planned resettlement of 350,000 Jews and 150,000 Poles from the newly acquired territories of western Poland to the General Government. It counted 46,535 Jewish adults and 18,945 Jewish children under the age of sixteen in Kraków and its environs.[27] With the rapid influx of refugees, however, the number of Jews in the city increased to 68,482 (including 787 known children) by the end of December 1939.[28]

———

Jews in Kraków experienced radical shifts in their daily lives under German occupation, starting with appropriations and evictions. A census that the German Construction Police (Baupolizei) conducted at the end of 1939 revealed 39,748 apartments in the city, of which the occupiers deemed only 20 to be appropriate for their needs.[29] The western part of the city, around the Wawel Castle and the Main Square (Rynek), was especially desirable. German civilians and officers were assigned individual rooms in Jewish homes, or commandeered entire apartments. Alicja Langer was eleven years old when the Germans appropriated most of her family's apartment in the coveted Smoleńsk Street, near the Wawel.[30] After her mother's staunch negotiations, the Germans allowed the Langers to inhabit one room while Nazi officers occupied the four others. It was both eerie and terrifying to share living space with their oppressors. The officers held drinking parties in the apartment and destroyed the family's furniture and equipment.

The behavior of German officers and clerks differed. In some cases, Germans accommodated in Jews' apartments exhibited civility, even kindness. The presence of a well-disposed German official affected a Jewish family's overall situation. Mieczysław Arzewski was a very young child when a German postal worker, Max Nagler, arrived in his apartment. From the beginning, Nagler showed compassion for the Arzewskis.[31] Ruth Salomon's parents were able to keep their prewar household help because she also served the German officers. The Salomons survived the harsh winter thanks to the German officers' supply of food and coal.[32] Adults who could converse in German had an advantage, as German officers saw these Jews as belonging to the same cultural milieu. Maurycy Sternlicht, ten years old, recalled that the officer who moved into his apartment warned the boy's mother against staying in the city. Maurycy remembered the officer warmly for still another reason—he brought him toys.[33]

Loss trumped gain, however. Appropriating Jews' real estate, the Germans also confiscated Jews' belongings. They embarked on an organized program of robbing Jews, which took various forms, from closing their bank accounts to grabbing their businesses. If children experienced these indirectly, degradation hit them directly. "I remember when they came to our house and they took our silver candelabras. They took off my mother's rings from her fingers. And

I remember my father being hit by a German. . . . I know we were all scared," Francis Immergluck, who was ten years old, recalled.[34] Plunder and violence in the space children considered safe frightened them.

Jewish children routinely witnessed the persecution of other Jews. "I saw the Germans rounding up the Hassidic Jews in the old part of town in Kraków-Kazimierz," Rena Ferber recalled. "They would cut their [facial] hair. . . . They would pull their beards. And then they would take them away."[35] Non-Jewish passersby reacted in many ways. As Francis Immergluck recalled, some mocked the Jews: "The Poles used to stand on the sides, applaud, and laugh."[36] Bearing witness to humiliation and crimes disturbed children and shook their sense of safety and stability. That feeling extended into the private realm when children were shocked by the disappearance of their loved ones. On the night of 8–9 November 1939, four Germans accompanied by two dogs burst into Ewa Heublum's house in search of weapons. The seven-year-old girl witnessed her father and grandfather being taken away. The blood on the walls of the building bore witness to the men's fate: they were shot. But their bodies were never found, prompting the family to believe that they were dumped into the Vistula River.[37]

Violence against Jews continued. The Germans cordoned off streets in Kazimierz on 5–6 December 1939. Ten-year-old Renate Leinkram recalled that the Germans ordered all windows shut while they went from house to house to pillage Jews' property. Renate peeked outside. She saw laundry baskets filled with various items, often silver, used for Jewish religious practice. A soldier also took Renate's doll, saying that a Jewish girl did not need one.[38] From stripping Jews of their belongings, the Germans turned to desecrating synagogues. On 5 December 1939, a Jewish Council clerk was ordered to set the Torah ablaze at the Izaak Synagogue. Then he was shot.[39] The Germans assaulted and murdered Jews in the district. The older children remembered this action well because it further eroded their feeling of safety. Fear or indifference prevented ordinary Poles and their leaders from interceding on behalf of the Jews. Reactions after the fact, including simple neighborly gestures or sympathy, from Poles were absent, too.

––––––––

Initially, Kraków residents shared the same restrictions. Everyone was a victim, and the war influenced the lives of all 250,000 Krakovians. Yet Nazi policies affected the 60,000 Jewish Krakovians and Jewish refugees differently from their Polish neighbors. Laws aimed specifically at Jews curbed their religious, social, and economic activities. Jews were the main targets of abuse. The Germans chose Jewish religious holidays to humiliate Jews particularly harshly. Abraham Englander recalled that on 23 September 1939 "it was Yom Kippur, and the first thing they [the Germans] did is to make all the Jews come out and cover the trenches that they built all around the city." All Jews over the age of ten had to appear on the streets on the holiest day in the Jewish religious calendar, a day when observant Jews are forbidden to work. The way the German officers treated these Jews shocked Abraham. "As I was there, some very tall SS men, three of them, came over to my father . . . and one of them pulled out a gun." Abraham recognized the gravity of the situation but could not understand why it was happening. "And I was a child. And [another German officer] said 'Leave him alone. Sooner or later we will put all of them against the wall.' So, they let him [my father] go. But it gave me like a cold chill."[40]

All Jewish Krakovians suffered from Nazi anti-Jewish laws. Children faced persecution aimed specifically at them when the Germans linked the definition of a child to one's ability to work. A law of 26 October 1939 required the registration and forced labor of all Jews between the ages of twelve and sixty, and in November the Jewish Council opened a labor office to avoid roundups. Jews on labor lists could either perform forced work themselves or pay the office for a substitute. Ester Spagatner, then around ten, sometimes replaced her father. The sight of young forced laborers bothered some Krakovians, and as she and other Jews plowed snow from streets, some Poles brought them hot drinks.[41] This small and rare act of individual resistance to the Jews' plight was important for the morale of young Jewish laborers such as Ester. The German authorities, too, gauged the atmosphere among Poles, who, as Slavs, occupied a low step on the Nazi racial ladder and themselves faced terror and deprivations. They encountered no meaningful opposition that would stifle the pace and intensity of Nazi anti-Jewish policy.

Jewish children continued to suffer restrictions. "When war broke out, of course right away all the schools were closed. And so our lives really changed," Celina Karp recalled.[42] Although it seemed to many children that education ceased immediately, it did not. The Kraków Board of Education halted its activity on 4 September 1939. However, teachers who remained in the city created a Temporary School Commission. The commission registered 217 teachers and 1,300 children of the over 20,000 enrolled in the Board of Education's schools before the summer vacation and opened thirty schools. By the end of September, almost all schools resumed their activities under German administration. According to Hans Frank's decree of 31 October 1939, Polish children, including Jews, were allowed to resume their education. In total, 15,897 children attended forty-two public primary schools, and 1,615 Jewish children were enrolled in five Jewish day schools.[43] But as of 11 December 1939, Jewish children were barred from all public and private schools. Renate Leinkram's teacher announced that all Jewish girls had to pack their books and leave.[44] Humiliated, she walked out of the classroom to the giggling of her classmates. The stability and normality associated with going to school collapsed for Jewish children.

Confronted with the end of formal schooling, Jewish parents initiated secret education for their children, bypassing the Germans' decree of 23 April 1940 that regulated education outside the school system. In doing so, these parents themselves resisted against Nazi policy on behalf of their children. For children, it meant assuming a concealed presence, to keep a low profile and engage in surreptitious activities. Rena Ferber and her friends attended clandestine lessons in different houses every morning. The girls' mothers took turns standing watch for German patrols. "If somebody had spied on us, they would . . . report on us to the Gestapo," Rena explained. "But we were so young. And our parents wanted to make sure that we were learning, because at that time they were still expecting the war not to last for too long."[45]

But the war continued, and so did the Germans' assault on the lives of Kraków's Jews, including imposing restrictions on their freedom of movement. Regulating where Jews could reside and the hours they were allowed outside affected Jews' social relations, economic activities, and religious observance. A May 1940 law marked the boundaries of Jewish presence in the city. Jews were banned from the historic Main Square and the Planty park that encircled it. However, they could walk on Planty between Hotel Royal, near the Wawel Castle, and the Main Post Office. They were allowed to cross streets cutting across Planty and to stroll on Planty along Dietla Street, at the boundary of the historic Jewish district of Kazimierz. Moving about grew increasingly difficult as Jews could only use designated areas in trams. They could use the railway only with a pass, which the German officials granted upon application for business, health, and other reasons they deemed eligible.

In addition to restricting mobility, the German authorities monitored Jews' every move with the institution on 1 December 1939 of a mandatory Star of David armband for all Jews over the age of twelve.[46] In effect, Jews were visible on the streets, as the white armband, worn on the right sleeve of an outer garment, had to be at least 3.9 inches wide, with a 3.1-inch diameter, and at least a 0.39-inch-wide blue ribbon for the Star of David. Square canvas patches with an edge length of 3.9 inches and a Star of David were introduced to cut costs on fabric needed for armbands and were in use until August 1940. The Jews had to purchase both the armbands and the patches. For younger children who lacked an understanding that the decree identified Jews and made them easy targets for harassment, the armband signified adulthood. Jakiw Klajner, then eleven years old, recalled, "I wanted to show that I'm a big man. Of course I made myself one, too." He quickly added, "I was a child, whatever."[47] Ten-year-old Leib Leyson recalled that in his house, a sign on the door reminded adolescents to slip on the armband upon leaving the house.[48] The punishment for failing to do so included prison and trial before special courts. According to official reports, at least 225 Jews (without age distinction) had been caught without armbands between April and July 1940.[49] The number of apprehended Jews would most likely have been higher if it included Jews who managed to pay off their blackmailers.

Separated, defined, and marked by Nazi decrees, Jews experienced ostracism from their Polish neighbors. If some Jewish children had been tormented before the war by their non-Jewish peers, others, especially those of early school age, did not recall such incidents. Perhaps this was because antisemitism became ingrained in the fabric of Jewish life and normalized. Or individual Jewish children truly were spared from verbal and physical intimidation before the Germans' arrival in Kraków. Francis Immergluck recalled her first experience of antisemitism. "[It was] one of my non-Jewish friends that I used to go to school with and play with. When I approached her, she said 'I cannot play with you anymore because you're Jewish.' And I came home crying. I wanted to play with her, and I couldn't. Because I guess she was told that she couldn't play with me."[50]

Confronted with weakening social ties and mounting restrictions, Jews explored their options. Jerzy Hoffman's parents decided to take on a non-Jewish identity. As he recalled, "What happened to us wasn't what happened to the Jews because we were not living as Jews. We were essentially living under false identity. . . . So whatever was happening to the Jews in 1940–41 . . . it didn't happen to us because we decided to lead a subterfuge."[51] Jerzy's family was in the minority. The majority of Kraków Jews continued to endure anti-Jewish laws as Jews. The losses they experienced, eviction from homes, and expulsion from the city ineradicably distinguished them from their non-Jewish Krakovian neighbors.

"I can no longer tolerate the mass concentration of Jews in Krakau. Therefore I order the resettlement of the majority of Jews from the city of Krakau."[52] With these words Hans Frank announced the expulsion of Kraków Jews to his subordinates in the four districts of the General Government on 25 May 1940. A week earlier, Frank had informed the Kraków city commandant of his plan and he, in turn, forwarded the order to the Jewish Council. To streamline the eviction, Frank introduced a definition of a "Jew" (based on the Nuremberg Laws) on 24 July 1940: a person descended from at least three fully Jewish grandparents by race or a mixed-breed (*Mischling*) who had two fully Jewish grandparents by race. According to the decree, a "racially pure Jewish" grandparent was someone who belonged to a Jewish community. Moreover, those who belonged to a Jewish community as of 1 September 1939, who had been married to a Jew, or who had married since the decree appeared were defined as Jews, as were the illegitimate children of those defined as Jews born after 31 May 1941. The racial law took effect on 1 August 1940. This law replaced an earlier law (18 November 1939) of the chief of Kraków District that defined a Jew as anyone of the Jewish faith, and anyone whose parent was Jewish. The governor's law was different in two ways. First, Frank's law applied to all Jews in the General Government, and not only to those in one of its four districts. Second, it enlarged the pool of those deemed Jews by mining people's genealogy.

Frank banished Jews from Kraków in order to mold it into the most representative city in the General Government and uphold what the Nazis believed to be its inherently Germanic character. Then too, German soldiers, officers, clerks, and businessmen arriving to staff the Nazi bureaucracy headquartered in Kraków could no longer share living space with Jews lest they contract diseases Frank believed Jews carried. The expelled Jews' apartments in desirable areas of Kraków were assigned to the newly arrived Germans.

Gazeta Żydowska (Jewish Newspaper) tells how the expulsion was presented to the Jews and how it was organized. The paper, published between 23 July 1940 and mid-1942, was the only media outlet that the Germans created and allowed for Jews in the General Government. While it served as a propaganda tool, its articles offer a wealth of information about Jews' daily lives. According to the newspaper, the German authorities wished to carry out the eviction and resettlement of Kraków's Jews "without unnecessary rigor and in a humanitarian way."[53] This was understood to mean that the Germans expected Jews' compliance. No baggage restrictions were placed on Jews who left voluntarily by 15 August 1940. Afterward, Jews were forcibly resettled and allowed to take 110 pounds of belongings per person (that allowance dropped to 55 pounds in December 1940). The Germans allowed Jews to settle in localities outside Kraków (but within the General Government) that the Jews chose or were assigned to, and waived a poll tax for expellees. Some Jews received aid from a resettlement fund created on Germans' orders, with money from blocked Jewish bank accounts.

To facilitate a smooth resettlement, the Jewish Council issued a request (14 June 1940) to the city commandant for permission to create a Jewish Order Service (Jüdischer Ordnungsdienst, also referred to as the Jewish police) to maintain order in Kazimierz, the Jewish district, and especially to monitor Jewish refugees. The council feared the image that refugee Jews conveyed to the Germans as unemployed aid recipients. Nor did the council trust the refugees. They were not originally from Kraków. And Kraków Jews took great pride in their tight-knit community and social networks that its members were part of. Eager to control that community, the German commandant of the security service in Kraków approved the creation of the Jewish patrol force as an auxiliary organ of the Jewish Council on 5 July 1940.[54] The Jewish Order Service undertook two types of service: internal service, such as keeping order in buildings and care institutions managed by the Jewish Council, and external service, such as delivering orders, enforcing decrees, controlling Jews' public life, and assisting in resettlement.

According to the resettlement law, only Jewish merchants, artisans, and skilled workers and their immediate families could remain in the city, provided they obtained residence permits. From the German perspective, these Jews would be useful for producing goods in advance of the war with the Soviet Union. In addition, Jews over seventy years of age, the sick, those incapable of travel, World War I veterans, orphans, and medical personnel could remain in the city with a permit. Jews submitted applications to the Jewish Council, which forwarded its suggestions to the city commandant's office, where a special commission issued final decisions. Some parents understood the need to present their children as "adults" over the age of fourteen and thus prove their children's usefulness as workers, at any cost. "We had to get a permit to remain in Krakow. . . . I was 10 years old. But they changed my birth certificate to make me 12," Rena Ferber explained. "I had to work. We all had to work."[55]

Both parents and their children resisted the expulsion decree. Yet the ruses they devised did not always guarantee safety. Jews slated for eviction were obliged to report to the Jewish Council's Resettlement Office at 21 Dajwór Street (which at some point moved to 5 Brzozowa Street). There they received identification papers, permits to use the railway, funds for travel and pocket money, clothes, and other help as needed. The Jewish Council and the city commandant disproportionally shared the costs of the operation.

Jews typically headed to localities where they already had relatives and friends, and to villages around Kraków. Thus geography and preexisting contacts mattered in Jews' strategies to respond to the expulsion law. However, many had no such connections, in which case the Jewish Council made the arrangements.[56] Preparing for resettlement, the Jewish Council had sent questionnaires to their counterparts in the region to assess living circumstances and ability to absorb expellees. By 1 July 1940, some 1.3 million Jews had lived in the General Government, representing 10.4 percent of the population. In Kraków District alone, 220,000 Jews formed 5.3 percent of the population.[57] The Jewish Council estimated 67,000 Jews in Kraków (including 11,000 Jewish refugees who arrived there at the beginning of the war) among a total population of 330,000, representing 21 percent. Between 48,000 and 52,000 Jews had to be resettled from Kraków at the rate of 1,000 per day.[58] The Kraków Jewish Council feared the consequences of the Jews' resettlement on the city's economy. Fewer community members meant less income from taxes that the council could use for their services. In order to limit the scale of the resettlement, the council voiced the need to make Jews productive and thus useful.

The repercussions of the resettlement action echoed in the cities, towns, and villages where Jews headed and settled. "The mass resettlement of Jews threatens those Jewish communities with complete ruin and catastrophe," the Kraków Jewish Council warned.[59] Council members feared that the influx of Kraków Jews in those localities would paralyze social welfare and spark the malevolence of the non-Jewish population. On the one hand, the resettlement order did become a source of enrichment for local people who charged the expellees exorbitant rents. On the other hand, many administrators outside Kraków refused to accept the refugees and threatened to evict them once they arrived. *Gazeta Żydowska* appealed to local Jewish communities throughout the General Government to show solidarity by welcoming newcomers, even if they differed in language, social status, and level of religious observance. "The injunction is to tell them 'come and be our guests until you find your own roof over your heads.' As the Book of Ruth says 'my house is your house.'"[60]

The efforts of Jewish leaders to mitigate the repercussions of this sudden shift in Jewish communal life, however, were not something to which children were privy. Nor did they receive much explanation from their parents. Still, they sensed an abrupt change in their lives, and interpreted and reacted to it based on their age-appropriate competencies. "All of a sudden there was a decree that we must leave Kraków," Roman Ferber recalled. "And we did." The Ferbers loaded their belongings onto a horse-drawn wagon and rented a house with another Jewish family in Borek Fałęcki, which to Roman seemed far away, but was a village outside Kraków. "I have some nice memories from that place," he reminisced.[61] He remembered the freedom that he experienced in the new environment as opposed to his very restricted life in the city. He viewed the transition into his new place of residence as rather smooth and claimed it was an adventure to a young boy. To Roman, events progressed fast and overlapped. In reality, the changes occurred in a rapidly developing process.

Jews felt rushed and hastened to leave. They had to find housing outside the city, settle their affairs, sort through belongings, pack, and arrange transport. Jerzy Biernacki, a non-Jew, observed in his wartime diary, "I was in the Jewish quarter today [8 August 1940]. Depressing impression! Over half of the stores are closed, and the others are hastily selling out the remaining items for close to nothing. They [Jews] load furniture and various household equipment—often very miserable—onto carts. By the way, poor are these people."[62] Biernacki acknowledged the German action against Jews as a major event in Kraków. The fate of Jews concerned some Poles like Biernacki on a personal level. But it did not affect non-Jewish Krakovians the same way as Jews. Daily struggles increased. Biernacki moved from mentioning the Jews' situation to discussing the price of eggs.

The Germans knew that non-Jewish Krakovians were occupied with other things. And they knew how to exploit and fuel negative emotions against Jews. The Germans presented the "Jewish problem" not only as a German issue but as a concern for all Poles in Kraków. The Germans promised that resettling Jews would solve economic, social, and moral problems. A number of Poles agreed. The city commandant's office received letters thanking him for expelling Jews. The author of one letter saw the expulsion as justice done on behalf of the Poles after years of economic and demographic subjugation by Jews.[63] For some Poles, the resettlement of Jews led to opportunities for enrichment—acquiring new apartments, taking over businesses, and obtaining various possessions that Jews stashed and could not take with them. In this context, the Poles adopted the euphemism of "formerly Jewish property" (po-żydowskie) to denote real and movable property that Jews had to leave behind when the Germans forcibly removed them from their homes and to which Poles now felt entitled to. Of course, the Germans sprang into action first to purloin items of value, like furniture. Those riches were for the Reich.

Gazeta Żydowska recognized the dire situation of Jewish Krakovians. "We stand at the turning point in the history of Jews in Kraków—before an evacuation of the Jewish population from Kraków."[64] By August 1940, 33,281 Jews had left the city. Among them were 12,711 children up to the age of fourteen, 19.5 percent of expellees.[65] Not satisfied with the number of Jews who left voluntarily, the Germans ordered an expulsion to begin on 16 August 1940. Pressed between meeting German demands and promoting a positive image of the Kraków Jewish population as productive and useful, the Jewish Council urged more Jews to leave by 13 August. The German authorities, too, understood the need to balance their desire to rid the city of Jews and their demand for Jewish forced laborers. By October 1940, 36,000 Jews remained in Kraków, while the Germans wanted to keep about 15,000.[66]

At first, Hans Frank intended to clear the city of unwanted Jews by 1 November 1940. But Jews continued to resist the expulsion order. They steadfastly remained in the city, and many returned after they had been resettled elsewhere. At that point, the categories of Jews allowed to remain encompassed a broad range of people, not only those with the labor skills the Germans desired. Confronted with such unanticipated resistance, the German authorities kept changing the deadlines. Then the district chief, Otto Wächter, ordered the registration of all remaining Jews between 2 and 11 December 1940. The purpose, he said, was "to de-Jewify Krakau and leave only those Jews, who, due to their particular work, are needed for the time being."[67] Jews received notices to appear with children under the age of fourteen at the Lubicz resettlement camp (*Aussiedlungslager*) at 1 Mogilska Street with fifty-five pounds of luggage per person, documents, and food sufficient for three days.

Still unwilling to leave, Kraków Jews continued their resistance to German expulsion decrees by submitting applications for permits to the city commandant to remain and to defer resettlement.[68] Parents usually based their appeal on their child's young age and medical condition. "My child suffers from a severe hernia and has also undergone various infectious diseases, which is confirmed by the attached physician's certificate. According to the doctor's finding, the child should be operated on and stay in bed for a longer time. For reasons stated, I would respectfully request a favorable decision to postpone the prescribed resettlement deadline," one letter read.[69] Other parents emphasized their children's contribution to the workforce. Some tried to appeal to the conscience of the letter recipients, especially in the face of the approaching winter. "I have seven children aged three to fifteen. My husband is a glazier by profession, but he is also working other odd jobs," one mother wrote. "My 15-year-old and 13-year-old daughters make sweaters and knit socks and contribute significantly to the family income. . . . The resettlement would be a great misfortune for [a mother] with young children, especially in the winter because we have neither the means to relocate, nor a place to go."[70]

Prospective or actual displacement posed hardships. But Jews who remained in the city also endured restrictions. According to the "First Decree about Limiting Jews' Presence in the General Government" of 13 September 1940, Jews who held residence permits could not leave Kraków unless they obtained temporary authorizations. This law was an important step in defining where Jews could live. Kraków Jews were aware of the situation in Warsaw, where Jews were confined to a ghetto as early as November 1940. Uncertainty and fear determined Jews' lives in Kraków. Seven-year-old Luiza Grüner attended religious services in one of the Jewish district's prayer houses during the High Holy Days in fall 1940. The weeping and mourning of attendees reflected the dire situation. "It made a tremendous impression on me. It was so intense that even as a young child I felt it."[71]

The fragile emotional state of Kraków Jews was also rooted in their deteriorating physical condition and decline in access to necessities. The Jewish Council assessed the living circumstances of the Jewish population in order to determine its health and to avoid epidemics. The council's Sanitary Commission deplored the conditions in which Jews lived. On average, two families, a total of around ten people, lived in a two-room apartment, and two or three slept in one bed. Workers observed that bathrooms were few and many were unusable.[72] Health care ranked high on the council's agenda. Its support for the Jewish Hospital at 6 Skawińska Street was of utmost importance to sustain children's health. In the first year of the German occupation, the hospital assisted 47,716 individuals, among them 3,639 children. The hospital also distributed 4,515 pounds of cod liver oil from the American Red Cross. From March to May 1940, 50 homeless children obtained the dietary supplement in the hospital's pump room. Children whose parents worked and were thus unable to bring them to the hospital received seven ounces of cod liver oil each.[73]

Efforts to provide medical care complemented endeavors to ensure proper nourishment for children. The Jewish Council dedicated a building at 7 Zielona Street for a children's kitchen in May 1940. However, once the renovation of the building had been completed, the city commandant requisitioned the building and some five hundred children were thus deprived of a place to receive meals. Still, the Jewish Council continued its efforts to assist youngsters. A feeding station for poor children opened in the Jewish Hospital on 12 November 1940, where 3,361 children received a breakfast of warm milk and a roll three times a week. Organizers were compelled to prioritize in light of shrinking resources. Only children aged two to fourteen from the poorest strata without access to other forms of welfare received this meal.[74]

Ensuring children's health and sustenance was one thing. Physically protecting children was another. A branch of Centos, the Central Organization for the Care of Children and Orphans, resumed activities in Kraków in May 1940 after a temporary halt due to the outbreak of the war. Centos, created in 1919 as the Section for Care for Jewish Children and Orphans in the Committee of Help for Polish Jews, became an independent entity in 1923. By 1939, Centos operated in 343 localities in Poland. Its Kraków branch cared for over 1,000 children in the region. A registration of Jewish children in fourteen shelters and four soup kitchens conducted in April 1940 by the president of Centos in Kraków, Dr. Józef Steinberg, identified 1,759 needy children.[75] To fulfill its mandate to provide both temporary and long-term care to Jewish youngsters, Kraków's Centos received support from multiple sources: its Warsaw headquarters, the American Jewish Joint Distribution Committee, the Kraków Jewish Council, the Jewish Social Self-Help, and ordinary Jewish Krakovians. Centos prided itself on involving members of the Kraków Jewish community in its efforts. Women in particular collected funds, clothes, and food; volunteered in Centos institutions; and recruited helpers.

Centos ran two care stations (*ośrodek opiekuńczy*): one in a shelter at 3 Podbrzezie Street (created by the Jewish Council in April 1940) and the second in the shelter at 10 Stanisława Street (opened on 9 June 1940). Centos also established a care station for children on 3 Krzemionki Street in Podgórze on 16 June 1940. That center, with its spacious building and courtyard, served as a summer day camp for about two hundred Jewish children from Podgórze and two hundred children mostly from Kazimierz. A central day care center for children opened on three floors of the former Jewish school at 3 Podbrzezie Street in summer 1940. Children received food and care, and educators taught children vocational skills. Girls in the day care exhibited their works (slippers, belts, drawings, and the like) in one of the halls to display their work capabilities.

Centos also was interested in introducing a comprehensive child welfare plan. The expulsion decree of May 1940 affected the most helpless among Jews in Kraków: refugee children, orphaned or abandoned in shelters by parents, who, as refugees, were the first to be expelled from the city.[76] Children in foster homes whose guardians left them at the Jewish Council or on the street were targeted too. Determined to assist those youngsters, Centos opened its own orphanage at 3 Podbrzezie Street, which it called a shelter (*schronisko*), on 1 August 1940. This was the second children's home in the city after the Jewish Orphanage at 64 Dietla Street. Children two to twelve years of age arrived in the Centos shelter in a miserable moral, physical, and hygienic state. "Therefore their guardians had a difficult task—they had to fight with dirt and habits, and often with illnesses, and moral savagery," authors of a Centos report observed.[77] The Centos shelter cooperated closely with a Jewish soup kitchen at 2 Mostowa Street, as well as with the Vocational Hostel for Jewish Orphaned Boys at 53 Krakowska Street. Children were channeled into work (and a new residence) once they reached the age of twelve. By the end of 1940, twenty-nine children had passed through the Centos shelter.

As Centos was expanding its activities, it struggled to keep its headquarters. When the Jewish Council requisitioned the building for a planned school in

November 1940, Centos searched desperately for new locations in Kraków to continue its work. It was forced to disperse in Kazimierz and settle in buildings that were not always appropriate for its activities. The shelter moved to 21 Dajwór Street, while one day care center for children aged four to seven was established in a small room in the Tempel Synagogue. Another day care, for children aged seven to fourteen, was transferred to the B'nei Emuna Synagogue. The latter also housed a warehouse and a central kitchen that catered to all three new Centos centers.[78] These moves affected Centos's expenses—more branches required a greater number of educators and increased resources. Between 150 and 250 children attended the day care centers. Centos staff deplored that "many children could not come to the centers due to a complete lack of shoes and warm clothing."[79] The extreme poverty of many children, the approaching winter, and the lack of care and attention youngsters received in their homes prompted Centos to open a day care center for children of Jewish workers at 1 Agnieszki Street at the beginning of November 1940. Two female educators cared for, fed, and arranged medical treatment for 59 children, aged four to fourteen.

While it concentrated on assisting Jewish children in Kazimierz, Centos was also mindful of the needs of young people in Kraków's Podgórze district. Pressed by medical personnel and activists, Centos supported the opening of a clinic (*poradnia higieniczna*) at 13 Limanowskiego Street on 10 November 1940. Poverty, overcrowding, malnourishment, and limited access to water posed a grave risk for epidemics. To prevent disease, six nurses visited homes in which children lived in Podgórze to appraise them, instruct parents on hygiene, and refer children for medical treatment to the clinic.

Embracing the importance of continuity, Centos emerged as the primary childcare organization. In addition to creating new child welfare institutions, it supported existing ones, especially those that fell under its umbrella before the war. Centos assisted the two Vocational Hostels for Jewish Orphaned Boys located at 6 Podbrzezie Street and at 53 Krakowska Street. Together, they cared for fifty-seven boys between the ages of twelve and eighteen, who worked in and outside the hostels, thus supporting the two institutions.[80] The youngest among them attended Centos day care, where they ate meals.

Although not a direct affiliate, the Jewish Orphanage at 64 Dietla Street received foodstuffs and other supplies from Centos, though its main source of funding came from the Jewish Council and Kraków Jews. The institution housed 125 orphans at the end of December 1940. The children received care from eight educators, three administrators, and nine assistants.[81] The resettlement of established and prospective funders, as well as the Germans' control of the institution's assets and the constant pressure to accept more children, plunged the orphanage into crisis. Women went from house to house to collect food. *Gazeta Żydowska* appealed to Kraków Jews: "Jewish society would not dare let the children starve! Everyone who knows the Jewish heart is convinced that despite the difficult time, Kraków Jewry will help the orphanage."[82] Ultimately, the orphanage carried on; the children continued to play, observe holidays, and learn, as an educational event in January 1941 for invited guests advertised. It showed decision makers on the Jewish Council that the orphanage fulfilled a vital role as a guardian of Jewish children and it offered children an opportunity to engage with their heritage.[83]

Educators took advantage of any chance to teach children when no formal schools existed. On 31 August 1940, the Germans tasked the Jewish Council with creating and supporting grade schools for Jewish children and training Jewish teachers. But the council was unable to fulfill its mandate in both regards. Buildings that had served as schools before the war had been appropriated by the Germans or allotted for other purposes by the council itself.[84] And schooling was not among the Jewish Council's funding priorities, as Jews were being resettled outside Kraków every day and the number of school-age children remaining in the city fluctuated greatly. Moreover, establishing schools required the Germans' permission. In September 1940, the Jewish Council's Education Department sent a request to the German authorities to open a few primary schools. It remained unanswered and the status of the 4,030 school-age children was left in limbo.[85]

All Jewish Krakovians remained in suspense as to what steps the German authority would take against them, but despite this uncertainty, Jewish community organizers drafted plans for extending child welfare in the city. They saw a future for themselves and their children. German plans, by contrast, envisioned the staged disappearance of Jews from the urban landscape. In tandem with the policy of expulsion of most Jews from Kraków, the Germans instituted a strategy of concentrating the city's remaining Jews either in Kazimierz or in Podgórze. But neither area was a ghetto in the Nazi understanding. That was where Jews, expelled from their homes throughout the city, tended to gravitate. That was where their relatives and friends resided. That was where other Jews lived, where Jewish institutions existed. That was where Jewish Krakovians felt safer—from the Germans and their Polish neighbors.

But the feeling of safety was an illusion. On 27 February 1941, the Germans invalidated Jews' work cards (*Ausweise*), except those issued by the chief of Kraków District. The German Labor Office began to allot identification papers to Jews aged fourteen and older on 1 March 1941. Children who reached the age of fourteen were in a peculiar situation, old enough to be regarded as adults (workers), but already included on a parent's identity card. They were in an ambiguous transitional state. But everyone was in an ambiguous state, and in early 1941, Krakovian Jews asked themselves, What would happen to their community? And to their families?

CHAPTER 2

Adapting to Life inside the Ghetto

The rumors circulating in Kraków about the creation of a Jewish quarter, similar to the separate living areas for Jews that the Germans had instituted throughout the General Government, had materialized. The order of the chief of Kraków District, Otto Wächter, published in newspapers and plastered throughout the city, established what the Germans called a Jewish residential district (*Jüdischer Wohnbezirk*) on 3 March 1941. Apart from separating Jews from Kraków's non-Jewish population for alleged health and security reasons, the law also aimed to solve the housing crisis that incoming Germans encountered.[1] Despite its official name and legal rationalization, the "Jewish residential district" in Kraków was nothing but a ghetto; an enclosed and guarded area in which Jews were forcibly concentrated, secluded, and persecuted.

The concept of the ghetto was completely new to Jewish children, and not immediately comprehensible. Thus, children who found themselves in the restricted area of their hometown experienced confusion, isolation, and loss. Older children realized that the move stigmatized them as different from other Krakovians.[2] Many children had no prior connection to the space that they and their families entered. Therefore, with the onset of ghettoization, children were suddenly and indefinitely sundered from their familiar surroundings. They were bereft of any remaining freedom of movement, their homes, their belongings, and often, too, their loved ones who had fled or been deported from Kraków.

The new situation demanded a response from adults, and produced a reaction from children, too. As this chapter explores, in Kraków, the strategies that Jewish children used and the ways that adults dealt with the situation of their youth resulted from the unique position of the city in the Nazi scheme for occupied Poland. The expulsion from Kraków in 1940 of Jews whom the Germans deemed useless in terms of their labor abilities determined the age, type, and number of Jews who later entered Kraków's ghetto. Children up to the age of fourteen were permitted to live there as appendages to their working parents. Neither parents nor community activists knew the Germans' plans for young- sters when they turned fourteen. Would they be separated from their families and forced out of the ghetto? Or would they join the slave labor pool in the ghetto? The Germans offered no clarity. Thus, adults preferred to keep children out of the Germans' sight so as not to attract their attention, and to create an illusion of absence. Nevertheless, children adopted familiar and new measures, both on their own and with the assistance of adults, to help them confront and adapt to the new circumstances. It is in this context that young people's and their guard- ians' efforts to grapple with Kraków ghetto conditions emerge.

———

The Kraków ghetto was established relatively late, one of 342 ghettos in the Gen- eral Government, and one of 71 ghettos in Kraków District.[3] Contemporary documentation suggests that the ghetto fell under the jurisdiction of different authorities, possibly to disperse responsibility and avoid concentration of power as different German agencies pursued their interests as they concerned exploiting Jews in the ghetto. At first, the Jewish Council answered to Othmar Rodler, the official for Jewish affairs in the Office of the Chief of Kraków Dis- trict.[4] Kraków's city commandant was also responsible for the ghetto. And in May 1942, the Kraków Gestapo and its unit IVB for Jewish affairs, headed by SS-Oberscharführer Paul Siebert, assumed governance over Jewish matters.

A local endeavor, the Kraków ghetto fulfilled diverse needs at different times: it held Jews in one place, solved housing problems, and exploited Jews' labor; later it served as a holding pen and transit site before deportation to camps. Hans Frank's "First Decree Regarding the Limitation on Presence in the General Government," proclaimed on 13 September 1940 and enforced eighteen days later, provided the legal framework for a ghetto in Kraków. Kazimierz, the city's historically Jewish quarter, was too close to the headquarters of the governor general in the Wawel Castle.[5] Podgórze, connected with Kazimierz by two bridges, was an area without a sizable Jewish population.[6] This site on the out- skirts of the city removed Jews from their homes, communal and religious institutions, and familiar surroundings, as well as their Polish neighbors. Barbed wire and a brick wall (built by Polish workers in April 1941) that resem- bled Jewish tombstones delineated the borders of the ghetto, as did bricked entranceways, doors, and windows that overlooked the Aryan side. Four gates regulated contact between Jews and non-Jews: on Plac Zgody, Traugutta, and Limanowskiego-Lwowska Streets. The Germans labeled the main entrance on Limanowskiego Street Rynek Podgórski with a sign in Yiddish.[7] Bordered by the Vistula River to the north, Krzemionki (flint mines) to the south, railway tracks to the east, and the non-Jewish section of Podgórze to the west, the area the Germans had designated was one in which Jews were both isolated and removed from the city center.

———

The Germans framed moving into the newly created ghetto as a privilege. Out of the some 20,000 Jews in Kraków, 16,036 applied for permission to enter the ghetto.[8] The majority of Jews surmised that the ability to remain in their hometown granted them an advantageous position. As the Germans branded the ghetto a Jews-only residential section of the city and entrance was granted only with German approval, some Jews thought it offered safety from the Germans' random violence and harassment by Poles. Other Jews referred to Jewish history in which ghettos had a precedent. The short window for moving into the ghetto mattered, too. Jews had little time to find housing outside Kraków. If they decided to hide on the Aryan side, they had to arrange shelter and procure appropriate documents quickly. Furthermore, the ghetto allowed Jews to remain a family unit and to be together with other Jews, and in the landscape they knew. Kraków is where they had familial and social networks. Then too, some Jews feared the consequences of disobeying German orders. In the end, only about 11,000 Jews the Germans deemed valuable acquired identity cards and work papers that allowed them to settle in the ghetto.[9] The rest either were expelled or left Kraków without requesting entry permits. For Jews who resisted and continued to stay in Kraków illegally, a German decree of 25 April 1941 specified a punishment of 1,000 złoty and, in case of insolvency, incarceration of up to three months.[10] The fee was equivalent to the cost of more than twenty-one geese purchased at the official maximum price set by the German city commandant.[11]

While the German authorities outlined their plan for the confinement and expulsion of Kraków Jews, they also introduced laws and procedures in preparation for the forced relocation. They limited Jews beyond the ghetto walls to individuals with identity cards issued by the Kraków District Office, and designated the Labor Department as the new issuer of such documents. This bureau now wielded control over the ghetto population. (This switch signified the new role for the ghetto as a pool of forced labor.) Tram stops were discontinued in the planned ghetto. And Jews were ordered to obtain permits from the German Office of the Trust Agency (Treuhand-Aussenstelle) to transport their belongings. Podgórze was divided into sections A and B, with section A covering about twenty hectares and consisting of some fifteen streets. Ethnic Poles had to move from their residences in section A to Jews' dwellings in Kazimierz. Jews were instructed to hand over their apartments to the superintendent or administrator of their building and to apply for new quarters through the Jewish Housing Office. Those who failed to move into the ghetto by 20 March 1941 risked eviction and restriction to only fifty-five pounds of personal property. Poles complained about the German decision to situate Jews in Podgórze, citing obstacles the move posed. The rector of Saint Joseph's parish, Józef Niemczyński, deplored losing his followers.[12] Such objections were to no avail.

The recollections of children who went with their families into the ghetto offer a glimpse into how the move progressed and what children encountered in their new quarters. Marcel Baral, nine years old at the time, began his description of the next stage in his life: "There was a decree that all Jews had to leave town and go to Podgórze across the river, the Vistula River, and that's where the Jews would be able to live freely. In fact, they would be protected against Polish antisemites." Presented this way, the ghetto promised to shield Jews against their non-Jewish neighbors and allow for the existence of a Jewish enclave. "That was the official story."[13]

Permit recipients had only seventeen days to prepare for the move, pack their belongings, arrange for carts, and settle any business and personal matters in the city. With experience living under German occupation for almost two years, some adults had acted with forethought by selling their valuables to Poles, thereby resisting the German policy of appropriating household items and valuables, and by entrusting other precious articles to Polish neighbors. What they loaded onto carts were the few items of daily use and furniture they were allowed or managed to take. Children took a couple of their prized possessions, like books and toys. While a number of Jews made their own arrangements, the Jewish Social Self-Help provided assistance to the needy for transporting their belongings.

Predictably, the busiest time for the move was just before the decreed deadline. According to *Gazeta Żydowska*, despite the commotion, agitation, fear of the unknown, and terror, "everywhere the moving proceeded in the greatest order, without rush or hampering traffic."[14] Marcel Baral confirmed that assessment. He recalled how well the Jewish Council planned housing assignments: "Everybody knew which room, which building, which street is allocated for them. It was in very orderly fashion. At least initially."[15] Photographs of the expulsion of Jews across the Vistula reveal a procession of people of all ages carrying objects, pushing carts, and riding on horse-drawn wagons. The images fail to document the responses of non-Jewish neighbors, but some negative reactions were etched into children's memories. Rena Ferber, twelve years old at the time, observed, "We just walked, and the Polish people stood on the sidewalk and they were yelling 'Good riddance!' 'Go! Don't come back!' Such hate."[16] Similarly, Jan Rothbaum, then ten years old, recalled that peasants came into the city to scoop up possessions Jews left behind, knowing they could not cart everything with them.[17]

While some children had experienced social distance from their Polish peers before the war, this division was clearly illuminated by their non-Jewish neighbors' reactions when they moved to the ghetto. For others, however, actual enclosure in the ghetto alerted them to their separateness. "That was the first time that I realized that we are different people from the others," Pinkus Fajnwaks, ten years old at the time, acknowledged. Geographic isolation and the external marking (which applied to Jews above the age of twelve) exacerbated his feeling of forced alienation from the outside world and instilled fear. "And being surrounded by barbed wire, and not being able to go out to the other side of the street.... All of a sudden it hit me that we are Jewish and that we are getting persecuted by the Germans, and I was very afraid of it."[18]

The forced living space defined children's new reality and heightened their sense of estrangement. Children were struck by their harsh living conditions, with crowded apartments and congested and noisy streets. The Germans crammed Jews into 288 residential buildings, which contained 2,273 apartments with 3,148 rooms. (Ten other buildings were allotted for nonresidential purposes.) On average, 41 people lived in each building, approximately 5 in every apartment, and about 3 people per each window.[19] Based on the Jewish Council's estimates of 1 May 1941, there were 10,873 Jews in the ghetto; 5,034 men (including 870 boys up to the age of twelve) and 5,839 women (including 912 girls up to the age of twelve).[20]

Living conditions became even more unbearable when the Germans incorporated thirty nearby communes (*gromady*) and parts of municipalities (*gminy*) into Kraków on 1 June 1941.[21] They forced Jews from those localities to register by 31 August 1941 and move within three days of receiving their papers. Hans Frank sought to concentrate Jews in the limited number of already active ghettos, not to establish new ones, a thought he expressed on 17 July 1941 upon the annexation of Eastern Galicia to the General Government. He grounded his approach in Hitler's statement of 19 June 1941 promising the removal of Jews from the General Government "in the nearest future." On 21 October 1941, Frank officially prohibited the creation of new ghettos, thereby straining the limits of the Kraków ghetto.[22] Newcomers arrived in the largest numbers during the High Holy Days, which caused an additional impediment for observant Jews. As of 14 October 1941, the number of inhabitants reached 15,288 (including 1,200 individuals without identity cards, and children and adults in care institutions). Children represented 20 percent of the incomers (1,000 people).[23] At this point, the ghetto was bursting at its seams.

To accommodate the arrivals, one-room dwellings now housed seven inhabitants; one-room apartments with kitchens housed ten people; two-room apartments, fifteen to sixteen people; and three-room apartments, twenty individuals.[24] Janina Fischler's description of her family's housing arrangements elucidates the dire situation, which worsened with every German action in the ghetto, with the borders redrawn and the area decreased. At some point, Janina, who was eleven years old when she entered the ghetto, was forced to move into a dilapidated house without running water or a toilet. The outhouse and communal water tap became sources of friction and misery. Residents struggled for privacy in the harried atmosphere of constant quarrels. They fought over access to water, a precious

commodity. But waiting in line for these basic services also provided information and instruction. Neighbors swapped rumors and circulated news. Older
children learned to conserve, measure, and recycle resources, and to be quick.
The kitchen, and especially the stove, were trigger points, too. Battling for a
burner, stealing food, and skimming off the top layer of food in others' sauce-
pans constituted only some of the offenses.[25]

The experience of ghettoization shocked children old enough to understand
the changes. For nine-year-old Celina Karp, the move into the ghetto shattered
her sense of rootedness and safety. "Life changed completely. You lost, not that
you ever had, a feeling of security, but as a child I did. And at that point I no
longer had that sense of security. It was totally replaced by the beginnings of
fear."[26] The debilitating new surroundings—as well as the prevailing uncertainty
and insecurity—instilled anxiety. The limited space and harsh restrictions
weighed heavily.

———

If at first children were crushed by their new living arrangements, in time they
acquired certain routines that allowed many to cope. Family life constituted an
important factor for keeping a semblance of normality for children in the ghetto.
Parents, and adults in general, often made efforts to orient children toward the
future, especially through education. Maintaining cultural tradition and religious observance also allowed some children to find solace and continue modes
of behavior they knew from before the ghetto. While adults introduced and
maintained routines for children, the young people, too, devised their own ways
of grappling with the circumstances of ghetto existence. They did what was
natural for people their age: they played, formed friendships, learned how the
world functioned, questioned the reality they endured, and rebelled against
adults and the conditions imposed on them.

"In the ghetto, there was [a] sort of normalcy to life because we still had our
family; it was intact. . . . We were safe then. We were still together."[27] In this way
Lucie Stern, a thirteen-year-old at the time, spoke about the importance of her
sense of family cohesiveness in the ghetto. In the eyes of children like Lucie, a
familial network ensured some measure of safety and domestic stability, which
made children feel cared for and protected. Looking back, many child survivors
credited their parents for their psychological and physical survival. In the early
stages of the ghetto, parents were still authority figures and breadwinners.
Children tended to overlook certain inconveniences in their new surroundings
because their parents offered emotional and material support. As Aneta Baral
reflected, "In the beginning the conditions were not too bad. I mean—for us
because our parents looked after us."[28]

The significance of family, or at least having a relative nearby, became evident upon relocation to the ghetto. Some children and their families had the rare

advantage of relatives already living in Podgórze. Able to stay with close family in familiar surroundings, they were spared the experience of moving into an apartment with strangers. Such a situation created a sort of continuity for children. In other cases, having relatives in the Kraków ghetto led families to flee their hometowns elsewhere and enter the ghetto clandestinely for the sake of joining their loved ones in times of crisis.

While entering the ghetto as a family unit or joining relatives there signified continuum, family life itself changed in the ghetto. Many mothers who had previously worked as homemakers now labored outside the home and were unable to devote themselves fully to the family. Then too, they were left without the assistance of gentile nannies and household help. In this situation, many children became caretakers of the home and of younger children. Ghetto conditions demanded that children mature more quickly than under normal conditions. Some older children found a sense of agency in their new roles. Eleven years old at the time, Ester Spagatner explained, "I felt I was becoming more mature. It was hard for me, but I understood the expectations and wanted to meet them."[29] While her parents were at work, Ester took care of her three-year-old sister, Lusia. In a number of homes, as we shall see later, children went a step further by becoming the breadwinners for their families as smugglers operating in and out of the ghetto and as clandestine workers inside the ghetto. With time, children's roles shifted family dynamics and often undermined parents' authority as providers.

Although children became more independent in a short span of time by performing roles traditionally relegated to adults, they continued to rely on their parents. Parental status on the ghetto social ladder also influenced a family's, and thus a child's, well-being. Some children acquired certain advantages by virtue of belonging to an esteemed family. The siblings Ryszard and Niusia Horowitz and their cousin Alexander Rosner were part of a renowned family of musicians. As local celebrities, the family enjoyed many contacts, which proved helpful in securing the temporary protection of its youngest members.[30] Other children were afforded a degree of advantage thanks to the "privileged" positions of their fathers, brothers, and uncles who worked in the Jewish administrative and enforcement echelons. Because of their roles and connection to the Germans, both the Jewish policemen and the Jewish Council members wielded some influence and possessed a degree of immunity, albeit temporary, for themselves and their immediate family members.

Acquiring a new social status affected family dynamics. Sometimes, the balance at home changed when fathers assumed greater leverage than they enjoyed before. Previously dependent on money from his in-laws, Dawid Szlang joined the Jewish ghetto administration and could therefore contribute financially to the household. His position and conduct, however, created tensions in the house, something new for his seven-year-old son, Norbert. Norbert's father owned a bar and restaurant in the ghetto, which served as a meeting point for German guards, and as a place where smuggling of food, people, and money was conducted. Norbert recalled that his father's status affected the decision to stay in the ghetto as a family instead of seeking shelter outside its walls.[31] In other cases, life in the ghetto magnified already existing familial tensions. Janina Fischler recalled the attitude of her father, an eternal bon vivant. He continued to spend his days in restaurants and cafés in the ghetto and lived mostly at his mother's relatively spacious apartment, rather than the crowded and dingy flat his own family of five occupied. He continued to avoid responsibility for his family, thereby forcing Janina to assume the role of breadwinner.[32]

These two examples suggest that despite the common idealized perception that all families continued as a unit in the ghetto, in reality the new pressures exacerbated extant tensions and led to familial disintegration. In some cases, ghetto conditions introduced ruptures that had not existed before. A number of families cracked. Faced with extreme life circumstances, some family members focused on their own survival, others were consumed by helplessness, and a few took advantage of their newly acquired status. Families fractured physically, too, when their members drifted apart once inside the ghetto or were separated because of the ghetto. Child survivors rarely delved into such issues in their accounts. Temporal distance from the events, the desire to remember their relatives in a positive light, and a series of tragic experiences that families suffered overshadowed domestic complexities.

If the myth of the united, mutually supportive Jewish family does not hold true in all instances, familial ties remained and served a key function. By staying together and implementing strategies aimed at adapting to the new living conditions, families fostered hope and oriented children toward the future. This expressed itself in transmitting social, educational, and religious values to children, as well as in ensuring their basic needs.

———

"I never remember being hungry. I think maybe towards the end things got bad, but I never really experienced hunger in the ghetto."[33] Tosia Sztahl's words resonate with the experiences of many child survivors of the Kraków ghetto. Images of starving and begging children presented in photographs and accounts have dominated the way we see child life in ghettos. Available sources do not document a similar situation in Kraków. Many children had a poor diet of potatoes, cabbage, and bread, supplemented occasionally with sausage, eggs, and milk. But they did not starve. This was due to the relatively small size of the ghetto population and a fairly well-developed social welfare system. Stores on the Aryan side and nearby farms where Jews bought or bartered for food, the laxity of guards at the ghetto gates, and outside work assignments facilitated smuggling of food into the ghetto, too.

Networks created by families, friends, and strangers assumed importance in procuring food. As Niusia Horowitz recalled, "People helped one another. In the ghetto there were still many such organized families that somehow managed. One could still buy bread and milk and a piece of margarine and some marmalade. In the ghetto people did not starve yet that much; they somehow helped each other." She pointed to the ability of individual Jews to exit the ghetto. "Besides, there was also outside help. People exited the ghetto, left with permits, one could always organize, steal, arrange for something."[34]

Although the Germans sealed the ghetto to sever contact between Jews and non-Jewish Krakovians, the separation was incomplete. This, in turn, opened a possibility for some Jews to obtain necessities. Polish utility workers entered the ghetto regularly, as did non-Jews who ran businesses there, such as the staff of Under the Eagle pharmacy and the employees of Spektrum glass factory, all of whom provided aid to Jews. Select non-Jews were allowed to enter the ghetto with a permit. Until 13 April 1941, Jews could leave the ghetto relatively freely. After that date, Jews had to secure a permit from the city commandant, which was granted only upon presentation of a delousing certificate, a procedure conducted once a month. Jews over the age of fourteen in outside work details held an especially advantageous position. Initially, Jewish workers were permitted to bring in goods in a quantity the Germans deemed sufficient for individual use only. Jews bartered or bought food on the Aryan side and smuggled it into the ghetto for their families to eat or to sell. Some of those bartering items derived from packages that Jews could receive from their relatives abroad until July 1942.[35] In April 1942, the city commandant's decree reminded Jews to reach their work sites using the shortest route possible. The Germans were aware that Jews separated from columns to run errands.

Such semilegal efforts to obtain food were indispensable for a steady in-flow of goods, as were the horse-drawn vehicles and garbage trucks loaded with food that, for a high price, entered the gates secretly at night. Both the individual activities and large-scale smuggling supplemented the meager official rations of one hundred grams of bread per day and two hundred grams of sugar and fat per person each month.[36] Jews paid one złoty per ration card, which the building superintendent collected and deposited at the Jewish Council's cash registrar. A ration card indicated the type of foodstuff one was eligible for. A letter marked every card to designate the store in the ghetto from which one was allowed to obtain such products. While child survivors recalled the relative availability of food during the beginning stages of the ghetto, they also remembered the supply diminishing toward the end. As time went on, the Germans tightened control of ghetto borders. They put an end to outside labor details in October 1942, and they threatened the Polish and Jewish populations with ever more severe punishments for transgressions.

Child survivors retained vivid memories about events and emotions associated with food. Mieczysław Arzewski's neighbors on the other side of the room partition made a living by baking and selling pastries. It was hard for him, a boy of about four, to savor the smell of these delicacies without being able to consume them. This situation created discord among families in the room (and in the apartment). "They couldn't give us food. I remember that. That was a big issue."[37] Some children were simply unable to control their hunger. They remembered those instances. Still others harbored more positive reminiscences. Six-year-old Anna Blatt's kosher-abiding family survived on a can of sardines eaten every other day. They nevertheless spoiled Anna with food considered extravagant in those circumstances. Perhaps Anna's parents felt that she, as a very young child, could be exempt from the dietary restrictions of Kashrut; she was growing up and needed nutrition. "The most wonderful memory I have of food was that there was a little bakery, and my mother took me there a few times, and for [a] considerable amount of money bought me a napoleon," Anna recalled fondly in an account she gave many years after the events.[38] During one such outing with her mother, Anna received a pastry as a "gift" right before she left the ghetto to hide on the Aryan side, and she accepted the treat without reservations.

Other children had qualms, seeing themselves as unimportant and an extra mouth to feed. As Chana Kleiner, who was between five and seven in the ghetto, put it, "I was a parasite. I was a child."[39] Perhaps this was Chana's assessment many years after the events, when she understood the lengths her parents had gone to in order to provide food. Possibly this was the way she felt about herself then. Even amid strangers, with whom children and their families shared rooms, children felt culpable for the mere act of biting into food, especially when provisions became scanter and the children fewer. Some acquired a manner of consuming food so as to not offend those around them—invisible and furtive.

Children continued to rely on adults for food, and many parents and relatives continued to try their best to provide it and to ensure the youngsters consumed it, just as they had in prewar times. Doing so, adults created a semblance of normal life. Felicia Vogler's family did not lack food, but Felicia, who was about seven at the time, admitted to having been a poor eater. "I remember how eggs, which must have come at such a high cost, were given to me, and I used to not want to eat them, and my grandmother would sit for hours trying to coax me to eat them, to keep me in good health." Felicia's grandmother acted as she would have under normal circumstances—she cajoled her granddaughter to eat. Felicia viewed this as her family's way to provide her with the comfort and freedom to be the child that she was. "So I was still their little princess, even in the ghetto."[40] Other children did not have the luxury of being treated that way. Some procured food to satisfy their hunger and brought it to their families. Hoping to find potato peels or bread, Marek Goldfinger, who was about six at the time, roamed the streets until he reached a bakery. He watched as people brought breads and cakes for baking and received stubs, and noted that after they received the product, the customers dropped their vouchers on the floor.[41] Marek, as did other children like him, exhibited courage, ingenuity, cleverness, and cunning. "I managed to get behind the queue and pick up one of those tickets. Then I joined the queue and I gave him [the baker] the ticket." Marek persuaded the baker that he had ordered a cheesecake. "Effectively, I stole it from someone, but it was the situation we were in."[42] *Stealing* was a relative term in the ghetto. Marek was simply acquiring food for his family to survive.

Children had to learn to cope with the challenges of their circumstances. To that end, they took the initiative to occupy themselves all day. Few recall specifically how they dealt with the situation, as their daily routine seemed trivial to them at the time. Still, there is a consensus among child survivors that boredom prevailed. "Most of the time there was nothing to do," Aneta Baral explained.[43] With little available to keep children occupied during the day and parents hesitant to allow them to go outdoors because they feared it was too risky, children were left alone while adults went to work. Not every parent had the advantage of leaving the child with another grown-up, with an older child, or in a care institution. Parents instructed their children to abide by their rules (do not go outside; do not go near the ghetto boundary; do not talk to strangers; do not start fights with other children). Most children obeyed; they did not want to be a burden, and they had a sense of obligation to be obedient. They understood the dangers.

Children had few options for passing their time in the ghetto. Nevertheless, their age-appropriate curiosity helped them cope. They directed their energies to writing, reading, and drawing. *Gazeta Żydowska* recognized the importance of adding a "children's corner," titled "Our Paper" (Nasza Gazetka). The aim of the section was to contribute to the mental development of the Jewish child and to prepare children for a future life. An editor explained, "We want ["Our Paper"] to be your real friend and for it to smile at you—in spite of all worries—with your own eyes; the eyes of children who do not want and do not like to be upset!"[44] The segment generated an enthusiastic response. Youngsters composed poems and stories, and editors offered advice and encouragement. Older children could engage in mental activities, such as crosswords and riddles. Younger children occupied themselves with anything they could find. Marcel Baral hunted for pigeons, which allowed him to forget about his life in confinement, at least for a while.[45] Other children used their imagination, looking through a window to observe people and life in the ghetto from a safe distance. Still others looked through the window all day waiting for their parents to return. This was not an action-based coping tool, but it worked on an emotional level, providing distraction from the complex and cruel reality outside the window.

Boys and girls who were allowed to remain outdoors during the day, forced by circumstances to spend the days in the street, or did so against their parents' warnings joined other children and formed groups. Jerzy Hoffman, who was between seven and nine in the ghetto, explained the purpose of such activity. "Roaming during the war is equal to looking for food. You're on the roam because you're hungry, you're looking for something or you're hiding from somebody, or you're running away from something." Games assumed a similar purpose. "Yes, you play games, but the games became games for self-support. If you're able to steal something, yes it's a game, but if you can use it—that's good."[46] Jerzy spent his days avoiding the Germans and the Jewish police. The survival tools that he gained served as a defense mechanism. His daily routine, especially after his parents had been deported, was to ensure self-preservation by finding a place to sleep and food to eat.[47] In roaming groups, children such as he received support from their peers and learned survival skills through the games they played, which became their response to daily life.

The depressing ghetto environment led some children to look for alternate places to spend time. Before the district was sealed, a number of children ventured to Krzemionki hills (which became part of the ghetto in April 1941), with its flint-stone mines. As the ghetto had few green areas, Krzemionki became a cherished meeting place where children sought entertainment, and where they felt free. As former mine dump, it was hardly appropriate as a recreational space. But the Jewish Council made efforts to beautify it, describing it as "the only place where one can relax and enjoy the air away from the dusty streets."[48] Yet, left without supervision during the day, children sometimes were exposed to danger. Twelve-year-old Adolf Teichman, for example, died after falling fifteen meters down the hill. *Gazeta Żydowska* urged parents to consider that accident a warning not to leave their children without supervision and to forbid them to play on Krzemionki hills.[49]

The Jewish Council looked askance at children's presence in Krzemionki. To the ghetto administration, children were a nuisance in the public sphere. One article in *Gazeta Żydowska* deplored that "unfortunately, some people, especially children, do not appreciate the useful green areas, and, crossing diagonally, they trample on the green areas and destroy the grass."[50] The Jewish Council appealed to ghetto inhabitants to respect every inch of green. Although the council and *Gazeta Żydowska* condemned the deleterious aspects of children's use of public spaces, their concern might have had more to do with protecting children against accidents and the Germans' capricious violence. To the Jewish Council, the children were better protected if invisible from the public view, tucked away in their homes, or entrusted into the care of institutions created specifically for them.

———

Eager for friendships, children roamed in groups and spent their time in the few available recreational spaces with their peers. This established a sense of belonging and companionship. At the same time, children were cautious about becoming emotionally attached because they never knew if, when, and how they might lose a friend. Children bound to their homes had few opportunities to find companions. To many, it seemed as if everyone was preoccupied and had no time or desire for socializing.

For those lucky enough to have a friend, the relationship helped to maintain a shred of normality. The structure of friendship itself served to overcome difficulties by offering the support of another human being. Some children had friends in the ghetto from their former lives; others made new friends with similar life experiences and common interests. Choosing a friend either was a product of coincidence—children whose families were neighbors or shared living space became friends—or resulted from a planned search. With their friends, children organized get-togethers and established friendship rituals. They sought to assure each other that everything would be fine. Francis Immergluck, then between twelve and fourteen, recalled, "We used to fantasize with the girls my own age. We used to fantasize when we grew up what we would do and where we would go." Dreaming and the idea of togetherness offered Francis and her friends a temporary refuge from reality and a way to look toward the future. "As a child I knew it wasn't normal, but I couldn't understand. I thought it would be fun to be together, with some of your friends, and children."[51]

With adults preoccupied, friends often became a key source of information for children in the ghetto. This alleviated some of the stress of loneliness and inadequate attention. Raymond (Roman) Liebling, who was about ten at that time, had a twelve-year-old friend named Paweł. "Paweł was my joy—my first companion and compensation for an increasingly constricted and fear-ridden existence," Roman recalled decades later. "This close relationship with someone outside my family circle was an educational as well as an emotional awakening."[52] Paweł was sort of a life guide for Roman. He explained how objects of daily use were constructed and how they worked. Paweł was deported in one of the German actions in the ghetto. This was a great loss for Roman. But he soon befriended a younger boy, Stefan, the son of the family with whom Roman's family shared a room. "We played together nearly all the time, and he became to me what I had been to Paweł: the eager recipient of all sorts of information."[53] Mindful of the advantages offered by the knowledge of an older child, Roman transmitted to Stefan what he had learned from Paweł. This proved beneficial for both children. Roman felt the satisfaction of sharing his knowledge and proving his importance in his younger friend's life. And Stefan had an opportunity to receive attention and to focus on aspects of life other than ghetto conditions.

———

Play, like forming friendships, is a natural activity for children. For children in the ghetto, play was a way of creating a sphere of normality within the skewed reality of ghetto life, as well as a form of resistance against oppression.[54] Play allowed children to retain their humanity and to find balance in their lives. It served as a way to help them deal with negative experiences by turning their attention to ordinary activities.

Play, apart from being a way to spend time, was also a physical activity. Left with limited options for venting energy, children turned to ways that they had known before, and that are normal for people their age. Girls played hopscotch; boys played soccer by substituting empty cans for balls. The harsh conditions in the ghetto, combined with danger lurking in all directions, restricted their range of play. However, they persuaded their caretakers, or took the risk without their parents' approval, and devised ways to stay physically active to release the tensions they endured. Without the structure of school attendance and with so many children in a confined area, there was more time and opportunity for children to play than under normal conditions. "Children played on the streets. They had to on the streets, because the houses were crowded. We were playing," recalled Emilia Heller.[55]

Children had limited items to play with. Toys were cherished treasures, and being in possession of them bolstered a sense of normality. They established a sense of ownership for the child and, for those old enough to remember, embodied memories from pre-ghetto life. They served as a distraction from misery and allowed the child's imagination to shape the reality. In this way, the toy served as a coping tool. Survivors have fond memories of their toys. Now-adult women remember their dolls with longing and regret their loss keenly. Girls desired dolls; modeling traditional female roles, girls took care of them. Then too, girls told their dolls their secrets; the toy became a friend whose silence comforted. During actions in the ghetto and in the course of evictions from their living quarters, the girls' dolls were mislaid or lost. Losing a doll shook the girl's sense of stability and continuity. The child was deprived of a confidant, toy, souvenir, and reminder of the life that once was.

In some cases, parents ingeniously "organized" toys for their children. Aware of the importance their daughters attached to dolls, mothers sewed them out of rags. Parents smuggled out scraps from work or gave their children items of daily use to play with. Children invented toys and games with whatever they could find or searched through possessions abandoned by people who had been deported. Playthings helped children retain a degree of emotional stability in the maelstrom of ghetto conditions.

Children sought to re-create normality. "Despite the limited freedom, our lives were not dominated by fear," is how Roman Liebling felt then. "During that time, I had moments of fun: I was sledge-riding, exchanged post stamps, ran with children my age."[56] These activities helped children manage in the only way they knew—to behave like children do in times of peace. Fascinated by cinema, Roman approached the barbed wire to sneak a peek at the German propaganda films screened for gentile Poles on Podgórze Square. During the film breaks, he saw Nazi mantras flashed on the screen: "Jews = Lice = Typhus." Marian Kwaśniewski's mother admonished him for going near the ghetto gate but, as Marian, who was around six years old then, explained decades later, the movies were his sole source of joy as a child.[57] In the absence of any entertainment venues, movies—with their dose of mystery and fantasy—offered a temporary escape from reality and contact with the outside world.

While older children dealt with the new situation themselves, the youngest had to rely on the resources and abilities of older children and adults to organize daily activities and keep them occupied. Children's corners helped youngsters cope and played an essential role in their intellectual and social lives. These were daytime meetings held outside, in courtyards, or inside buildings. Some teenagers assumed the task of organizing such meeting places. Seventeen-year-old Rela Weinfeld and her friend Ester opened a children's corner (dzieciniec) when one child educator, known as Mrs. Maria, died and the corner she ran ceased to exist. Essentially, the girls set up a shelter for abandoned children. In order to learn educational methods, especially those of the German educator Friedrich Wilhelm Froebel, they took classes from teachers.[58] Froebel's educational method for children emphasized the value of play in young people's development and promoted play in places designed specifically for children. This reliance on Froebel's approach highlights the value that experienced educators and passionate amateurs placed on providing the best possible care for children. In doing so, their charges were allowed to exercise their status as children.

———

Wanting their children to continue life as usual, a number of parents tried to create the illusion of normality, which, they hoped, would maintain the children's sanity. Many parents showered their children with love, sheltering them from much of the tragedy occurring around them on a daily basis. Some parents, for example, continued to celebrate their children's birthdays, a ritual from the pre-ghetto time. Celebrating lifecycle events honored children as individuals and provided a future-oriented routine. It afforded an opportunity to socialize with family and friends in a joyful atmosphere and offered a way to teach children the modes of behavior that adults believed children would need when they resumed life after the war. "We were waiting for the war to finish and go back to our normal lives," Rena Hocherman recalled. "And while that was happening, they [parents] wanted us to have as normal [a] life as possible."[59]

One way of normalizing the situation was to provide educational opportunities for young people. Elsa Biller, who was about ten years old in the ghetto, spoke decades later about the importance her family attached to her schooling. "They were living with hope that the war would end and how would I ever amount to anything. And that [education] was very important."[60] Continuing

their education in the ghetto established a ritual and gave the children something to look forward to.

At first, education efforts in the ghetto were disorganized and based on individual initiatives. Before the June 1942 action, Janina Fischler belonged to a
children's library led by a middle-aged couple. After that first action, the library
closed, but, eager to learn and to escape the reality, Janina tracked down the
librarians and continued to borrow books.[61] Halina Nelken, then a teenager,
undertook to educate an eight-year-old girl, Rita, and other children under her
care. In her diary (lost during the war but re-created later), Halina lamented the
lack of educational tools. She took action. "So I dragged out my own trusty, worn
volume of children's stories, typed out several poems, and drew and colored some
amusing illustrations to give to Rita and also to the other children in our house."[62]

Shortage of reading materials made books prized items, although they were
not always age-appropriate. Stella Müller, then about eleven, learned on her own
and for a short time from older girls who gave her reading and writing assignments. It was only a temporary solution to the lack of formal schooling. In the
end "nothing came out of reading and writing, nobody had the time nor the
mind to take care of that." Hungry for knowledge and eager to pass time, Stella
reached for books that her parents considered too mature for her age. "I began
my reading from the so-called prohibited books. My education progressed in
this way, but not in the direction that my parents would have wanted it."[63]

The issue of schooling sparked a lively debate in the pages of Gazeta Żydowska.
The discussion referred primarily to the situation in Warsaw, but its echoes rever-
berated throughout the General Government. In the editorials, Jewish educators focused on the language of instruction: Hebrew or Yiddish. Polish was
rejected outright. In prewar Kraków, the majority of Jewish children learned in
state schools in the Polish language.[64] Even in the Hebrew School, students
learned in both Hebrew and Polish. The author of one of the newspaper articles,
however, agonized over what he believed a "tragedy" for such children: the
detachment from Jewish culture, worldview, and spirit. This commentator considered Hebrew to be the language of spiritual treasure, durability, unity, and
the rebirth of Israel. Yiddish, on the other hand, signified the language of literature and the masses. The writer urged readers in all of the General Government,
including those in the Kraków ghetto, to educate their children in Hebrew and
Yiddish in an effort to think forward; to cultivate a knowledgeable future generation and prepare it for emigration after the war. Education led to salvaging
the Jewish people and ensuring a Jewish future. It would imbue a strong Jewish
identity in children even after they had endured the emotional, cultural, and
spiritual degradation of their current life in the ghetto. According to the author's
reasoning, "Polishness" was never theirs. If young people ever felt Polish, they
should have lost that sense already.[65]

While language and identity formation dominated the discussion about education in the early stages of the Kraków ghetto's existence, the social aspects of schooling marked the discourse later. Articles in *Gazeta Żydowska* continued to refer to the situation in Warsaw in this matter. But these articles were read by Jews in the Kraków ghetto, too. Parents understood the value in educating their children, and they enabled mainly private schooling for them. The need for children to remain inconspicuous might have been one reason for facilitating such endeavors.

Gazeta Żydowska writers, however, admonished parents for displaying their supposed indifference toward their children's future by either keeping them at home or sending them to work instead of to an organized school. One commentator reminded parents that Jews had always respected education, even in the most difficult of times, and explained that such an attitude determined Jewishness and Judaism. That same author diagnosed parents' unwillingness to ensure their children's education as resulting from misunderstanding and ignorance. "Therefore the masses ought to be informed about the importance of education for children; about its meaning for the individual and the general." Citing efforts to create schools in ghettos, the author noted, "Mass enrollment of children in schools—this is the task that the community is currently faced with."[66]

It was no longer up to the parents to decide about their children's life track; in the ghetto, education became a community obligation. As the author of another article in *Gazeta Żydowska* proclaimed, "A school cannot be replaced. Even the best private education cannot equip the child with what is needed." According to this author, the outcomes of education, discipline and solidarity, constituted the pillars of society. The writer praised the work of schools in the Warsaw ghetto, which managed to rescue abandoned and orphaned children. The school thus acquired a new role, becoming a refuge from persecution, loneliness, and rejection. In the Kraków ghetto, however, Jews focused on maintaining an illusion of the children's absence. Jews did not want to expose young people to the Germans more than necessary. A school was considered too visible a place in which youngsters would gather. Still, Kraków Jews struggled with the need both to create educational opportunities for their youngest members and to provide safety. The author of the *Gazeta Żydowska* article called for adults to situate all young people in schools to keep them off the streets (and thus safeguard them from arbitrary violence), develop positive behaviors, and demonstrate their usefulness to the Germans by teaching them skills in preparation for work. "No sacrifice is too great on behalf of any community to achieve this aim." Referring to a principle on which the community had agreed, the author went on, "Besides, care for young people is one of the branches of social welfare. The old truth holds that the community that best helps itself takes best care of its youth."[67]

According to *Gazeta Żydowska*, Jewish activists and educators tried to continue the work and legacy of the Chaim Hilfstein Hebrew School in the ghetto. Between 18 and 20 July 1941, an exhibit showcased the work of the school's pupils during the 1940–1941 school year. The entrance fee served as a donation to the Jewish Social Self-Help, so the event assumed a charitable function. A festive close to the school year took place on 15 July 1941, complete with a requiem in memory of Theodor Herzl and Chaim Nachman Bialik. The commemoration honored the school's Zionist orientation and encouraged young ghetto residents to persevere to ensure that Jewish life would endure and overcome the current challenge to its existence, as it had so many times in the history of the Jewish people. Final report cards were distributed to students three days later, on 18 July 1941 (although the exhibit continued to run for another two days).[68] Then the school closed, ending formal education in the Kraków ghetto.

Recognizing the need to educate the youngest ghetto inhabitants, the Kraków Jewish Council pledged a large building on Limanowskiego Street for use as a school in April 1941. This plan never materialized because of high costs and legal hurdles. News from Warsaw described issues educators and activists faced. In the Warsaw ghetto alone, the cost of sustaining forty thousand children in schools was estimated at 250,000 złoty a month, meaning 6.25 złoty per child.[69] Such a sum seemed beyond reach for the leadership in the Kraków ghetto when other problems, such as poverty, housing, and hunger, loomed large. In order to open a school, the Jewish Council would have had to clear a number of administrative barriers: form an education department and a school council, register teachers and students, develop a curriculum, and organize teaching supplies. A German law of 3 May 1942 reiterated the Jewish Council's responsibility for creating and sustaining schools in the ghetto—with the Germans' approval—in case the council wished to offer such. The Germans would still regulate all aspects of schooling. They also continued to control private lessons, specifying the tutors' skills and granting them permission for one year that could be revoked at any time.[70]

The absence of an organized school system and the obstacles posed by the Germans were circumvented by the creation of a clandestine education network. Adults from a range of social, cultural, and professional backgrounds could no longer pursue their work in the ghetto. Some in this group were scholars and teachers; others had the ability and passion to educate and transfer their skills to the ghetto's young people. Educators taught a wide array of classes and recognized the importance of developing useful professional skills for children. Although there were children who did not have any schooling, some attended informal learning groups, others were fortunate enough to have their own tutors, and still others studied independently. In general, language study (Polish, German, Hebrew, and English) was popular. For many children, language and literacy were combined with learning other subjects, such as math, Jewish history, music, and dance. Francis Immergluck learned ballet from a dancer and actress. "It felt good; it felt that pretty soon I'd be able to perform in the free world. I was learning. I was looking to a bright future."[71] Although illegal and punishable, secret schooling allowed children to receive basic education, kept them occupied, and instilled hope that they had a future.

Education initiatives embodied resistance in the ghetto. The spiritual and material mobilization needed to carry on education programs was a form of active defiance of physical and cultural disappearance.[72] Adults refused to accept German policy. They planted hope and a mission in the children. The youth would be the natural bearers of Jewish heritage and the Jewish people. But first, adults in the ghetto needed to prepare children for the task. They strove to ensure that their children received the education possible in those circumstances. The knowledge children acquired would give them the tools to exercise resilience both during the war and in its aftermath. Children assumed an active role in those endeavors. Education granted a much-needed respite from the harsh ghetto life. Oriented toward instilling knowledge and skills that children could use in practice, education also sparked their imagination about the places they had yet to see, the extent of information they would still acquire, and the individuals they would become. Education thus allowed children to dream about a life that awaited them. Therein lay the refusal to succumb to the plans that the Germans held for Jews.

———

Many children received Jewish religious education in the ghetto in addition to pursuing secular studies. A number of children came from observant Jewish homes. Others had received some religious education before being forced into the ghetto. No matter where the family fell on the religious observance spectrum, introducing concepts of Judaism or Jewish studies often enabled children to look for answers to their current predicament in religion and Jewish history, and to help them cope with ghetto life.

Many parents wanted either to introduce their children to Judaism in the ghetto or to continue the children's religious education there. Some did so for religious reasons, others to instruct children about their cultural or ethnic identity and to foster a sense of pride in it. Lazar Panzer, a prewar director of Yesodei Hatorah, an Orthodox school in Kraków, together with Rabbi Schein Klingberg, organized clandestine religious education in the Kraków ghetto for boys aged five to eighteen.[73] Some boys studied either in a religious school (cheder) or with a rabbinical student in preparation for bar mitzvah. Maurycy Sternlicht was one such boy who celebrated this major religious lifecycle event in the ghetto. Maurycy was not fully aware of its significance at the time. He described his bar mitzvah: "It was something my mother wanted me to do. It was important for her. And I did it."[74]

The Germans did not approve religious education in the ghetto. Nor, with few exceptions, did they allow for Jews' religious observance.[75] Nevertheless, both children and adults contravened German policy. Children attended religious services, prayed, and observed Shabbat and at least some holidays. "We would pray. We were not allowed to have *shuls* [synagogues] and temples, but we would pray in apartments and get together without this," Roman Ferber, who was between eight and nine then, recalled.[76] Celebration of Passover and the High Holy Days remain especially clear in child survivors' memories. Perhaps because of the specific rituals associated with each holiday and the message each carried, now-adult children remember them clearly. Passover focuses on the move from slavery to freedom; and the High Holy Days center on atonement and renewal. For children from Orthodox homes, religious activities maintained a familiar structure when everything else seemed devalued and changed. For these children, religion offered continuity and stability.

Performing religious rituals clandestinely, children staged resistance, knowingly or not, against their persecutors. They defied German laws against prayer and religious observance in the ghetto. And they continued to embrace their own humanity. In celebrating holidays and marking lifecycle events with their children, adults imparted values to their children that fostered a sense of belonging to family, community, and religion.

Children who came from either less observant homes or assimilated families, or those who had limited exposure to religion before entering the ghetto, harbored different attitudes toward the practice of Judaism in the ghetto. Not all children were at ease with their Jewish identity. Having seen and experienced the conditions in the ghetto, and the atrocities committed by the Germans, some children began to question their religion, or the religion because of which they were isolated from the rest of society, and the religion that, in the children's eyes, caused their persecution.

Some children found solace in the Catholic religion of their prewar caretakers. Anita Kempler, who was about six years old, and her younger brother Bernhard had received Catholic medals from their prewar nanny. Anita believed that Catholicism, not Judaism, offered protection and that the medals made them less Jewish.[77] Other children showed contempt for Jewish holidays, and observance in general. During Passover, when Jews are forbidden to eat leavened food, Stella Müller mocked observant Jews by ostentatiously holding and pretending to devour a slice of bread. She despised the Yiddish that she heard on the streets, and did not understand and was annoyed by Orthodox boys who exhibited their religious identity by keeping their side-locks.[78] Her behavior might have been a child's rebellion against people who insisted on practicing the religion that, in her understanding, led to their tragedy. Distancing herself from the religion she perceived as having contributed to her isolation from the larger society and prompted persecution might have served as a mechanism that helped her (and others like her) cope with the new situation through self-deception; they persuaded themselves that they really did not deserve to be there. They were not like those religious people.

———

Children who were old enough to experience life before being forced into the ghetto, or who had some memories of that time, quickly realized the differences in and degree of deterioration between their pre-ghetto and ghetto lives. While most children soon understood that the ghetto signified an end to their childhood, they also pursued their (stringently restricted) agency to create a niche for themselves amid the dire conditions created by the Germans. Adults assisted them in their endeavors. In doing so, many children managed to retain their humanity and exercise resilience. Despite the issues affecting Jews' lives, and often precisely because of them, children in the Kraków ghetto engaged in activities, individually and collectively, that were crucial for their own survival and for the well-being of their families. As we shall see next, many children assumed responsibilities in the ghetto that reached far beyond expectations.

CHAPTER 3

Clandestine Activities

Janka Warszawska engaged in black-market trade when she was about twelve years old, meandering between Kraków, her hometown, and the nearby towns of Brzesko (or Bochnia), where she stayed, and Wieliczka, where the rest of her large family lived. Before the liquidation action on 28 August 1942 in the Wieliczka ghetto the Warszawski family had dispersed and eventually reunited in Kraków by sneaking into its ghetto. Once there, Janka continued her covert activities, exiting and reentering the ghetto, smuggling in various items and food and running errands on the Aryan side of the city for her own family and for other Jews.

Submitting her postwar testimony at age sixteen, she explained, "Did I have a choice? We didn't have what to live off in the ghetto so I had to become a provider." She joined forces with her one-year-older sister, Halina. The Germans regarded slinking out and smuggling as criminal activity and, as Janka pointed out, "it was very difficult to get back into the ghetto with merchandise. We had to be very careful and watch that a policeman didn't grab us and take any merchandise. It would take weeks to recoup that which was lost."[1] With the impending German actions in the ghetto, Janka's tasks extended to smuggling out children to the Aryan side. She recalled the first time she took out a boy. "I didn't know what to do with him. Aside from that, I myself was still a child and didn't know what to do to get him to listen to me. When we got close to the fences I was so frightened that I pleaded with him not to cry. To this day I still feel the fear."[2] Janka's familiarity with the geography of Kraków, her ease with navigating outside the city, her bargaining acumen, and her connections with Poles supported her clandestine activities and helped her maintain a concealed presence.

Janka Warszawska's testimony provides a glimpse into the smuggling operations of both goods and people, and the associated dangers. More than that, her story, as this chapter illustrates, conveys how covert activities led to children's (often only temporary) survival. The German regime's policy toward Jews and the living conditions inside the Kraków ghetto meant that Jews' lives had to assume a circumspect form. Jewish children, their parents, and their caretakers realized that deception, evasion, and disobedience were tactics necessary for, but not guaranteeing, the children's existence. Children were routinely encouraged by their own families to undertake surreptitious endeavors. At other times, young people took their own initiative, unbeknownst to their parents.

Enlisting for adult work assignments, hiding inside the ghetto during German raids, sneaking in and out, smuggling food and other goods, and escaping permanently all constituted forms of illicit activities in which children engaged both passively and actively. In so doing, children resisted—consciously or unknowingly—German efforts to destroy Jewish life. Despite their young age, children who were in the position to do so refused to succumb to the deprivation of life in the ghetto. They retained their humanity by attempting to preserve their own lives, and by extending their (already constrained) efforts to help others, even at the risk of death.

Located in the Podgórze district near industrial plants, the ghetto served an important function by offering the Germans a pool of labor. The German Labor Office (Arbeitsamt) at 10 Józefińska Street registered all Jews over the age of fourteen, issued work stamps in their identification cards (*Kennkarten*), and coordinated forced labor assignments.[3] As we have seen from the previous chapter, some Jews marched in columns under German guard to work outside the ghetto. With a dose of luck and appropriate contacts, they could purchase goods on the black market on the Aryan side and smuggle them into the ghetto for their families to use or to sell.[4] Work outside the ghetto also offered opportunities to establish contacts with non-Jews and to maintain communication with relatives and friends on the Aryan side; all done in secrecy from the Germans. Other laborers toiled in German-owned factories inside the ghetto, such as Oskar Schindler's Emalia and Julius Madritsch's uniform-sewing company.[5]

Work status served an essential purpose, starting with resettlement into the ghetto, when the Germans allowed only Jews with work permits to live there. Thus, the Kraków ghetto was restricted in size, population, and the type of Jews who entered it. The Germans treated work unrelated to their war effort as inconsequential. Therefore, there was a difference between work that warranted an official stamp in a Jew's identity card and employment to earn a livelihood. By fulfilling work assignments, Jews proved their usefulness to the Germans. In the case of Kraków, that factor carried weight during selections and deportations. Bernard Offen, who was between twelve and fourteen when he lived in the ghetto, explained: "Lots of people believed at that point in time, if you have a job, make yourself useful for the Germans, that they would not deport you. And that was true to some extent; in the beginning."[6] A number of adults took the initiative to include their underage children in the ghetto labor pool, despite the illegality of such procedures. They hoped that an official proof of work would shield their children. This was no easy task; it involved forming and using connections with Jewish clerks in the ghetto, approaching appropriate German officials, and possessing the money or valuables to bribe them.

One method of entering children on the official work registry involved falsifying their birth certificates. Janina Ast's mother obtained a forged document for her daughter by bribing an official in the ghetto's Jewish administration. Janina spoke about that experience many years after the events. "I was eleven, looked like I was going on five, and was passing for a sixteen-year-old."[7] Another practice consisted of making children look older than they actually were. For girls this involved changing their hairstyle, applying makeup, and wearing adult clothing.

Children who worked—and they were very much in the minority—did so in a wide range of jobs, both in German-run factories and in Jewish workshops.[8] Celina Karp, around ten years old at the time, recalled, "For a while I worked in the ghetto at a paper cooperative. They only employed children really; licking envelopes, making envelopes."[9] Luiza Grüner, who was about eight years old, got a job in the same workshop as Celina. Apparently, the deception techniques were successful inasmuch as children often failed to recognize the presence of other workers their own age. Even fifty years after the war, Luiza still believed she was one of only two children employed in the workshop: "I think there was another child, and I. We were the only children."[10] In fact, more children below the age of fourteen worked in the paper workshop (*Papiergemeinschaft*). Often, work stints were short. Celina, before her parents secured a post for her as a seamstress at the Madritsch factory, worked as a brush maker. She recalled what her job entailed: "Sticking bristles into brushes and pulling it with a wire."[11] Maurycy Sternlicht, who also performed such work as a twelve-year-old boy, explained the task in detail: "I had to drill the wood on a drill press. I had to take a little bit of pig's bristle, take a piece of wire, and twist it around the center of the bristles and then pull that through the hole that I had drilled; the bristles would fall and form one; then trim and cut that. I was making brushes."[12]

Forced labor of all types was dangerous for children. Their age, exhaustion, and stress made children prone to injuries in the workplace. The benefits associated with their work capability category, however, often outweighed the disadvantages and risks. Because of their status as laborers, children received food rations. In this way, children helped contribute to their family's well-being. Official work assignments also could offer protection against deportation.

———

Misleading through age distortion and appearance camouflage allowed some children to lead furtive—yet open—lives in the ghetto as working adults. These methods of safeguarding children from deportation began to be pursued either immediately before or during the first major German action in the ghetto. Such efforts intensified before the second raid and the final dissolution of the ghetto. Selections and deportations defined children's existence in the ghetto and were etched into their memories. As Tosia Sztahl, who was between seven and eight years old at the time, recalled, "The only thing that I seem to remember are the deportation days. And they were pretty bad; a lot of crying, a lot of screaming, a lot of mothers trying to protect their children. That was quite tragic."[13]

The first action in the Kraków ghetto confirmed the link between labor and permission to remain in the ghetto for many Jews. On 29 May 1942, the Germans surrounded the ghetto and ordered everyone to line up at the Jewish Social Self-Help building at 18 Józefińska Street.[14] Connections and bribes, as well as randomness and luck, played a role in the selections. Only those who worked in German factories and employees of the Jewish Community and Jewish welfare institutions (and their immediate families) automatically received work stamps. Those Jews who were not granted work stamps by 31 May received an order to appear on Plac Zgody, which served as a collection square. Both the German special police (*Sonderdienst*) and the Jewish police inside the ghetto combed apartments in search of Jews who did not have official approval to remain in the ghetto. Torn out of their apartments and assembled on the square in the scorching summer heat, Jews were then marched in columns under German guard to the railway ramp in the Płaszów district. There they boarded cattle cars headed to the death camp in Bełżec.

Unsatisfied with the results of the human harvest in the first days of the action, the Germans pursued Jews with greater fervor. On 6 June, they ordered all Jews to appear once again at the Jewish Social Self-Help office with their identity cards and proof of employment in hand. An additional document, a blue card (*Blauschein*), authorized select Jews to remain in the ghetto. The Germans directed those who did not secure such cards to a square by the Optima factory on Węgierska Street. From there, German units marched them to the ramp in Płaszów two days later. When the German forces left the ghetto on 10 June, the population had been decreased by the some seven thousand Jews deported to Bełżec and the approximately six hundred people killed inside the ghetto.[15]

Protected by their work cards, the remaining Jews in the ghetto were safe for the next four months. Then, on 27 October 1942, the commissar of the Jewish Council, Dawid Gutter, returned from a meeting with SS-Oberführer Julian Scherner, the chief of Jewish affairs in Kraków District.[16] The Jewish Council verbally notified the ghetto inhabitants of the order to appear on 28 October at the council's building together with their work details.[17] Rumors about another possible German action spread quickly. German units surrounded the ghetto that evening. Some Jews attempted to take their children with them to the registration site, a plan quickly thwarted by German officers conducting thorough selections. At this point, a work stamp meant nothing in the face of the officers' capriciousness. In the course of a day, the Germans transported some 4,500 Jews to Bełżec and murdered about 600 Jews inside the ghetto. "All previous deportations were brutal and bloody, but the action of October 1942, through its barbarity, bestiality, and cruelty, exceeded everything that Jews in the ghetto had experienced until then," Aleksander Biberstein recalled.[18]

He observed, "The October deportation demonstrated most clearly that no work for the Germans affords guarantee and protection against deportation, and worse—against separation from one's family."[19] The Jews' identity cards lost validity after the raid. Jews received passes (*Judenpassen*) in the form of squares, worn on the left side of one's outer garment. The pass, bearing the stamp of the chief of SS and police, displayed letters signifying the type of performed work: W (*Wehrmacht*—for the armed forces), R (*Rüstung*—for the armament industry), and Z (*Zivil*—for civilian workers). To further mold the Kraków ghetto technically into a labor camp, the German authorities divided it on 6 December 1942 into "ghetto A" for working Jews and "ghetto B" for the unemployed. The latter also confined Jews sent there in the wake of actions throughout ghettos in Kraków District.[20] Some German factories removed their Jewish workers from ghetto A and placed them in barracks in their outposts. Jewish workers sent to build a camp in the Płaszów district were placed in the barracks there.[21]

Impatient with the gradual resettlement of Jews from the ghetto into the Plaszow camp, the German authorities ordered the transfer of all able-bodied Jews from ghetto A on 13 March 1943. A written announcement delivered by the Jewish Council appeared that morning. Events progressed quickly. The Germans surrounded the ghetto and ordered Jews to leave their children (up to the age of fourteen) in the day care center (*Tagesheim*), falsely promising that both children and belongings would be delivered to the camp the next day.[22] Realizing the impending dissolution of the ghetto, some parents desperately sought to save their children. The day the ghetto was closed, Renate Leinkram was a few months short of her fourteenth birthday. Her mother cut her braids, dressed her in adult clothes, and shoved her in the middle row of five short women so that she, a rather tall youngster, might pass as an adult worker in Plaszow.[23]

––––––

If masquerading as adults served as one survival tactic, physical concealment constituted another. And many of those who had secured hiding spots understood their advantageous position. They heard the screams and cries. They knew the fate they managed to avoid. Older children were well aware of the risks associated with hiding and, potentially, discovery. Most younger children, by contrast, did not, although they realized that it was necessary to hide.

In the ghetto, many Jews created spaces within the geographically confined and legally restricted area to hide from the Germans. Such hiding places were a temporary solution. Jews hid until the danger passed. They sometimes chose their hideouts instinctively and haphazardly, especially when faced with instant threat. Or their choice resulted from careful and purposeful preparation in antic- ipation of danger. In the latter case, Jews needed to search for and arrange the hiding place, organize food and water, and plan how to handle their hygienic and bodily needs when leaving the hideout was not an option. Regardless of whether they hid individually or as a group, their hiding endeavors required ingenuity, secrecy, and luck. Despite all the problems that hiding posed, remov- ing oneself from the Germans' immediate purview was necessary. Emilia Heller, who was between nine and eleven while in the ghetto, explained: "We hid. Because whenever we hid, we bought ourselves more chance."[24]

Hiding was a constant in the lives of a number of children in the Kraków ghetto, and finding hiding places was an endeavor in its own right. For some, their own dwellings in the ghetto served as short-term hiding places. They stayed in rooms until their parents returned from work. Then too, places throughout the apartment, and even the building itself, served as "safe" nooks in case of sud- den danger. Both adults and children identified creative and ingenious shelters: behind cupboards, inside ovens, under tables, in attics and cellars, under heaps of potatoes, or in laundry baskets. Parents instructed their children to remain silent and hide in case of commotion. Children, for their part, understood that their lives depended on staying invisible. They knew, as did Luiza Grüner, that their "job was to hide, not to be seen."[25]

While some children were fully aware of the absolute need to hide and the reality of their secret existence, others were less conscious of it. Some children lived under the illusion that they led their lives in the open, when in fact they were hidden. Henryk Haber, who was between eight and ten years old when he lived in the ghetto, claimed even half a century after the war that he had "worked as a secretary" at his uncle Artur Peckner's medical office. Henryk's perceived role as an office assistant occupied him during the long hours before he returned home with his parents. Henryk's daytime location offered protection and shel- ter. He admitted, "I don't remember any contact with other children."[26]

Although it was common for children to hide either alone or together with other children, some families hid as a unit for the duration of an action. Hiding in a group was often necessary because limited concealment opportunities existed in the ghetto. Families wanted to remain together, especially in the face of mortal danger. While hiding as a family offered emotional support, their con- centration in one place also compromised their chances of survival. Indeed, some families separated. Some parents placed their children with other Jews (rel- atives, friends, or neighbors) hiding in the ghetto. In other cases, families split because they identified multiple hiding places within their apartment building.

Some children concealed their presence during actions in previously arranged places that their parents or caretakers considered relatively safe and others that would serve as a meeting point for the family after the roundup. In the ghetto, one such "safe house" was the Jewish police building.[27] As Jerzy Aleksandrowicz, then an eight-year-old boy, explained, "It was like an island; whoever reached it was already saved."[28] When the Germans surrounded Jerzy's building during the October 1942 action, he admitted, "I didn't get scared at all because I simply didn't know what awaited us."[29] Seizing an opportune moment, Jerzy and his mother escaped. When their previously arranged hiding places failed, they rushed to the Jewish police headquarters. They were let in thanks to a prewar acquaintanceship between his father, the prominent prewar physician Julian Aleksandrowicz, and a Jewish policeman.[30]

Jerzy was lucky to have his mother beside him. Children whose parents were at work during an action were left to their own devices. The rapid and chaotic course of events often required children to think and act swiftly, not always strictly according to a plan. During the same action, Janina Ast realized something major was taking place outside. Curious and wanting to leave her small room, she ran toward the assembly place, Plac Zgody. Seeing what was happening, she went to the predesignated safe house. Unable to reach the place (where her father's friend, a Jewish policeman, lived), Janina hid in a garbage can that stood in the courtyard of the Jewish administration headquarters. She was petrified. After several hours, Janina reached the safe house and reunited with her parents.[31]

A connection to the privileged Jewish police, whose members and immediate families the Germans spared during actions, sometimes served as a lifeline for ordinary Jews, including children. Marcel Grüner began his postwar account, "This is what I remember: when we came to the ghetto, Daddy became an OD [Jüdischer Ordnungsdienst] man, a Jewish policeman." Hersz, Marcel's father, understood the personal and familial benefits that such service carried since his brother was also an OD man. Marcel alluded to the belief that Jews in the ghetto held about the OD's power, and pointed out the reality. "Different people came to Daddy asking for intercession [protekcja]." Hersz took advantage of his privileged position and permit allowing him to exit the ghetto, and took his son with him. His son served as a "safety passport" when Hersz ran errands for himself and for others, including helping his friend imprisoned in the criminal police jail on Szlak Street. There, "you paid a Ukrainian at the gate and you could pass on a package."[32]

Yet an encounter with OD men could also turn disastrous for those seeking shelter. Tasked with fulfilling German orders, the Jewish police was responsible for ferreting out people who evaded actions. During the liquidation of the ghetto, Aron Geldwert, his wife, and their three children, together with eleven others, hid in an attic. Aron described that space: "Our hiding place was walled in, invisible from the outside; we had a water supply, toilets, and foodstuffs. The bunker was about 30 meters long and 12 meters wide."[33] Among those in hiding was a brother-in-law of an OD man, Mojżesz Brodman, who came for his relative the next day and promised he would rescue the group. "However, we all felt that we were doomed, because we were convinced that Brodman will denounce us." Aron was right. The next day, as the OD men began uncovering the bricks leading to the hiding place, cries broke out; people, frantic, uttered prayers. Pushing the Jews into the courtyard, the Germans warned them that if anyone tried to escape they would be shot. Aron knew the warning was real—the day before, the Germans had caught about one hundred people in another bunker and shot them. Aron's group was taken to the Jewish police jail. Unguarded, the men eventually cut through the door with a file and freed the women and children. The Jews dispersed to various hiding places in the ghetto.[34]

Hiding in the ghetto was fraught with constant risk of exposure and death. The atmosphere inside the hiding place affected everyone. Hiding individually or with a group, children were overwhelmed by the fear of ensuing danger, the brutality of the persecutors, and possible discovery. Still, most children exhibited unusual composure for people their age. Older and more religiously observant children in particular, anticipating death, prayed. While many children did not recall precisely what transpired in their hiding places and what their exact responses were at the time, they remembered their emotions under extreme distress. Many years after the event, Roma Liebling, a very small child at the time, recalled the feelings associated with a specific incident. During one raid, when the Germans entered their apartment, her grandmother hid her under the table. The girl, numb with fear, covered her ears so as not to hear her grandmother's screams as she was taken away. After the action, she knew that something terrible had happened, but she did not ask questions and no one explained the events to her.[35] Her young age did not make her immune to trauma. Silently and privately, she wrestled with her anguish upon witnessing (hearing and seeing) her loved one violently pulled away.

The ability to remain silent and still constituted an important factor during the hiding process. Small children thus posed a risk of discovery. The ideal of solidarity sometimes crumbled in face of danger. Fearing that noise made by young children would expose everyone, some adults denied children entry to group hiding places. During the October 1942 action, thirteen-year-old Aneta Baral hid in a nook with approximately thirty people, including two babies. When they started to cry, the mothers were compelled to smother their own children.[36] Older children, such as Aneta, understood that infanticide, however horrible to witness, had nevertheless saved their own lives and the lives of other people. This was but one of the tragic scenes many children witnessed while hiding with others. They saw adults fall apart mentally, and they saw individuals commit suicide. They lived in the presence of corpses, as there was no way to dispose of bodies without detection. Still, children were expected to behave like adults.

––––––

Hiding and being hidden in the ghetto was one part of the experience of removing oneself from view in order to survive. Another factor consisted of dealing with the post-factum reality. Jews understood that eventually they would have to emerge from their hiding places and continue the clandestine life as someone who managed to evade deportation. Hiding had an impact on the psyche of those who were able to conceal themselves during raids, as well as on the attitudes of those whose loved ones were deported. During the October 1942 action, Luiza Grüner descended with four other people into a sewer located under her apartment building. They heard the screams of a woman who had just returned to her apartment to find her children gone. "We just felt horribly ashamed; in a way ashamed that we were still there," Luiza admitted. "You are almost afraid to show your face, crawl out to show them you had made it, that you had survived this particular episode." She ended with a statement that was either her postwar analysis or a thought filtered through an adult's expression at the time: "But I thought it was important that, as terrible as the event was, we were still capable of feeling guilt and we had a conscience, which the Nazis did not have."[37]

Guilt was but one of the emotions that children experienced upon emerging from their hiding places. Irena Joachimson was ten years old when she managed to evade the October 1942 deportation. She recalled her own reaction and that of people like her. "We did not believe we were alive. We touched each other and the furniture. So we are really alive? We savored the thought that we were alive; life seemed the greatest value to us." She juxtaposed her family's happiness at surviving to the sorrow of others: "There was joy at our house. And mourning around us. People returned to empty homes. One man, out of despair, bit into the wall and the floor. Until then, life buzzed in the ghetto; on that night morbid silence, broken by cries and laments."[38] To Janina Fischler, twelve years old at the time, the atmosphere in the ghetto was steeped with anxiety. She quickly understood that in an extreme situation, some people became numb and others focused only on survival. Confronted with the absence of her own family members, Janina yearned for a gesture of understanding or comfort, neither of which she received. Janina recalled, too, that while some mourned their losses, others looted abandoned belongings to obtain items they could use or sell.[39] Callousness, a survival strategy brought on by German violence, as well as daily hardships, defined Jews' lives in the ghetto.

––––––

Despite German actions, many Jews paradoxically perceived the ghetto as the safest place to live. They reasoned that it was the only area the Germans formally (and specifically) sanctioned as a "Jewish space" within the city. Children without official permits to live in the Kraków ghetto either were smuggled in or sneaked in and joined parents or relatives already there. They entered through an unguarded passageway, through a hole in the ghetto wall, through one of the ghetto gates, or under a barbed wire. The existence of those who slipped in was rarely, if ever, recorded. Hence, their entire presence in the ghetto was clandestine.

More often than not, children (sometimes together with one or both parents) sneaked into the ghetto following unsuccessful hiding efforts on the Aryan side in Kraków and elsewhere. Theirs was a reaction to the risk of exposure or the inability or unwillingness of non-Jews to hide them any longer. After hiding at her father's friend's house for one night, eleven-year-old Ida Jakubowicz and her family had nowhere to go. Mixing in with the crowd of Jews returning to the ghetto from work, Ida slipped inside. "And from the place we were running away we were now begging to go back," she recalled.[40] Seven-year-old Jacob Baral entered the ghetto in winter 1942. After spending a night at a non-Jew's house, he was dropped off in front of the ghetto the next day and wormed under the barbed wire. His mother and brother sneaked in separately. Jacob's memory about the exact course of events is vague. But, he remarked, "I do know for a fact that we had to come back because of the hostility of the population. We knew we would not survive on the outside."[41] Trying to live in an atmosphere of constant terror and amid threats of denunciation was nerve-racking for children and their families (and their aid givers). The feeling of being hounded often translated into real situations. Zygmunt Gelband, a boy between ten and twelve years old at the time, entered the ghetto after his mother was caught on the streets of Kraków.[42] He was left without alternatives for shelter on the Aryan side.

Older children quickly understood the tangible difference between life on the Aryan side and inside the ghetto. Younger children often perceived that distinction on an emotional level. Mieczysław Arzewski, about four years old when he and his family entered the Kraków ghetto in 1942, recognized a change in routine between hiding on the Aryan side and living in the ghetto. He no longer had to hide, but moved around a room divided by sheets to mark the living quarters of three families.[43] Other children, having lived in other ghettos or localities, noticed a variation in living conditions that contributed to their feeling of relative safety. Elsa Biller's mother, concerned with the well-being of her ten-year-old daughter and herself in Lwów, decided to join her relative in the Kraków ghetto. Elsa did not remember how they came to Kraków, but she interpreted a change. "I did sense a difference. And the difference was, I think, that my uncle had a little better quarters. . . . There were more people around . . . so the family was a little more extensive." As an "illegal" incomer to the ghetto, Elsa's mother initially stayed mostly indoors to avoid control on the street. For Elsa, her mother's presence offered stability. "There was a little more security for me in the ghetto than when I was in Lwów, because there I was left by myself, and my mother wasn't with me most of the time," Elsa explained.[44]

———

While some children (sometimes with their parents) sneaked into the Kraków ghetto for an indefinite period of time, others entered temporarily because it appeared a safer alternative to the smaller ghettos in the vicinity. In the Kraków ghetto they waited until raids in "their" ghettos passed and the situation calmed down. The story of ten-year-old Mendel Feichtal exemplifies this point. Hearing rumors of an action in the Brzesko ghetto, where they lived at the time (about thirty-three miles away) in spring 1942, Mendel's mother sent him with a Polish woman to the ghetto in Kraków. Once he reached the gate, Mendel bribed an OD man with around 3,000 złoty and entered with Jewish workers. He stayed there with his aunt for about two weeks, until it was rumored that the raids had stopped in Brzesko. To exit the ghetto, Mendel once again bribed both a Jewish and a Polish policeman with money and a gold watch.[45] The Polish policeman then escorted him to the railway station so that Mendel could return to Brzesko.[46]

Mendel's story demonstrates the Jews' desperate search for safe havens for their children, including in other ghettos. As a medium-size ghetto, Kraków offered opportunities to melt in with the crowd, something difficult to accomplish in the Brzesko ghetto, because of its small population and area size. Mendel's illicit entrance into the Kraków ghetto illustrates, too, that mobility was possible despite German efforts to curb it. Certainly difficult and dangerous, even life-threatening, Jewish secret—and thus illegal—entry into the ghetto was often facilitated by bribery, but also depended on timing. Mendel entered the ghetto before the October 1942 action. Following that action, German monitoring intensified and outside labor groups were abolished, thus limiting opportunities for sneaking in and out. And the Germans dissolved most ghettos in the area by the end of 1942, concentrating the remnant of Jews in select ghettos of the General Government, including Kraków.

Parents responded to the evolving situation and the danger that German actions posed as best as they could with the means available to them at that particular time. While parents sent their children into Kraków's ghetto, others sent them out of it until the situation in Kraków calmed down. Tipped off about impending actions, the father of the siblings Niusia and Ryszard Horowitz arranged for their children and their cousin Alex Rosner to be taken out of the Kraków ghetto and to the Bochnia ghetto, where their uncle served as the president of the Jewish Council. Once the danger in Kraków passed, the children were brought back.[47]

———

From the beginning of the Kraków ghetto's existence until its liquidation, many children refused to recognize the boundary dividing them from the outside—

Aryan—world. Although officially sealed, the ghetto remained porous for those children who found secret passageways. Sneaking out of the ghetto provided an opportunity for a number to experience a different life in a place where they believed they belonged. Driven by curiosity and seeking relief from the pressures of daily life, a number of children regularly slipped away.

Furtively exiting the ghetto provided both a physical and emotional escape, albeit temporary. Maurycy Sternlicht, then about thirteen years old, ventured out twice. "I just wanted to go out, see what was happening on the other side of the wall." Maurycy compared conditions inside and outside the ghetto. "I went to places I used to go and I was amazed life continued normally."[48] Of course, life did not proceed as usual. Roman Liebling, about eight years old then, was flabbergasted at the sight of what appeared to him to be ordinary life outside the ghetto. "It was like walking through a mirror and emerging on the other side—entering a different world complete with streetcars and people leading normal lives."[49] Life for non-Jews under German occupation was not and did not resemble life as usual. But it seemed so in contrast with the ghetto. However pleasant conditions on the Aryan side appeared, Roman always returned. "It wasn't until I was back inside the ghetto, after slipping through the wire again, that I felt entirely safe," he admitted.[50] Fearing denunciation by Poles, or random selection by the Germans in a roundup, children saw the ghetto as the safest place.

If some children stole away to experience life outside the confines of the ghetto briefly, others sneaked out in order to sustain themselves and their families. Once the Germans staged raids in the ghetto and abandoned outside work details after the October 1942 action, the task of smuggling shifted almost exclusively to children. Some children thus became the only link with the world outside the ghetto walls, thereby contributing to their families' well-being. They risked their lives to venture into the Aryan section of Podgórze or cross the Vistula River to obtain goods. As children, they tended to arouse less suspicion. Then too, children learned to adapt to situations in and outside the ghetto that changed instantly. They used cunning when leaving and reentering the ghetto and planning their routes, as well as ingenuity once they returned to the ghetto and parceled out their products. They exhibited courage: even if their actions (deemed illegal by the German authorities) frightened them and they were terrified of the consequences, they exercised responsibility on behalf of their families. Their role as smugglers required them to become independent, resourceful, and manipulative.

In some cases, adults pushed children to take on smuggling. Other children made independent decisions. Sometimes, prewar life and the early war years prepared children for their ghetto roles as smugglers and breadwinners. Janina Fischler learned the meaning of smuggling at an early age. Few landlords were willing to rent a flat to a family of five with unstable earnings. So her parents smuggled Janina and her youngest brother into apartments. She soon learned, too, how to care for the family, as she was responsible for grocery shopping. When her relatives were forced into the newly created ghetto, the ghettoization order did not yet apply to Janina's own family. She capitalized on her less stereotypically Jewish features and moved freely in the city, bringing the food that her family spared for her relatives in the ghetto.[51] While some children, like Janina, were motivated by expectations or experiences, others acted out of obedience to their parents. As David Zauder recalled, "At eleven, I was not concerned with anybody except my family and what my father told me to do." He viewed smuggling as his task, saying, "My job was to bring in the contraband."[52]

When recalling the reasons why children became involved in smuggling, survivor accounts point to the relevance of age. Jews under twelve were not yet required to wear the armband. The wording of the regulation opened a legal gap. On the one hand, the Germans restricted Jews' presence to the ghetto. On the other hand, the regime exempted children up to the age of twelve from being visibly identified as Jews. When exiting the ghetto, child smugglers formally broke only one law—the prohibition against existence outside the ghetto. They did not need to remember to remove the armband upon leaving the ghetto and put it back on upon reentry, or to worry about the armband accidentally falling out of their pocket or being discovered in a random search.[53] This loophole also allowed children to use public transportation, which expedited their smuggling missions and made them less susceptible to vigilant eyes.

If few remembered why they took up smuggling, many recalled whence they obtained bartering goods. In the beginning stages of the ghetto, most families still possessed some belongings. Upon resettlement to the ghetto, the Germans permitted Jews to take possessions that were not marked for requisitioning. Some Jews managed to conceal valuables that they would later barter for food (jewelry, currency, clothing, fabrics, furnishings, and silver religious objects). On the other hand, Jews who entered the ghetto "illegally" by sneaking in possessed even fewer or perhaps none at all. At times, Jews entrusted items with Poles (whom they thought they could trust), planning to retrieve valuables on a need basis. They could not anticipate that possessing bartering articles weighed on the thin line between life and death. Some Jews had already gained black-market experience in the first year of the war and knew that while money lost its value, gentiles were ready to engage in an exchange of items.

Possessing items to trade—or knowing where to obtain them—children took advantage of the guards' silent consent or sensed a moment of inattention to slip out. Janina Fischler recalled, "Slipping in and out of the Cracow Ghetto was quite simple; one did not even have to have an official pass—I never did have one. One just had to know the individual policemen. Most of them were decent, kindly men."[54] With or without the assistance of German, Polish, and Jewish policemen guarding the ghetto, a number of children waited for an opportune moment to sally forth. Young people devised intricate methods of leaving, as well as finding their way back in. They exited through sewers, holes, or a gate on their own accord or by blending in with the crowd. One maneuver involved using a passing truck or tram as a cover, which required children to time their exit and entry carefully. The Aryan-only tram passed the ghetto without stopping. Yet the opportunity to jump on and off the tram arose when the vehicle slowed upon nearing a very sharp turn, and right before it straightened out and accelerated again.

When caught by a Polish or Jewish policeman, the little "criminal" usually received a few slaps on the buttocks. If spotted by a German, however, the child could be beaten or shot on the spot. In order to pass undetected with their booty, child smugglers employed a range of techniques. Bernard Offen remembers how he transported his loot: "And I being young, quick, nimble, took a pack on my back or these knickers. . . . They were tied in the bottom and were great for stuffing with things that I traded for, and to bring it back to the ghetto."[55] Hiding food underneath clothing provided limited space. Bags and rucksacks, on the other hand, while conspicuous, offered enough room for food.

Frequently, Jewish child smugglers believed they were proceeding clandestinely, when in fact Poles noticed their efforts. Janina Stefaniak, a Polish girl of about eleven at the time, witnessed recurring scenes from her apartment at 30 Lwowska Street, located right outside the ghetto, such as of a girl dragging a bag with potatoes and squeezing through a hole dug out under the wall, or a boy carrying a rucksack on his back and a large pot in his hand, hiding near the ghetto gate and waiting for the tram to approach.[56] Stefaniak's observations, carved into her memory, point to the smuggling activities of both Jewish boys and girls, the frequency and modes of smuggling, and the extent to which the phenomenon of child smugglers was visible to non-Jews.

Prompted by need, two types of child smugglers emerged. The occasional smugglers slipped out to obtain specific goods, primarily for their own families. David Zauder belonged to this group of "food suppliers." He ventured out once or twice a week to buy bread, meat, and jam.[57] The second variety were "professional" child smugglers, as Janina Fischler called herself. Janina found a window of opportunity after the June 1942 deportation. "I was the link between the outside and the inside because of my age, my appearance, and my business acumen. I was a smuggler really; I was in and out, bringing food in." She grew into a professional. "People gave me commissions," she explained.[58] This allowed her to become the family's breadwinner. With time, many youngsters extended their range of services. Abraham Blim, a boy of about eleven then, for example, procured specific items considered luxurious in wartime, such as live chickens for wealthy Jews in the ghetto. He also smuggled letters between members of what he termed the "underground organization" (the Jewish Fighting Organization, Żydowska Organizacja Bojowa; ŻOB), to which his older brother belonged, and a brush maker on Starowiślna Street.[59] He served as a messenger between Jews in the ghetto and Poles on the Aryan side, dealing with both the sale and barter of items and arranging for potential hiding places.[60]

Children engaged in what Abraham Blim called a "trade career" on their own, or joined forces with others. At times, with their inconspicuous appearance and owing to their young age, they served as "security passports" or stood on lookout for adults on missions. Sometimes, mothers and their young daughters engaged in smuggling activities together and relied on their nonstereotypical Jewish features to obtain food and other necessary products to survive in the ghetto. Sophia Śpiewak's mother used her, about a five-year-old girl at the time, as a safety passport to detract attention. With Sophia's blue eyes and blond hair, neither she nor, by extension, her mother was taken for a Jew.[61] Siblings sometimes participated in joint stints outside the ghetto. Pinkus Fajnwaks, then between nine and eleven years old, and his brother sneaked out once or twice a week, usually in the early morning or evening, to buy groceries, mainly bread, flour, potatoes, and vegetables.[62] In other instances, children made connections with youngsters in a similar situation and treated them as business partners.

The direction of smuggling goods was mostly from the Aryan side into the ghetto. Some children, however, engaged in the reverse path. Janina Fischler was commissioned by her aunt to deliver lunch to another relative imprisoned in the Montelupich prison in winter 1941. Janina's "Sunday job" consisted of slipping out of the ghetto to carry a three-course meal to the prison across town. Each week, Janina battled with her conscience, wanting to devour the lunch. The pungent smell of the food tormented and tempted the hungry girl. As a professional smuggler, however, she did not succumb and continued such missions until spring 1942.[63] Children like Janina faced expectations from adults, who relied on young people to undertake tasks they themselves were unable to complete. Children often obliged. But they also experienced age-appropriate impulses. Yet children's life circumstances demanded that they mature immediately.

Responsible for their families' welfare, children recalled that their initial apprehension disappeared in the face of food scarcity. Older children understood the significance of their position as providers. They knew that without them, their families would be left in dire straits. Perhaps the passage of time influenced their ideas when questioned many years later about their attitudes to wartime experiences. Or that was indeed what they had thought at the time. Some, like Luiza Grüner, who stuck live chickens through the barbed wire so that her grandmother could check whether they were appropriate for cooking, considered such missions ludicrous. Luiza admitted that it was foolish and that she was terrified, aware that she could get caught and killed.[64]

Other child smugglers considered the mishaps they experienced during their missions as silly. Maksymilian Perlmutter, who was about nine at the time, ran smuggling errands for his mother and for other people. "The last time this happened I tried to get back and did a very foolish thing." He failed to notice a German policeman at the gate and tried to reenter the ghetto with the help of the Polish officer he knew. To save face, the Polish policeman stopped Maksymilian and, with the German officer, dragged him to the police station. "I was never so frightened in all my life. I was shaking with fright," Maksymilian recalled. Upon release, he pleaded with his mother not to force him to engage in smuggling ever again. Although his role was valuable for those who solicited his "expertise," he saw his activity as absurd.[65]

Children like Luiza and Maksymilian acted out of necessity, pushed by their guardians to fulfill specific tasks. And yet, their smuggling missions, however idiotic they might have seemed to the children themselves, were grounded in adults' refusal to accept life conditions in the ghetto. Even if most children did not perceive their role as exceptional, many acknowledged deriving a certain self-worth in their newly found mature role. Maksymilian recalled at first, "No, I didn't like to do this [smuggling] because it was very unnerving," admitting in a second, "OK, I mean it gave a little sense of importance and accomplishment because at the age of eight I was running across."[66]

Opportunities for procuring food from the Aryan side decreased as the number of restrictions multiplied and actions intensified, making sneaking out and in more difficult and dangerous. With the imposition of Hans Frank's decree of 15 October 1941, Jews who left the ghetto without a permit, and non-Jews who assisted them, risked the death penalty.[67] After the June 1942 action, the Germans intensified control of the ghetto borders and curbed contacts between Jews and non-Jews even more. A law of 28 July 1942 prohibited Jews, and non-Jews acting on their behalf, from making purchases in stores outside the ghetto. Only members of Jewish organizations with special permission from the city commandant were allowed to shop in the city. Store owners were forbidden to sell anything to Jews, at risk of punishment, which included fees, arrest, and closure of the business.[68] The Germans anticipated Jews' efforts to leave the ghetto to supplement their rations and recognized the opportunities that barter with non-Jews afforded Jews seeking hiding places on the Aryan side. The new decree was meant to thwart such activities. Still, some child smugglers knew the exact spot on Józefińska Street where the wire was cut and where the strands could be drawn apart to escape. Driven by sheer necessity, they continued to push their way out.

While some children engaged in smuggling throughout the existence of the ghetto, others undertook that mission for a limited time. An action was but one reason why children stopped smuggling. For some, being caught in the act or recognizing the dangers they incurred caused fear, and hence a child's unwillingness to pursue smuggling. For others, the timing of their activities was influenced by the availability of bartering items. The degree of smuggling depended, too, on the situation among non-Jews. Bernard Offen remembers that Polish informants posed the greatest threat to him on the Aryan side. "I always, always, had to be on the lookout for Poles who were called *shmalcovniks*;[69] they were who betrayed Jews especially. . . . So, I had to be on the lookout for them when I did my trading."[70]

Children's missions assumed more dangerous proportions with the switch from the smuggling of goods into the ghetto to the smuggling of other children out of the ghetto.[71] Recognizing that the situation in the ghetto was worsening steadily, parents realized that whereas bringing in goods to sustain the family worked on a temporary basis, slipping children out to the Aryan side could lead to their prolonged survival. Knowing escape routes, confidently treading on the Aryan side, being familiar with the geography of Kraków, and possessing connections in the city, Jewish child smugglers were in high demand.[72]

At thirteen years old, Janka Warszawska was known for her successful smuggling skills. She received a request from a Mr. Neuman to smuggle his two children out of the ghetto. Neuman had learned, as had a select number of Jews in the ghetto, about what turned out to be the October 1942 action. Janka recalled Neuman's motivation. "He was terrified for the safety of his children and didn't see any other solution than this."[73] Pushed by her father, Janka took on the task. She mustered even more courage to smuggle out other children and her own siblings, and to show the exit to numerous strangers. Boys, too, undertook these risky endeavors. Aware that Abraham Blim knew secret passageways, parents brought their children to him in the hope that he could lead them to safety outside the ghetto. Most of these children already possessed addresses on the Aryan side. Abraham's "job" was to get those children out.[74] Children's role as smugglers thus extended from that of providers to that of rescuers.

Escaping the ghetto to hide on the Aryan side was another way for Jewish children to survive. Despite the strict German law, parents searched for ways to slip their children out and looked for prewar friends, acquaintances, coworkers, housekeepers, nannies, teachers, neighbors, building supervisors, or even strangers to keep the children in a secure place on the Aryan side. Both parents and prospective caretakers envisioned this as a short-term solution, until the situation in the ghetto calmed down.

Eight-year-old Janek Weber left the ghetto for the duration of the June 1942 action. He knew he would return. "In a few days I came back to the ghetto where it was safer because it was legal to be there," he recalled.[75] Janek's story shows that escape for the sake of hiding on the Aryan side was only a temporary means of children's survival; at least until the October 1942 action, and most certainly until the liquidation of the ghetto, when survival meant placement in a long-term shelter. The risks for non-Jews associated with harboring Jewish children, the fear of accidental discovery or denunciation by a neighbor, the parents' refusal to part permanently with their offspring, and even a child's unwillingness to live away from family all contributed to seeking out short-term rescue options. While some children did indeed return to the ghetto according to plan, others, once smuggled out and placed with non-Jewish caretakers, stayed on the Aryan side either for a longer period of time or permanently.

Arrangements were made in a variety of ways, both before and during the Jews' enclosure in the ghetto. In some cases, Jewish women who lived on the Aryan side or left the ghetto for the purpose of finding potential rescuers solicited non-Jews willing to take care of a Jewish child until a raid was over and prepared exit and reentry routes. Jewish men who worked in outside work details established contacts to smuggle children out of the ghetto. More often than not, parents themselves approached potential rescuers. Before March 1943, Salo and Eda Kunstler established contact with a Mr. Sendler (his first name could not be established), a Pole who worked as a driver for the German authorities, taking Jewish workers from the ghetto to work on the Aryan side of the city. The Kunstlers arranged with Mr. Sendler to shelter their baby daughter, Anita. In a letter that Eda passed to Mr. Sendler's wife, Zofia, she not only appealed to Zofia's maternal instinct and religion to assume the role that Eda was denied but also instructed Zofia on the baby's care rituals to create continuity for Anita.[76]

If some non-Jews extended their assistance upon the request of a child's parents, others offered their help voluntarily. An inspector from the electrical company, Józef Jaskier, came to the ghetto once a month to read the meters. Hearing rumors about the imminent dissolution of the ghetto, Jaskier offered to help the Heublum family. A day before the ghetto was liquidated, the family's ten-year-old daughter, Ewa, approached the main entrance of the ghetto. A Jewish policeman created an artificial commotion, shouting at her in Polish: What was she, a Catholic, doing inside the ghetto? Sidling out, Ewa crossed the street to a prearranged meeting place.[77]

In yet another case, the permanent presence of the only Pole permitted to live in the ghetto proved indispensable for a number of Jews. Tadeusz Pankiewicz ran the Under the Eagle pharmacy (Apteka pod Orłem) located at 18 Plac Zgody.[78] Pankiewicz was instrumental in arranging for the exit of a few children from the ghetto, including the two Perlman children. Their father met Tadeusz Skrzyński, a Pole who was in charge of Jewish workers who left the ghetto daily to work on the Aryan side in a carpentry workshop. Perlman enlisted the help of Pankiewicz, who, in turn, arranged for false papers for his two children, Mosze and Dziunia, and for Skrzyński and his wife to care for them.[79]

Channels established through work connected parents and, by extension, their children to avenues of rescue as well. To save a child from the ghetto often required stitching an intricate network. Róża Kwiaśnicka established contact with an acquaintance, a Polish woman named Danuta, who worked in the Labor Office in the ghetto. Danuta, in turn, made arrangements with her own acquaintance, Katarzyna Zabierzowska, a supervisor in a metal factory that employed workers from the ghetto. When Róża and her little daughter Miriam left the ghetto through the sewers on the night of 12–13 March 1943, they received assistance from Katarzyna.[80] Both Polish women worked for the German war effort, but they chose to help a Jewish mother with a small child when the threat to the lives of the latter became imminent. Perhaps their firsthand observation of Jews' life conditions prompted them to arrange for assistance—but only once the Jewish mother and her child escaped the ghetto on their own.

Quite unusually, one exploiter of Jewish labor in the ghetto, an Austrian named Julius Madritsch, participated in endorsing and forming such rescue chains too. Working in tandem with his factory manager, Raimond Titsch (also an Austrian), Madritsch arranged to have a few of his workers and their children smuggled out of the ghetto.[81] Witnessing the plight of Jews sparked the businessmen's activities. Perhaps that was the reason too for the German policeman Oswald Bousko's facilitation of Jews' escapes.[82] Ewa Lewi was six years old at the time of the October 1942 action. She and her five-year-old sister were ready to leave the ghetto on a truck when their aunt interceded with a German officer, perhaps Bousko, to allow the girls to disembark. The two girls and their aunt then hid in an attic with three other people. A further unidentified man retrieved Ewa's group and informed her father of their whereabouts. Ewa's father, in turn, made contact with his Polish coworker at Madritsch, Lucia Pawlak, who maintained a relationship with Bousko. Lucia then placed the girls with her parents.[83]

Once appropriate contacts in and outside the ghetto had been secured, an avenue of escape needed to be devised. Escape routes mirrored those used by smugglers. Often, however, children were physically camouflaged and removed from the ghetto, carried out in knapsacks or baskets. At other times they were given a sleeping medicine to reduce noise and thus avoid disclosure. Roma Liebling's parents, for example, realized that the Germans targeted children during actions, and they gave Roma a tranquilizer and put her into a suitcase. Her screams before their administering the medication, however, were too much to bear.[84] Roma's story demonstrates the lengths adults were prepared to go to save their children from immediate danger. It also illustrates the emotionally wrenching decisions that parents wrestled with when faced with exposing their children to the unknown.

Smuggling children out of the ghetto depended on timing too. During times of relative stability, escape strategies required less refined planning. Yet such temporary stability deceived many a parent. Unwilling to part with their children, most parents waited until the last moment before an action, a period especially dangerous for child smugglers like Janka Warszawska. She was upset with the lack of consideration of one parent, a Mr. Neuman. "He didn't give them [his two children] to me when it was quiet, but rather he kept them with him until the last minute."[85] Children's functions as rescuers intensified with the impending liquidation of the Kraków ghetto. A number of parents made the desperate decision to relinquish their children permanently in the hope that their lives might be spared. Right before the final liquidation of the ghetto, Neuman begged Janka again to save his children, and she did.

Faced with the final action in the ghetto, some children managed to sneak out on their own. Roman Liebling recalled his escape. "On the day the Kraków Ghetto was finally liquidated, March 13, 1943, my father woke me before dawn. Taking me to Plac Zgody, to a blind spot just behind the SS guardhouse, he coolly snipped the barbed wire with a pair of pliers. He gave me a quick hug, and I slipped through the fence for the last time."[86] Finding the door locked to the apartment of the Polish Wilk family, whom he knew, Roman decided to return to the ghetto. He saw a marching column of Jewish men, among them his father. When Roman finally got his father to notice him, his father hissed, "Shove off!" Roman explained the reason for his survival: "Those two brusque words stopped me in my tracks. I watched the column recede, then turned away. I didn't look back."[87]

Escaping through the sewers was another common method of leaving the ghetto at the last moment. As Abraham Blim explained, "I knew that the only way to survive was the sewers; no other option remained for me." Together with his friend, Abraham jumped into a manhole on Węgierska Street. They found people already lost in the darkness. The two boys instinctively headed toward the Vistula River. "Water flowed in the middle of the tunnel, and sometimes there was a strong current. We walked sideways; it was muddy and very slippery."[88] They exited in Podgórze. Poles saw them, but none reacted.

Some children escaped with their families or as a group. Helpless, Jerzy Aleksandrowicz and his parents noticed people hurrying toward manholes, and the family followed suit. Treading through the sewers was a memorable experience for this young boy. "We walked along a main corridor on narrow walkways. Papa, who had a small flashlight, guided the group. We were walking in the direction of the flow of sewage toward the Vistula River." The group gradually dispersed "so that we and one other man were left by ourselves." The Aleksandrowicz family had to find a way out fast. "We exited at the last moment because German police were shooting close behind us."[89]

During the liquidation of the ghetto, some parents, unwilling to separate from their children, attempted to bring them into the Plaszow camp in backpacks or under their coats. A number of other children were smuggled out of the ghetto in carts among furniture or medical equipment. Janek Weber's father understood that children had bleak chances for survival. He put his son in a suitcase and placed it on a cart going to Plaszow. Janek recounted the incident half a century later. "I felt, surprisingly enough, that it was an adventure, and I don't recall being frightened. My luck, there is luck in such circumstances, is that I was sufficiently adult and grown up, mature enough to cope with the situation but unable to grasp the tragedy of it all."[90] Other children tried to leave the ghetto with columns of prisoners marching to the camp. In the commotion, individual children managed to escape the guards' attention.

Only a small number of children survived the liquidation and continued to hide in the then dissolved ghetto until an opportune moment to escape presented itself. They either were subsequently smuggled out or sneaked out to the Aryan side. Eight-year-old Janina Feldman, her older sister Ewa, and their mother hid in a wooden outhouse. After two days in the lavatory, the mother looked through a crack and saw a German soldier standing at ease. She gave him the little remaining jewelry she had and they escaped to the Aryan side.[91] On 14 March 1943, Roma Liebling came out of her hiding place in a cellar. Her mother whispered to her that her last name was now more Polish-sounding—Ligocka. Both were among the last to be smuggled out of the now defunct ghetto in a cart transporting Jews' confiscated belongings.[92]

———

Many parents supported children's clandestine activities and concealed presence throughout the existence of the ghetto. Most children, however, had neither the means nor the opportunity to engage in such survival strategies. The parents' resourcefulness for the sake of their children and the children's inventiveness for the well-being of their families and themselves depended on the outside assistance of Poles. Yet these efforts were framed both by the sense of uncertainty about how such relationships would develop and by the pervading danger of death upon discovery. Children's presence in the ghetto and their survival demanded an organized plan to protect them and remove them—to the extent possible—from the Germans' purview. Therefore, as we shall see next, Jewish children's activists and members of child welfare institutions inside the ghetto engaged in a range of relief efforts tailored to the availability of resources and the timing of Nazi anti-Jewish policy.

CHAPTER 4

Child Welfare

Efforts to assist children were meant to ensure their survival, and thus the future of the Jewish people. Concurrently, such efforts were meant to improve the morale of the ghetto population in two ways. First, by giving people hope and renewed confidence in a time of desperation. Second, by fostering a semblance of normal life in which communal organizations existed to support the less fortunate. As we will see in this chapter, theirs was a difficult task, shaped by the constant deterioration of living conditions; sacrifice on the part of the Jewish population; deceit of the German authorities; and financial, structural, and power limitations. The Jewish Council and Jewish police fulfilled German orders. German policies, in turn, framed the activities of Jewish organizations and the lives of ghetto inhabitants, including children. Food and other goods distribution, the fate of child welfare institutions, definitions of who was considered a child, and deception of Jews throughout were beyond the Jews' realm of influence.

As we trace the welfare activities pursued on behalf of children in the Kraków ghetto, we observe not only the challenges that the activists faced but also how they found inspiration in the past and adapted those solutions during stages of the ghetto's existence. In doing so, child welfare advocates also continued their practice from the first year and a half of the German occupation of keeping children out of German sight. Sites established specifically for children served that purpose.

———

Drawing on Kraków Jewry's history of philanthropy, and with the assistance of international aid, the Jewish Social Self-Help (Żydowska Samopomoc Społeczna; ŻSS) and its affiliates provided care for children in the Kraków ghetto.[1] ŻSS remained the central Jewish welfare authority in the General Government, with headquarters transferred into the Kraków ghetto and located at 18 Józefińska Street. In Kraków, ŻSS operated through its local institutions. Kraków's official agency was the Jewish Welfare Committee of the City of Kraków (Żydowski Komitet Opiekuńczy Miejski w Krakowie; ŻKOM). From March 1942, ŻKOM consisted of two branches. One was the Department for the Care of Children and Teenagers, or Wydział Opieki nad Dziećmi i Młodzieżą (formerly the Association for the Care of Children and Orphans—Centos [Centrala Towarzystwa Opieki nad Dziećmi i Sierotami—Centos]). The second was the Department of Sanitary and Hygiene Care, or Wydział Opieki Sanitarnej i Higienicznej (formerly the Society for the Protection of Health—Towarzystwo Ochrony Zdrowia [TOZ]).

Efforts by Jewish relief workers to organize help for children in the Kraków ghetto fall into three stages. From the inception of the ghetto on 3 March 1941 until the culmination of the first German action on 8 June 1942, Jewish organizations underwent a process of adaptation. They had to transfer their activities into the new surroundings and adjust them accordingly. They obtained new locations and tailored them to their needs, moved their staff and equipment, accommodated their charges, and assessed and responded to the needs of children in the ghetto. In addition, Jewish organizations devised ways of obtaining funding and goods, such as food, clothing, and medicine, in a new situation of confinement. They struggled to streamline their work, especially in light of the influx of Jews into the ghetto from the areas surrounding Kraków, and simultaneously to meet both German demands and pressures from the Jewish Council.

Members of Jewish organizations redefined their activities and recalibrated the hopes they had held for sustaining normalized living conditions for children in the Kraków ghetto following the German action of June 1942. In this next stage of mobilization (which lasted until the second major action on 28 October 1942), children's activists intensified their efforts by introducing structural changes to their work. Compelled by orders from the Jewish authorities as well as ever-increasing German restrictions, Jewish organizations merged child welfare institutions. Mindful of the first large action, the Jewish personnel reconsidered their approaches to care. They marshaled the available human and material resources to introduce forms of aid that corresponded to the constantly deteriorating conditions, and they placed greater emphasis on ensuring children's health.

The Germans' action of October 1942 crushed the efforts and aspirations of Jewish child welfare activists, and heralded the third—and last—stage of Jewish organizational endeavors on behalf of children in the Kraków ghetto, marked by desperation. Faced with Jewish authorities' interference in their activities and evaporating resources, Jewish social activists merged their meager assets to provide basic care focused on one institution that catered to the remnant of children left in the ghetto. They managed to keep the children alive until the Germans dissolved the ghetto on 13–14 March 1943.

———

When the Germans created the ghetto in the Podgórze district of Kraków, some Jewish child care institutions, previously located in Kazimierz, either ceased their work or were forced to seek new premises inside the ghetto and transfer activities there. This was no easy task in an already physically crammed area, and with the Jewish Housing Office working assiduously to accommodate 10,487 Jews (including 1,959 children up to the age of fourteen).[2] In light of these difficulties, the Jewish Council appealed to the Germans (successfully) to postpone the move of a few institutions.

One of those, the Department of Care for Children and Orphans (Centos), relocated to the ghetto six days after the deadline, on 26 March 1941. After a daunting search, Centos moved into a building at 37 Józefińska Street, which contained several rooms, including a kitchen, a dining hall, and a laundry room. Part of the garden adjoining the building served as a playground. Transferred to the ghetto were the two Centos "children's corners" (ogródki opiekuńcze) for about two hundred youngsters, which had been located at 17 Meiselsa and 1 Podbrzezie Streets in Kazimierz. Under the Centos umbrella were also a shelter for twenty-five orphaned and abandoned children ages one and half to twelve (at 2 Józefińska Street); a soup kitchen specifically for children (at 5 Węgierska Street); and two day care centers (świetlice), one for youngsters three to seven and the other for those seven to twelve years old (at 22 Rękawka and 5 Węgierska Streets). Centos resumed its activities on 8 April 1941. Under the care of committed women educators, Centos charges spent their time on play, arts and crafts, and tending the garden. These endeavors helped some children by diverting their attention, at least temporarily, from the misery of daily life. Recognizing the growing demand for day care, Centos raised its admittance rate from two hundred to three hundred children and extended its hours of operation to keep children off the ghetto streets. It also opened a sewing workshop for older girls to help them acquire work skills. Still, infectious diseases were such a great problem that Centos accepted children into its institutions only if a physician certified that they were clean and in good health.[3]

In light of the new demands on parents in the ghetto, as well as forced labor, Centos broadened the range of its care. First, it offered a nursery for children whose parents worked to fulfill the labor requirement imposed by the Germans. Knowing that their children were fed, clothed, and cared for, many parents were relieved of additional worries to some extent. And children had a place to go while their parents were at work, and where they could socialize with their peers. Centos also took on the task of promoting hygiene and health among children and their families. Its clinic at 13 Limanowskiego Street served as a consultation and vaccination point.

Under the leadership of Rachela Mahler, a prewar social activist and educator, Centos served a crucial role because it created and supported institutions whose goal was to spare children the detrimental physical and emotional effects of the ghetto. Centos addressed, too, the challenging life circumstances of the children's parents in the ghetto. Mahler proceeded to implement familiar solutions that had worked in the first year and a half of the war. The activities of Centos illustrate that the fate of its youngest members was a priority for Jewish organizations.

Another institution, the Jewish Orphanage (Żydowski Dom Sierot), directed by Anna Feuerstein, also was allowed additional time to transfer to the ghetto.[4] It moved from a five-floor building at 64 Dietla Street in Kazimierz into a one-story building of the Wasserberg Foundation at 8 Krakusa Street. Thanks to his job in the German Office of the Trust Agency, Rafał Morgenbesser (an orphanage board member) obtained building materials to renovate the children's home in the ghetto and adapt it to fit their needs. As of 12 May 1941, 115 children lived in the orphanage, including 54 girls and 43 boys ages seven to thirteen, and 14 girls and 4 boys ages fourteen to eighteen.[5]

Faced with a growing demand for assistance, both the Jewish Orphanage and Centos struggled to make ends meet. Documents of ŻSS and ŻKOM relate an urgent need to help children in the Kraków ghetto, repeatedly thwarted by a lack of funding. A perpetual sense of uncertainty about the future and of helplessness ruled. Children's activists agonized over keeping their institutions afloat to provide a full range of child care. Disputes erupted over possible mergers. Children's activists questioned the effectiveness of conglomerate agencies. Could these continue to offer tailored solutions to specific groups? Or would their carefully devised methods be absorbed into uniform responses to the children's plight? Still, the good of the children stood at the forefront on all agendas. In order to prevent duplicating efforts, and make their work efficient, Jewish child welfare organizations in the ghetto met on 8 April 1941. According to their arrangements, Centos continued to act as an "emergency care center" (*pogotowie ratunkowe*) for homeless children and as a shelter (*przytulisko*) for children under seven years old, while the Jewish Orphanage accepted children seven to fourteen years old, and the Vocational Hostel for Jewish Orphaned Boys admitted youngsters over the age of fourteen.[6]

The Jewish Council implemented yet another solution to the problem of orphans and abandoned children. It allocated a monthly budget of 2,000 złoty to pay not only Jewish families inside the ghetto to serve as foster parents but also Catholics, with whom children were placed on the Aryan side.[7] The fact that an official Jewish agency was prepared to entrust Jewish children to the care of non-Jews outside the ghetto, even risking a child's loss of his or her Jewish identity and without control over the quality of care, illuminates the community's desperation to save its children at all costs.

And the price of keeping children alive often exceeded all budgetary projections. The Jewish Orphanage relied on external funding. To illustrate its dire situation, in April 1941, donations to the orphanage amounted to 3,000 złoty, which enabled it to provide care to only forty children, leaving a monthly deficit of 10,000–12,000 złoty (with a cost of care of 1.80 złoty per child per day).[8] Exacerbating the problem, the orphanage initially fell beyond the scope of ŻKOM. As Jakub Sternberg, president of that committee, expressed to the president of the Jewish Orphanage, Aleksander Biberstein, "The orphanage belongs neither to the Jewish Welfare Committee nor to the Jewish Council, but is an institution of Krakovian society."[9] Members of the Jewish community joined forces to organize and administer the meager resources that they managed to obtain legally and illegally. The orphanage, then under the aegis of ŻSS, limped along thanks to the donations of ghetto inhabitants, as well as nominal subsidies afforded by Jewish welfare organizations. Articles in *Gazeta Żydowska* promoted the work of the orphanage and encouraged Jews to contribute what they could. The orphanage board organized various collections within the ghetto community, charity concerts, and street fund raisers. Older children earned money by assembling brushes in a workshop at the orphanage that were then sold. The Germans had to approve all these efforts, which points to the degree to which they dominated all aspects of Jewish communal life and child relief efforts.

Similarly, Centos leaders worried about their inability to provide adequate care to all needy children because of limited resources and personnel shortages. The budgetary allocation from the various sources to Centos changed each month. Faced with insufficient funding, Centos nevertheless consistently found the necessary resources to care for the community's youngest members. In the critical months between January and April 1941, Centos relied on its Warsaw branch, ŻSS, the American Jewish Joint Distribution Committee, and women's committees for money, food, hygienic care items, and coal.

ŻSS recognized the role women volunteers and teenagers could play in developing and initiating child care efforts. Women's circles prepared and distributed meals, mended clothing, checked the houses of their charges, organized fund raisers, and led clothes and food drives. Youth circles collected food, wood for heating, clothing, toys, and scraps of materials that children used for their crafts activities in day care. The activities of such committees factored into communal solidarity in the face of oppression, but also provided more tangible results by complementing official help.

Child relief efforts were undertaken on individual initiative as well. Matylda Karmel, a member of the Women's International Zionist Organization and a prewar children's activist, created and ran a children's corner in the ghetto. Her charges received care, along with Jewish education. Karmel spearheaded the

Centos program "Slice of Bread for the Hungry Child," which offered extra bread rations for the poorest children, and she grew vegetables and fruit that children in day care received for breakfast.[10] Similarly, despite personal hardships, Ewa Heublum's grandmother continued her prewar Friday evening ritual of distributing soup to women and children in need, and giving money to the poor.[11] Individual women and those acting within groups took action for the sake of the community, and especially its youngest, most vulnerable members. Their wide-ranging efforts gained urgency with the influx of children into the ghetto.

The forced relocation of Jews from surrounding areas to the ghetto in Kraków between June and October 1941 caused a surge in its population. As of 14 October 1941, official statistics noted 15,288 people in the ghetto.[12] The resettlement action increased the pressure to help children. Some 1,200 children already lived in the ghetto, about 400 of whom attended the three main care institutions (the Jewish Orphanage, Centos, and the Vocational Hostel for Jewish Orphaned Boys). The arrival of an additional 1,250 youngsters, with an estimated 300 in need of assistance, created an extra set of challenges for Jewish welfare organizations.[13]

In October 1941, the orphanage confronted another problem—that of accepting ten foundlings ages two to twelve, some of whom were of unconfirmed background. The Nazis considered such children Jews. Previously, these children had been under the care of either the Jewish Council or Centos, or had been in non-Jewish foster homes. In accord with Hans Frank's decree of 15 October 1941, all Jews found on the Aryan side risked the death penalty. Children whose background could not be validated and who were housed in closed care institutions, nurseries, institutions for the disabled, and Catholic institutions located on the Aryan side had to be transferred to the Jewish Orphanage. ŻSS and ŻKOM tried to ascertain the backgrounds of these children in order to apply to the German city commandant for their birth certificates. These were mostly either orphans or abandoned children of refugees or of parents unable to take care of their offspring.[14]

The Jewish Orphanage took another ten children at the end of 1941 or beginning of 1942, this time at the city commandant's order. They had formerly lived in a Catholic day care and nursery on Koletek Street in Kazimierz.[15] All of them had been raised according to the tenets of the Catholic faith, and they had difficulty adapting to life among Jews in the ghetto. How the German authorities discovered these children is not clear, but the fact that they were indeed found, selected, and sent to the ghetto sheds light on the Germans' attitudes toward children suspected of being Jews, and how important it was for them to remove even alleged Jews from Aryan life. It also draws attention to the way the perpetrators viewed Catholic orders. And it indicates the degree to which the Germans suspected, were informed of, and knew about the activities of nuns in sheltering Jewish children.

The number of children in the orphanage increased, too, when Poles began to return Jewish children who until then had remained under their care. Some feared the consequences of harboring Jewish children; others lacked the means to continue caring for them. Still others realized that sheltering Jewish children was not temporary, which opened a set of questions about finances, parental rights, and risks.[16] The Germans also ordered the return of Krakovian Jewish children placed in other institutions outside the city. Sabina Mirowska recalled the difficulties that order created at the orphanage: "Not to mention that this influx of children was difficult for the orphanage, but it was hard to deal with children, raised by nuns, now in an institution led by Orthodox Jews. Besides, Catholic women, with whom Jews had lived before the resettlement and with whom they had left their children, now brought those children to us, so that the orphanage was overcrowded, to the point that often five children had to fit on a single bed. This resulted in the deterioration of children's health and hampered care."[17]

Attempts to ameliorate children's lives centered on providing them with shelter and basic care, supplying food, and addressing the problem of poverty. One factor that may explain the relative stability of food supply for children in open and closed care institutions is that child care was centralized in Kraków. Only three recipient institutions relied on funding from ŻSS. Leaders of child care establishments also arranged for the smuggling of basic foodstuffs into the ghetto from the Aryan side. And Kraków Jews prided themselves on a long tradition of helping those less fortunate, including children. Still, it was difficult to obtain the food needed for the proper development of children. Because Jews in the ghetto had little or no income, donations for child care institutions dropped to cover barely 57 percent of their monthly budgets, making hunger a constant.[18] In its report, ŻKOM lamented the "particularly poor appearance of children in the orphanage," but hastened to emphasize that this had resulted from malnourishment rather than negligence.[19]

Faced with food shortages, scarce financial resources, and the growing number of children in the ghetto, organizations devoted to child care raised funds in the only way they could and were allowed to: by appealing to the conscience and values of the ghetto population. The Warsaw headquarters of Centos organized a "Month of the Child" campaign in November 1941, hoping the sentiment would spread throughout the General Government. The plea to action was straightforward: "We must exert all our energy, combine all forces to save children—the joy and delight of families, the future and hope of the society— even at personal costs. The children must survive! Let's save the children!" In the Warsaw ghetto, the stakes were high. Centos catered there to fourteen thousand children and incorporated thirteen dormitories and orphanages, ten soup kitchens, twelve children's corners, twenty-two day care centers, and two care stations for babies, as well as 410 house corners for eleven thousand children.[20]

In Kraków, ŻSS and ŻKOM organized the "Month of the Child" campaign to support the collective interests of Centos, the orphanage, and the hostel. Their proclamations referred to notions of continuity: "A child is not only a parent's joy, but first and foremost a link between one generation and the next, and therefore a mainstay and basis of a society." The campaign evoked the community-established values of social responsibility: "Every good person is interested in the fate of a child and loves it [sic]. Care for the child stands at the center of social issues."[21] Jews were urged to participate actively in building a network of assistance to children. "Kraków Jews hold a centuries-old tradition, with a respectable history of service. The child has always found devoted caretakers, and its [sic] needs have always been properly understood." In light of the inability of parents to devote total attention to their children and feed them, "the community must assume the role of parents and take care of the children generously, wholeheartedly, and with real parental love."[22]

The "Month of the Child" campaign was an adult initiative, but the participation of children was crucial for moving adults to donate vital funds despite their poverty and need to support their own families. The program included a performance entitled "Children for Children" by charges from the orphanage and the Centos nursery. Children, together with the artistic director, prepared ten song-and-dance vignettes.[23] If for adults the program was a fund-raising event, for the children it served as an opportunity for release and self-expression. As group-based art therapy, the performances provided a way for children to feel important and for adults to engage them in creative activities, as well as to impart an appreciation for art, music, and dance. The preparation for the event also served as an opportunity for children to learn about Jewish heritage through Yiddish songs and to gain a deeper appreciation for their identity as Jews.

The "Month of the Child" campaign sensitized the Jews to the destitute situation of their community's youngest. In October 1941, ŻKOM's monthly budget equaled 958 złoty, rising in December to 1,300 złoty, which reflected the growth in the ghetto population, and an increase that can be attributed to the "Month of the Child" campaign held in November. The augmented sum still fell short, but it enabled the agency to allocate 550 złoty for the care of children as part of its mission to support child care institutions.[24]

As an umbrella organization for relief efforts in the Kraków ghetto, ŻSS argued that it was vital to consider the factors necessary to sustain child life when allocating funds. The organization's protocol called for spending 55 percent of the budget on food, 35 percent on direct aid to children, and 15 percent on hygienic and medical help.[25] These allocations reflect the Jewish leaders' preoccupation with child relief efforts and ensuring that appropriate amounts were invested in children's well-being.

Medical surveillance and hygiene checkups also claimed attention and resources. ŻKOM feared that overcrowding, poor sanitary conditions, and varying levels of hygiene among the newly arrived ghetto residents would lead to an epidemic outbreak. The committee called for raising the number of female sanitary workers from eleven to forty in December 1941, and up to fifty in January 1942. This increase in personnel, it argued, would allow for greater effectiveness in monitoring children's hygiene and their housing conditions.[26] The committee estimated 2,500 children at the peak of the population surge in mid-December 1941, including those who lived at home and those in the orphanage and the shelter.[27]

The Jewish Council's Sanitary Commission conducted its own survey.[28] Evidently, the commission wanted to reach and record as many children as possible to document their and their families' living conditions. Possibly, it planned to use its findings to establish an action plan. But the commission's activities supported the German occupying authority in its efforts to repress Kraków's Jewish population. The commission's monthly reports landed on the desk of the German official in charge of it. He thus had a count of the Jews in the ghetto, including children, their places of residence, and an assessment of their overall health conditions. Notwithstanding the caretakers' wish to veil the children's existence to minimize their presence in the Germans' sightline, the German official learned, for example, that in January 1942 the survey reached 264 houses and registered 4,494 families, including 2,607 children.[29] But the registration was partial, as the ghetto encompassed 288 residential buildings. It most likely took into account only those Jews who lived in the ghetto legally and not those who sneaked in.

The over two thousand children in the ghetto received assistance from organizations created specifically to provide relief for them, as well as from others, such as the Infectious Disease Hospital.[30] Its pediatric patients suffered from illnesses including typhoid fever, hepatitis, scarlet fever, measles, and inflammatory diseases. The hospital workers and volunteers showed special sensitivity to the children. Halina Nelken, a student nurse at the hospital, wrote about the one child she cared for and remembered best: "Among the many children, there is one severely retarded five-year-old boy who is like a small, helpless animal, unable to speak, sit up, use his hands to eat. He just lies there without making a sound, even when he has wet himself." She recalled what perhaps other staff members had to face. "I fed him, with aversion at first, but when he politely swallowed the food and looked at me with such trust in his big eyes, I felt tenderness for this beautiful, unfortunate child and caressed his smooth cheek."[31] Children such as that boy required a special kind of attention and dedication. Witnessing human tragedy on a daily basis could have desensitized the staff. The example of Nelken shows, however, that there were individuals who may have had contradictory feelings but in the end maintained respect for the youngest and the most defenseless.

Nelken joined Centos as a volunteer hygienist in May 1941. "The work consists of checking the housing and health of children," she wrote in her diary re-created after the war. She found it particularly painful to witness ailing parents and children. "It is heartbreaking to see small anemic children with hollow cheeks huddling around their sick mothers."[32] In light of the rampant diseases, Centos issued an appeal in July 1941 urging parents of children under the supervision of the Department of Sanitary and Hygiene Care to seek advice on all matters related to their children's health and upbringing. Centos catered to two separate age groups, three-to-seven-year-olds and seven-to-twelve-year-olds, and offered parents separate appointment days, suggesting recognition of different age-range problems. Perhaps social workers identified these issues as they observed children's behavior and scrutinized their living conditions. Possibly the advice hours started in response to popular demand. Centos explained the goal of its program as helping parents meet their children's needs.[33] This call to parents reflects the preoccupation of Centos with sustaining a cohesive family unit and indicates concern for family life in general, and that of the child in particular.

Other efforts to improve child health were contemplated, and some launched. ŻKOM set up a pump room (pijalnia) at 11 Józefińska Street, where children received cod liver oil and milk to supplement their meager rations.[34] In April 1942, a proposal to start an infant clinic received enthusiastic support from ŻSS. Directed by a Dr. Guttmann, the plan was for the baby clinic to join the already existing clinic located at 13 Limanowskiego Street. It would open for two hours a week to examine newborns. A registry of babies obtained from the two clinics (the second was located at 13 Rynek Podgórski) would give the staff an idea of the number of newborns in the ghetto.[35] That such a clinic was even discussed reflects the fact that children continued to be born in the ghetto, emphasizing both a hope for the future and an incomplete picture of Nazi policies.[36] Another clinic was opened by the general hospital. Situated at 14 Józefińska Street, it offered daily medical services specifically for children.[37] Recognizing the need to raise awareness about health, Gazeta Żydowska published articles instructing pregnant women and mothers on how to care for themselves and their newborns.

If hygiene and health remained high priorities for Jewish organizations after the forced resettlement of Jews from the vicinity of Kraków into the city's ghetto, so did food provision. The Jewish Council was responsible for arranging the food supply into the ghetto. These meager rations were supplemented with the assistance of international organizations such as the American Jewish Joint Distribution Committee (JDC). Still, the German authorities controlled food supply into the ghetto even when food products arrived from international organizations. These international supplies went first to the ŻSS Kraków headquarters, and then were distributed to other cities throughout the General Government.

International food supplies did not last long, however, as they fell victim to global politics and warfare. With the U.S. entry into the war in December 1941,

JDC was unable to continue its direct aid work in the General Government. Nevertheless, it managed to channel assistance—money, clothing, medicine, and food—into the General Government clandestinely under local auspices.[38] This was crucial in ensuring children's well-being.

Jewish children's activists found ways of overcoming the obstacles constantly placed in their way. The continued existence of two soup kitchens specifically for children exemplifies these efforts. It also illustrates the potential for abuse of power in extreme circumstances. On 10 March 1942, an inspector from ŻKOM's Department for the Care of Orphans and Teenagers visited the soup kitchen at 5 Węgierska Street.[39] Sponsors had collected enough money and food to feed approximately 230 children, although not all of them showed up on a daily basis. The dinner and supper they received was insufficient to satisfy their hunger or to facilitate their physical development. But it provided them with the bare minimum of nutrition. The inspector reported that the soup kitchen's ten-member staff received more nutritious, two-dish meals. He expressed his dissatisfaction with that, as with the fact that while the staff ate their meals, their charges were required to leave the premises. Perhaps this rule was instituted to avoid adverse reactions by the children and suppress guilt on the part of staff for eating while many children were still hungry after they had left the table. More probable is that, as the inspector feared, the soup kitchen staff, earning little themselves and lacking supervision, invited mismanagement that ultimately harmed those the kitchen was designed to assist in the first place.

In addition to providing food under straitened circumstances, the Jewish Council and Jewish welfare organizations recognized the problem of homelessness among the ghetto population, including children. The Jewish Council set up a shelter (*azyl*) at 7 Węgierska Street for thirteen adults and four children. Inhabitants included legal residents of the ghetto, meaning they possessed identity papers but they had yet to receive housing. The Sanitary Commission also assigned a doctor for them. In order to gain admittance into the shelter, candidates applied to the Jewish Council and awaited assignment by the Housing Office. Another shelter for over forty people was located at 36 Limanowskiego Street and served two specific groups of homeless ghetto residents: those referred by various organizations and those who sought temporary refuge. Among the residents of that institution were ten children under the age of twelve, who remained under the care of Centos. All of the inhabitants received assistance in the form of food and clothing from ŻSS, while their food came from the Jewish Council's soup kitchens. Some of the residents worked and were thus able to sustain themselves. Still, demand exceeded space, as the planned expansion of the shelter indicates.[40]

Despite the efforts of ŻSS, ŻKOM, and the Jewish Council, the situation of children worsened steadily. In December 1941, Rachela Mahler, the inspector in charge of the Department for the Care of Children and Teenagers, examined children's living conditions in the ghetto, especially in the shelter for homeless newcomers. Her observations presented a harrowing picture of life in the private sphere of the shelter, hidden from public view. Mahler's report testified to the abject poverty that some newly arrived families in the Kraków ghetto faced, as well as their deplorable living conditions. Children were singularly affected by destitution, and their dire situation required them to spend their days at home, not able even to go outside. Mahler reported on the newcomers' ominous condition: "Both children and adults live in inadequate hygienic conditions; children are malnourished, weak, and often huddled to their tuberculosis-ridden mothers."[41] Such a situation undermined morale, both for those who experienced it and for those who witnessed it.

Jewish children's activists, social workers, and medical professionals recognized that the quality of child life was inextricably linked to that of mothers. In advance of Mother's Day (26 May) and Child's Day (1 June) in May 1942, *Gazeta Żydowska* issued an appeal to the Jewish community reflecting on the role of the child in society, especially during that difficult time: "A child—this is our future, so it [sic] deserves the necessary support. Before, it was the mother's job; today, society has assumed this task. But society has the same responsibility toward the mother also." It was no longer sufficient to provide assistance solely to children. Recognizing the difficult position of the children's mothers was important too. *Gazeta Żydowska* called for greater understanding for mothers, both married and alone, who could no longer care for their children, and for sympathy for those who lost their sons and daughters. The appeal ended with a call to action to "combine our care for children, who are our future, with the care for mothers, who by giving us those children laid the foundations for this future."[42]

If Jews saw children as a continuation of the Jewish people, the Germans viewed Jewish children as perpetuation of the Jewish race. Jewish institutions in the Kraków ghetto sought to shield children from the adversities of daily life, starvation, disease, and death. They tried as well to safeguard them against the brutality of the perpetrators and moral degradation caused by it. But the children's fate rested with the perpetrators, not with the Jews. The Germans continued to search for Jewish children, or those of unconfirmed and thus suspect background, and concentrate them in the ghetto. Thus, in May 1942, the Jewish Council ordered Centos to vacate the building at 22 Rękawka Street to accommodate nine toddlers from Catholic orphanages.[43] The Jewish identity of these children could not be established in all instances, but the Jewish Council was compelled to comply with the German order. The displaced children, who had until then attended the nursery at that location, were transferred to the second day care center at 5 Węgierska Street, which was overcrowded by that time.

The Węgierska Street center was open for a short time, between two o'clock and four o'clock in the afternoon, and catered to children whose parents worked during the day. There children participated in activities under the care of educators, while parents were assured that their offspring remained in a relatively safe place until they returned from work. Homeless children were encouraged to come there between nine in the morning and five thirty in the evening, thus reducing their exposure to the dangers that awaited them in the ghetto streets.[44] Educators offered these children shelter, as well as involvement in activities that fostered a sense of community. In effect, by offering a somewhat peaceful place, care, and methods of engaging young minds, the center extended its role to mediating the debilitating influence of ghetto life and improving the morale of its charges.

At this point, children's activists could not understand why the Germans hunted so vigorously for Jewish children outside the ghetto walls, except that the law explicitly restricted Jewish life to the ghetto. Nor could children's activists fathom why the Germans were so determined to concentrate Jewish children in officially sanctioned institutions inside the ghetto. Members of Jewish organizations continued to care for their charges. When the Germans unleashed the first major anti-Jewish action in the Kraków ghetto (30 May to 8 June 1942), the Jewish Orphanage and Centos evaded the deportations thanks to the intercession of the Jewish Council under the leadership of Artur Rosenzweig, a fact that was not widely known at that time.[45] Following the German raid, organized child welfare continued, but it morphed from the stage of adaptation into one of mobilization whereby children's activists were compelled to consider and pursue ideas they had been hesitant to employ thus far and to strategize new solutions.

———

Gazeta Żydowska reaffirmed the importance of sustaining child life after the first action in the Kraków ghetto and issued a call to all Jews in the General Government to muster all their resources to provide the needed assistance. "The problem of care for the abandoned child, the orphan, and the street child occupies a top place in our social life," an editorial proclaimed. The care the commentator referenced included ensuring basic needs, like food and clothing, as well as educational endeavors that would train children as future workers. The article reminded social workers, educators, and all others that lonely children without moral and material support could acquire debilitating traits. "Such characteristics include a feeling of inferiority, social lethargy, egoism, lack of moral restraints, feeling of humiliation. All this can turn the child into an asocial and even anti-social element."[46]

However, the resources needed to continue child relief work in the Kraków ghetto became ever more difficult to obtain. After the June action, a census taken by the Department of Sanitary and Hygiene Care revealed that at least eight hundred children required immediate assistance.[47] Exacerbating the difficult situation, the effectiveness of the Department of Care for Children and Teenagers diminished at that time, strained by a lack of facilities, an insufficient number of qualified personnel, and food shortages. In light of this drastic change in young people's situation, ŻSS called for a radical shift in the way it approached child care. Activists recognized the demand for a practical approach to address children's needs in the ghetto. A memo prepared by ŻSS proposed mobilizing personnel and resources and intensifying care of the ghetto's children. The memo argued that this approach "will help to stop the spread of moral savagery among children. . . . This would be the first step towards putting a stop to the catastrophe that is threatening us, and which holds dangerous consequences in the long run."[48] This short document reflects recognition of an existing problem, and the importance that Jewish organizations attached to child relief as a way of building morale among children and the rest of the ghetto population. What emerges from the text is a genuine interest in the fate of children and the urgent need to take action, especially in the aftermath of the German-perpetrated action.

Jewish welfare organizations took the appraisal of children's situation seriously. In July 1942, employees of the Department of Sanitary and Hygiene Care visited 95 percent of homes inhabited by children (1,085 of 1,142 apartments).[49] They examined 33 percent of children (641) to assess their health status. The major hygienic issue was lice, a problem especially prevalent among girls because of their long hair. Social workers attributed the dreary state of children's hygiene condition to the absence of mothers in their daily lives. With adults either deported in the first action or drafted for forced labor, children remained without adult supervision for most of the day. Hygienists took up the work that had previously fallen to the children's caretakers: washing children's heads, combing and cutting hair, clipping nails. They also instructed both children and (if available) their mothers about hygiene. In addition, hygienists helped educators in the Centos day care center and carried out vaccinations.[50] Despite the unsanitary conditions in which Jews were forced to live, and the increasing persecutions, combined with deportations, Jewish organizations in the ghetto continued to pay attention to the welfare of children. They found purpose in their activity as guardians of children's health and the well-being of the remnants of the community.

In order to extend the network of open care for children, despite decreased ghetto space after the June 1942 action, ŻSS proposed "children's corners," led by educators. These were set up outdoors in the few existing fenced-off squares and courtyards. An educator was responsible for her group of children. The group was further subdivided, with each subgroup tended by an older child. This system was based on the scouting model of substituting adults with younger people and a program of self-education of youths. Children whose parents worked, as well as abandoned and orphaned children, thus received care. This measure served as a temporary solution until ŻSS was able to allocate proper space.

If daily child care ranked among Jewish organizations' highest priorities, sufficient quantities of food became ever more problematic. The policy adopted by

ŻSS specified that parents had to provide food for their offspring who attended day care. Only children without any means were fed by the institution. Eventually, the German authorities forced a blanket policy when they forbade (on 4 July 1942) extra feeding of children who already received food at home or in soup kitchens.[51]

Impelled by the increased need to support children and their parents, Centos opened "a sort of nursery" (*pewnego rodzaju żłobek*) for children over two years of age. Located at 13 Rynek Podgórski, the new Centos initiative cared for some 250 children in August 1942. Open from six in the morning until five in the evening, the nursery supervised children and fed them three times a day. In makeshift condition, the new building was not suited to serve permanently. Yet as *Gazeta Żydowska* reported, "The day care is one of the most important institutions in the Jewish District today, because it allows mothers to fulfill their work requirement while alleviating their concerns about their children."[52] Children were divided into groups and, taking advantage of the summer weather, spent most of their time outdoors in the garden of the Vocational Hostel for Jewish Orphaned Boys at 35 Józefińska Street and in a private garden at 5 Limanowskiego Street. Gardens, as precious and rare areas in the ghetto, offered children a place where they could be relatively safe and carefree. On rainy days, children spent their time in the spacious dining hall in the hostel. The situation demanded that children's activists devise and implement ingenious solutions to create a semblance of normal life for children.

Ongoing challenges inhibited the work of child care institutions. For example, following the June 1942 action, the Jewish Orphanage moved to a new location at 31 Józefińska Street. The building had a garden that had previously been used by Centos, so children could continue to take advantage of play space.[53] However, overcrowding posed a threat to the effectiveness of the institution's mission. About 150 children and twenty-five staff had to be accommodated in fourteen rooms totaling 220 square meters. "This alone shows the extent to which children's living conditions had yet again deteriorated," Biberstein, the orphanage board member, observed.[54]

The decline of the Jewish Orphanage reflected the situation in the Kraków ghetto and in Kraków District in general. The decrease in the population of the ghetto after the June 1942 action drastically reduced donations for child care. To add to the already dire financial status of Jewish welfare organizations, ŻSS (as an umbrella welfare organization) struggled to support numerous child care institutions in twenty-six locations in Kraków District. Kraków had the most child centers (three) and the highest proposed subvention—1,500 złoty, a sum that could not be met and that was not allocated by ŻSS.[55] When the Germans dissolved ŻSS on 29 July 1942, providing a full-range of help to children proved ever more difficult.[56] Possibly, that is when Centos was forced to stop its activities.[57] Another change that affected child welfare was the Germans' appointment of a new Jewish administration for the ghetto, with Dawid Gutter as its head (called commissar), after the June 1942 action. Henceforth, all issues related to welfare and child care fell under the jurisdiction of the Jewish Council. And the council, now essentially a commissariat (department) subordinated to the Germans, fulfilled German orders dutifully.

Nevertheless, the Jewish Orphanage pursued its mandate with ever greater fervor. Lacking resources to ensure physical health, the staff turned to safeguarding children's spiritual well-being. In these circumstances, Jewish identity loomed large. As a June 1942 *Gazeta Żydowska* commentary noted, "Among all educational elements, the religious factor—one of attachment to faith, tradition, nation, its language and spiritual goods—is undoubtedly one of the most important. It gives the child strong spiritual support; it acts—in the first place—as a moral restraint."[58] Dawid Kurzmann, responsible for education at the orphanage, focused on maintaining religious observance among children. In that realm, celebrating Shabbat and keeping Kashrut assumed great value. At the request of Symche Spira, the Jewish ghetto police chief, the orphanage also served as a prayer house during the High Holy Days of 1942. In the spirit of the Jewish New Year, he promised financial assistance for the institution.

But Spira proved perfidious. He commandeered the building to accommodate his Jewish policemen and their families.[59] Immediately after Yom Kippur on 21 September 1942, Spira ordered the Jewish Orphanage to relocate to a building at 41 Józefińska Street, which had served as a day care center run by nuns before the war. Children and the orphanage staff lived in an area with one larger room and five smaller rooms. When the charges in the Vocational Hostel for Jewish Orphaned Boys were forced to vacate their building and move into the 41 Józefińska Street premises, the two institutions—the orphanage and the hostel—were fused together and housed over two hundred children.[60] "And this was the beginning of an end," Sabina Mirowska, formerly a secretary and then an educator at the institution, observed. Two to three children slept on each level of the bunk beds. The overcrowding, food shortages, and inadequate sanitary conditions took a toll on the youngsters' physical and psychological health. "A great dejection ruled among the children, as if they sensed what awaited them," Mirowska noted.[61] To demonstrate the usefulness of the children to the German authorities, ten older girls were employed as nurse aids in the Infectious Disease Hospital and the boys from the hostel continued to work.

Exacerbating this already dire situation, the number of children kept increasing. The Germans hunted for Jews, including children, who were hiding or passing as non-Jews on the Aryan side. With German actions clearing Jews from ghettos and towns in Kraków District, more children found their way into the ghetto in Kraków. Poles continued to drop off unwanted children whom they had previously agreed to shelter. "Gestapo also brought in children who had been caught on the Aryan side, who were at times of non-Jewish origin," Regina

Nelken (Halina Nelken's mother), an educator at the orphanage, explained in a postwar testimony.[62] Lili, a seven-year-old child of a German soldier and an allegedly Jewish woman, was one such example. She was placed in a boarding school in Jaszczurówka near Zakopane in the Tatra Mountains, but since her father died in the war, the money for her tuition stopped. Upon discovery of the girl's ostensibly Jewish roots, Lili was brought to the Kraków ghetto.[63] Witnesses recorded Lili's predicament. Not knowing Polish, she could not communicate with the other children. She sang German songs and carried a photograph showing men in German uniforms. In the end, "she met the same fate as the other children," Sabina Mirowska recalled.[64]

On 27 October 1942, Jews in the ghetto sensed looming danger. Concern spread among children and staff at the institution, who anticipated another major action. Sabina Mirowska remained at the orphanage until ten o'clock that night. "Still, we each held a glimmer of hope that the orphanage would be spared this time," she recalled.[65] They were right to be worried. In the early morning hours of 28 October 1942, the Germans began a selection of able-bodied Jews in the ghetto. In the meantime, medical personnel tried everything in their power to save their patients, including the youngest ones, at two hospitals in the ghetto. While eighteen sick children were discharged from the Infectious Disease Hospital into the care of their parents, the hospital staff hid several other children in neighboring buildings. When questioned by a German officer about the lack of patients, a Polish policeman, who had witnessed the rescue mission, confirmed the hospital director's version that no patients had been recently admitted. The Germans' fear of infectious diseases stopped them from conducting a thorough inspection. From the general hospital, on the other hand, the Germans took a woman in labor and two children, and murdered an unknown number of other patients.[66]

Around noon, the Germans surrounded 41 Józefińska Street and parked trucks by the building. A number of boys from the former hostel had saved themselves by leaving the building via the roof.[67] Yet some three hundred children from the orphanage and their caretakers were trapped inside. The Germans cleared the orphanage violently; they threw small children into baskets that stood on the truck platforms. Sabina Mirowska recalled, "Lorries with small children left the ghetto. It was rumored later that those little ones were killed somewhere outside the city, because they evidently did not arrive at the cattle cars."[68] The Germans led the older children together with the orphanage personnel onto Plac Zgody.[69] Once on the assembly square, the Jewish police attempted to release the key personnel of the child care centers. Chaskel Entenberg, the hostel manager, was set free, but others declined to accept the offer.[70]

After the war, and equipped with the knowledge of what had transpired in the Warsaw ghetto, Aleksander Biberstein, the director of the Infectious Disease Hospital and board member of the Jewish Orphanage in the Kraków ghetto, described Dawid Kurzmann, the director of religious education at the Jewish Orphanage, as the "Janusz Korczak of Kraków."[71] This reference and his depiction of the children from the orphanage marching in rows with their dedicated educators leading them peacefully and assuredly toward their almost certain death have served as the single source referenced by writers dealing with the Holocaust in Kraków. His words resonate with the now iconic procession of children from the orphanage led by the famous child educator and activist Janusz Korczak in the Warsaw ghetto during the Great Deportation on 5 (or, according to some sources, 6) August 1942.[72] The comparison between the two child educators shows that Kraków, too, had its own hero. Kurzmann, as did most other educators from the orphanage, decided to accompany the children he cared so much about. But so did the director of the orphanage, Anna Feuerstein, and her husband.

———

In a testimony she submitted in 1945, Sabina Mirowska vividly remembered the orphanage, stripped bare of life. "The day after the deportation of children, the orphanage presented a blood-chilling view. Here and there lay individual little stockings, small shoes, and other child clothing items, which were not taken amidst the chaos; and the house, recently full of commotion and life, stood empty and silent, and filled with dread."[73] If the orphanage stood silent, the ghetto groaned in pain. "Apartments were plundered, screams everywhere, and cries over those lost."[74]

From that point forward, it was clear that it was best for children to be as invisible as possible. It was the end of an era, in a way. After ninety-six years, the Jewish Orphanage ceased to exist. Looking back, Aleksander Biberstein observed, "If the transfer of the orphanage from [64] Dietla Street to 8 Krakusa Street was a catastrophe, then moving it yet again to the building at 31 Józefińska Street was a blow, and to the former [Catholic] day care center—an almost deadly blow." Biberstein claimed that "everything leads to the conclusion that the destruction of the orphanage was decided upon its transfer into the [formerly Catholic] day care center."[75]

Few children remained after the October action, and the question then arose: What to do with them? Thus began the third, and last, stage of child care efforts in the Kraków ghetto, that of desperation. As Regina Nelken recalled, "It was understood that assembling children in one place caused terrible consequences." Yet "the Jewish Council was forced to create something like an orphanage which was then called 'Tagesheim' [day care center] because it was supposed to be a place that kept children during the day, and in the afternoon parents were supposed to take them home after work."[76] A few days after the October action, the Germans issued a (most likely) verbal order to the Jewish Council commissar, Dawid Gutter, and the Jewish police chief, Symche Spira, to open a Tagesheim for the remaining children in the Kraków ghetto. Initially located at 15 Limanowskiego Street (in the former Hospital for the Chronically Ill), it was moved to a building on the corner of 22 Józefińska and 17 Krakusa Streets in response to the influx of children when the ghetto was divided into two parts on 6 December 1942. Marek Bieberstein and Jakub Kranz assumed co-responsibility for the institution.[77]

The Tagesheim both departed from and drew on the legacy of child welfare activities undertaken in previous years. It certainly was not a direct continuation of the dissolved orphanage. Created on the Germans' order to assemble the remaining children and in anticipation of the arrival of more children into the ghetto, the institution apparently had no statute or rules to guide the admittance policy.[78] Sabina Mirowska understood this was a new trap. "I instantly realized that the Germans purposefully wanted to gather together all orphans, to facilitate the next action and so I accepted this work unwillingly."[79] At the same time, the Tagesheim was the only institution sanctioned by German authorities specifically for children in the Kraków ghetto. Its role mirrored that of then-dissolved Centos and the Jewish Orphanage combined. And educators and children's activists continued to strive desperately to assist children in need.[80]

Jews in the ghetto distrusted the motivation for the Tagesheim, especially in light of the Germans' previous treatment of such institutions, staff, and children. Nevertheless, many parents and guardians in the ghetto placed their children there out of necessity. Half a century later, Henryk Zvi Zimmerman, a member of the ghetto underground, the Jewish Fighting Organization, remembered the tragic situation of children. "One had to have a lot of love and emotional strength in order to help these kids." He went on to explain the underground members' worries about the children's safety. "We were afraid to assemble them in one place, because we knew what the risk was." The underground was skeptical about the idea of a group home, "but soon we received information that Gutter, Streimer, and Spira were working zealously to create a Kinderheim [children's home]. They wanted to persuade the Jewish community through this zeal that they were caring activists. Children up to the age of fourteen were supposed to be housed in this place." The Jewish Fighting Organization saw the undertaking as assisting the Germans, enabling them to destroy the lives of children under the veil of relief efforts. "From trusted people we knew that this was being done by order of the German superiors. Gutter and his aides wanted to incorporate the activity of this facility into the activity of our social welfare organization. We wanted to avoid participation, not wishing to contribute to an enterprise which aimed to deceive children who trusted us," Zimmerman explained in a memoir written after the war.[81]

Postwar testimonies by witnesses and those submitted by the few charges of the institution who had survived tend to use the term Kinderheim interchangeably with the word Tagesheim.[82] This conflation of terms may be connected to the formation of the labor camp in the nearby district of Płaszów. As the number of children in the ghetto increased, and as many mothers were moved to the Plaszow camp, a need arose to expand the Tagesheim to place children there permanently—in a children's home, a Kinderheim.[83] But the switch in terminology may have been adopted from the Germans' vocabulary. The Germans "promised" the Jewish workers, whom they planned to transfer from the ghetto into the camp, that their offspring would be allowed to join them and would be placed in a special barrack for children—a Kinderheim—in the Plaszow camp. The Jewish Council and the Jewish police reaffirmed the Germans' promises, and it appears that many Jews in the ghetto accepted this reassurance. To add to the confusion, in his postwar account, Aleksander Biberstein mentions the existence of two child care institutions in the Kraków ghetto following the division of the ghetto on 6 December 1942: a Tagesheim, a day care center, in ghetto A for children whose parents worked, and a Kinderheim, children's home, in ghetto B for orphans.[84] No other documents corroborate his description, however. Yet his brief mention of the alleged two child care institutions affirms the real need to offer shelter and care to children in the aftermath of the October 1942 action.

Indeed, the Tagesheim served both as an asylum for the homeless, abandoned, and orphaned children whose parents had been deported or killed and as a day care center for children whose parents worked. As we have seen, when Hans Frank declared the General Government free of Jews on 14 November 1942, he nevertheless sanctioned the existence of five ghettos, including one in Kraków. The areas in which Jews were allowed to live in Kraków District shrank. Thus a number, including children, flocked into the Kraków ghetto. And children of unknown origin continued to be brought to the ghetto's sole child care institution. A girl named Janina Tarlińska (or Tarłowska) was one such child. She claimed her parents lived on Dietla Street and asked her caretaker, Regina Nelken, to contact a Protestant pastor outside the ghetto to take her out. Giving her testimony in the immediate postwar years, Regina was still uncertain whether indeed the child was placed in the ghetto by mistake.[85]

Children placed in the Tagesheim experienced a steady deterioration of life. Six-year-old Bronia Bruenner was smuggled into the ghetto and placed in the institution when her aunt, who lived on false papers on the Aryan side, could not take care of her anymore. Bronia recalled that the sanitary conditions in what she referred to as the Kinderheim were horrendous. She was full of lice and her braids had to be cut off. She regarded the institution as an enclave where children could stay together and off the streets. There was no one to take care of them in the institution's final days. The adults had been taken away in German actions, and there were just not enough educators. Children had no activities, but they still had to keep themselves occupied somehow. Bronia's testimony illuminates the feeling of an impending end. Her aunt must have sensed it too. Hearing rumors about yet another action, she smuggled Bronia out of the ghetto.[86]

The feeling of doom prevailed. Children were miserable despite the efforts of educators to provide the best care they could in such a hopeless situation. Children were nervous and sleepless, and they often cried. Their activities reflected what they observed in their daily surroundings. As Regina Nelken recalled, "The children in the *Tagesheim* play strange games. They do not laugh but they shout, do not play but fight each other, give orders, deport, hang or rob each other; almost always these games end with an adult having to intervene."[87] A contradictory assessment of children's responses to their situation was provided in an account by Pearl Benisch, who recalled a conversation she had with an educator at the Tagesheim. "'I often work with these kids at night,' Ruchka [Reinchold] once told me. 'They baffle me. They're four or five years old. They rarely wake up at night like normal children, and when they do, they don't cry. They don't ask for anything. They just lie still or talk to themselves quietly. There's no one to cuddle them. No matter how [hard] Dr. Bieberstein tries to make them feel like children, they're just haunted little Jews, scared, frightened, always on the watch. Knowing little Jews.'"[88]

When the safety of the children was concerned, the Tagesheim personnel took rumors seriously and responded accordingly. At one point, there was a rumor in the ghetto that children who had jobs would be treated as adults and would be spared deportation. In response, the Tagesheim set up a stationary workshop that specialized in making envelopes. Regina Nelken testified about the situation of the little ones. "The children worked till they dropped. They would return home with their heads aching, sad, exhausted, and resigned." Because of their age, "there were some children whom it was impossible to persuade to work; they would run out into the yard at every opportunity so as to be able to play for a moment, playing tag, swinging on boards, and so on. Others ran away back home and declared categorically that they would not go to work."[89] Roman Liebling, a ten-year-old boy at the time, remembered that in the final weeks of the ghetto, children, including him and his friend Stefan, were put to work in the Tagesheim. They received one meal a day and an hour of tutoring. Their work consisted of making paper bags, folding and gumming sheets of brown paper.[90] Jewish educators meant to protect children through their work in the day care center, but the workshop eventually served a purpose for the Germans. It was a means to record the number of children left in the ghetto.

Regina Nelken recalled that speculation about the imminent destruction of the Kraków ghetto increased exponentially. "Meanwhile, rumors spread about the final liquidation of the ghetto and here it was known that a terrible thing will happen." On the morning of 13 March 1943, Nelken was at the Tagesheim when the news spread. By order of the commandant of the Plaszow labor camp, Amon Goeth, who led the final action in the Kraków ghetto, children were to gather in the already crowded Tagesheim, irrespective of whether they had parents or were orphaned. Goeth "promised" that the children would be brought to Plaszow the following day. "Mothers and fathers came with children; some of them said their goodbyes, while others went completely mad [and] left their children and ran away; heartrending scenes took place," Nelken recalled. She remained with the scared and crying children until Dawid Gutter, the commissar of the Jewish Council, entered the Tagesheim and ordered all employees to leave the premises.[91]

The Germans murdered the majority of children from the Tagesheim on Plac Zgody. Their bodies were brought into the Plaszow camp and buried there. A small fraction of the children managed to survive by hiding in the ghetto. Some of them later entered the camp by sneaking in, were smuggled inside, or were permitted to enter the camp owing to the privileged positions their parents, then Plaszow prisoners, had held in the Kraków ghetto. The experiences of these children compose the next chapter of the Germans' persecution and the Jews' efforts to protect them.

CHAPTER 5

Concealed Presence
in the Camp

For Ewa Ratz, who was six years old when she entered the Plaszow labor camp, the difference between the ghetto and the camp was that in the camp violence was visible and regular, and the Germans were constantly present.[1] Not immediately apparent in the camp was the presence of children, who, because of their age, were considered dispensable. Despite the Germans' ban, children slipped into Plaszow, where they traversed the new landscape of their persecution. Regina Nelken, a child educator in the Kraków ghetto and later an inmate in Plaszow, explained, "And here, too, they [children] had to be either in hiding or counted among adults, and so toil in workshops. . . . They had to be constantly kept hidden from the authorities."[2] This chapter explores the concealed presence of Jewish children in a camp whose purpose and operation intertwined with the how the Holocaust evolved in Kraków District, as well as with the larger Nazi anti-Jewish policy in the General Government and beyond.

The creation of the Plaszow camp was connected to the resolutions of the Wannsee Conference (20 January 1942), at which Heinrich Himmler, the leader of the SS and chief of the German police, secured authority over "the Final Solution to the Jewish Question" and assumed control over Jewish slave labor.[3] The emergence of Plaszow was also tied to the dissolution of ghettos in Kraków District. Himmler's order of 9 October 1942 paved the way for concentrating all Jews—who until then had worked in and outside ghettos—into camps. The Plaszow camp originated as one of three *Julags* (*Judenlager, Zwangsarbeitslager* or *ZAL für Juden*), or labor camps for Jews in Kraków.[4] SS-Unterscharführer Horst Pilarzik supervised the construction of the Plaszow camp. SS-Oberführer Franz Josef Müller took over as commandant of Plaszow and its two satellites, Prokocim (Julag II) and Bieżanów (Julag III), in January 1943.[5] SS-Unterstürmführer Amon Goeth became the commandant of Plaszow a month later. In conjunction with the liquidation of the Kraków ghetto on 13 March 1943, the camp, officially called Forced Labor Camp Plaszow of the SS and Police Leader in Kraków District (Zwangsarbeitslager Plaszow des SS und Polizieführers im Distrikt Krakau), inaugurated its operation as a site solely for Jews.[6] It fell under the jurisdiction of Oberführer Julian Scherner, the chief of SS and police in Kraków District.[7] It also became subject to the SS Main Economic and Administrative Office headed by SS-Obergruppenführer Oswald Pohl. When Pohl transformed (on 22 October 1943) Plaszow into a concentration camp, its name changed to Concentration Camp Kraków-Plaszow (Konzentrationslager Plaszow bei Krakau) on 10 January 1944. Some twenty-five thousand prisoners passed through Plaszow.

Deliberate planning dictated the geography of the Plaszow camp, which served as a continuation of Kraków's ghetto.[8] The camp spread over three districts (Płaszów, Wola Duchacka, and Podgórze) and encompassed two Jewish cemeteries.[9] The fact that it was walking distance from the ghetto (1.8 miles, meaning about a thirty-five-minute walk) eliminated the need for intricate logistics upon its liquidation; able-bodied Jews were transferred with ease. The camp's position near railway tracks allowed for the swift transport of robbed goods and of products made by prisoners, just as it expedited the deportation and transit of human cargo. The workshops, factories, and warehouses that existed inside and outside the ghetto, and whose inventory was transferred to the camp, as well as the Krzemionki stone quarries, effectively exploited all resources: human and material. From an initial stretch of approximately twenty-five acres, the camp expanded to two hundred acres by September 1943.

The interior site was divided into three parts: administration, labor, and living areas. Surrounded by a double set of barbed wire on the outside and electrified wire on the inside, the perimeter was guarded by Germans and Ukrainians. Prisoners assumed policing roles. Individual members of the Jewish police (Ordnungsdienst; OD) from the ghetto, as well as new men designated in the camp, supervised their fellow prisoners. Wilhelm Chilowicz, the OD chief, served as camp elder, while his deputy, Mietek Finkelstein, served as commandant of the order service, and Chilowicz's wife, Maria, supervised the women's section of the camp.[10]

Although the Jews' transfer to Plaszow did not constitute radical displacement in the sense of geography, the living conditions imposed on them destroyed family and communal life. Still, together with the workshops, the hierarchical and neighborly, collegial, and familial structures from the Kraków ghetto shifted to the camp. Plaszow emerged both as a continuation and a disruption of the forced patterns of wartime existence of Kraków's Jews. Children constituted an immediate target. The Germans perceived them as a hindrance to the efficiency of Plaszow as a slave labor center. However, Jewish children's existence there demands investigation into how wartime chronology and stages of the camp's evolution influenced the children's experiences, adult responses, and German actions. Focusing on children's experiences in Plaszow illuminates the multi-functional character of the camp as a site of concentration, labor, and exploitation; a holding pen, transit camp, and prison; and a site of annihilation, execution, and mass graves.[11]

———

Marcel Haber, a young boy, began his letter to his sister with the following words: "I write because I have nothing to do. I will tell you how I got to the *lager* [camp]."[12] On 13 March 1943, unable to exit the Kraków ghetto with his parents, and prepared to hide in case of such a situation, Marcel took some bread and, entering a carpentry workshop through the roof, hid in its attic. From his vantage point he spied two Ukrainians and two Jews who came to retrieve goods from a kitchen near his hiding spot. When he saw the four men drinking vodka together, Marcel decided it was safe to emerge. Heavily bribed and persuaded by the two Jews that they would receive more if they complied, the Ukrainians agreed to take Marcel to Plaszow. Marcel's story exemplifies the few choices available to children once they were separated from their parents. It also highlights the prevailing loneliness and desperation that eventually led some, like Marcel, to seek to enter an even more restricted place than the ghetto.

Faced with a strict prohibition against bringing children under the age of fourteen into the camp, some parents smuggled their young children into the camp under coats or in rucksacks, falsified their documents, or pushed them into columns of adults heading out to Plaszow. During the liquidation of the ghetto, ten-year-old Jerzy Hoffman's OD uncle placed him among workers lined up at the exit. "Until this day I do not know how it happened that I managed to survive," Jerzy recalled.[13] Luck, chance, and his uncle's fast action allowed Jerzy to leave in time, as did his uncle's privileged position. In fact, some OD men used their special status to smuggle in their own children, as well as those of their relatives, friends, and even strangers.

Other children hid in the then defunct ghetto and waited for an opportune moment to enter the camp clandestinely. Eleven-year-old Roman Ferber and his brother hid on a cart wheeling possessions from the former ghetto into the camp.[14] Other children remained in a group hiding place that was identifiable by their loved ones who were already in the camp. That information was passed on to members of the *Sauberungskolonne*, a squad composed of about fifty Jewish prisoners from Plaszow, who were brought in daily to sort possessions left by Jews and clear the area of the former ghetto. Ignacy Markiewicz joined such a group the day after the ghetto was liquidated. He discovered that his two sons and his niece survived in hiding. After eight days, he smuggled the children into Plaszow.[15] Other workers undertook such initiatives also, risking their lives to do so.

If some children relied on adults to reunite with their parents in the camp, the longing for their family, as well as the pervading sense of loneliness and fear of denunciation, drove others to initiate action. "Everyone was in the camp—my parents, sisters, brothers, acquaintances. Only the two of us—Halina and I—were in the city. We were drawn to the camp, to our loved ones, to the Jews," fourteen-year-old Janka Warszawska recalled. Yet Janka had little comprehension of what that new holding place for Jews actually was. "In general we had no idea what it was like inside the camp. We thought it was like a kind of a ghetto."[16] Janka and her sister approached the wires to bring food to their family. They went undetected quite a few times, until a Polish boy denounced the two sisters. Once in the camp, they paradoxically experienced a sense of relief. No longer forced to endure hardships associated with passing as non-Jews on the Aryan side, they were finally able to stay with their family. Like other children who joined their loved ones in Plaszow, they recalled their sense of overwhelming joy at unification. Twelve-year-old Rena Hocherman, who entered the camp with a group through the intercession of her OD uncle, remembered what she felt upon seeing her parents: "This was by far the most happiest day in my entire life."[17] Being with their parents and relatives, and simply among other Jews, gave some children an enhanced sense of personal security.

While a number of children remained in the camp once they found their way in, some sneaked out or were smuggled out soon after arrival. Faced with extreme conditions in the camp, and realizing the dire situation of children who were too young to work and whose parents or caretakers were not privileged prisoners, some parents or guardians made a desperate decision. Some relinquished their children in the hope that they would have a better chance of survival outside the camp. Others decided to find their way out together with the child. Each option, however, involved its own set of challenges.

After a short time in the camp, seven-year-old Marian Kwaśniewski fled from Plaszow with his mother. Under the cover of night, the two approached the camp gate, where Marian's mother bribed a German guard to let them out.[18] Most likely, Marian's mother had previously arranged the escape. Jews in the camp knew about many a guard's venality. They were aware of the repercussions for their acts. Unless they were in the camp "illegally" (they had been smuggled in) or another prisoner took the place of the escapee, adults registered in the camp as workers endangered the lives of other inmates by escaping. Penalties ranged from beatings to shooting every tenth prisoner in a line. During the first, more chaotic stages of the camp's existence, prisoners who found the courage, had the valuables, and possessed the contacts on the Aryan side, or had a plan as to what to do once there, had more leeway to escape.

Another method of escape involved a more concealed approach. While this method might not have involved a guard's silent consent and payment, it did require previously secured contacts on the Aryan side. This points to the existence of communication channels between the camp and the city, and between Jews and Poles, primarily through outside work details. For example, twelve-year-old Pinkus Fajnwaks merged into a column of workers leaving Plaszow. He had previously left his hiding place on the Aryan side to join his parents in Plaszow and, with the help of adults, was thrust into the line of workers marched into the camp.[19] By the time of his escape from the camp, Pinkus could retrace his path in reverse. Other children employed an even more covert way of escape. Nine-year-old Helen Ungar either already knew or was pointed to an exact spot where she crawled under the barbed wire. Once beyond the perimeter of the camp, Helen met a woman on the Aryan side, who took care of her.[20]

If some children left the camp permanently, a few exited temporarily. Stella Müller's case is perhaps unique. Her father, a former OD man in the ghetto, arranged for his thirteen-year-old daughter to be smuggled out of and then back into the camp with the ghetto-clearing crew. At that time, some 160 Jews, including members of the Jewish police, Jewish Council members, German informants, foreign Jews, and employees of the Jewish Aid Agency in the General Government (Jüdische Unterstützungsstelle; JUS), and their immediate families were allowed to remain in the dissolved ghetto area. The Germans confined them to the Jewish Council's administrative building.[21] (The remnant ghetto ceased to exist on the night of 14–15 December 1943, when members of the OD and Jewish Council were loaded onto trucks, brought to Plaszow, and shot.)

Stella desperately wanted to bathe. Privileged Jews, her family's friends, lived in the remnant ghetto, and she went to them. Stella's short absence from the camp had a soothing effect on her; she was bathed, clothed, and fed. This, she later explained, restored her humanity. At the same time, leaving the camp allowed Stella to observe the reactions of ordinary Krakovians to their former neighbors. Stella recalled a range of responses from Poles—from those who pretended not to see her, to those who stopped and shook their heads and wept. While adults tended to look the other way, or expressed support for the prisoners, children and teenagers reacted with cruelty, yelling at the Jewish prisoners and throwing snowballs at them.[22] Ironically, for children like Stella, the camp offered protection from the dangers that Jews endured in the city. Plaszow was the only place where she was allowed to be legally.

———

Stella entered Plaszow as a child. She was able to remain there as an adult prisoner and a slave laborer after her mother registered her as two years older than her actual age. Many Jews had already realized the importance of work during their time in the ghetto. In the camp, classified as able-bodied, children such as Stella had a chance to stay alive.

Children who worked and lived openly in the camp were subject to the same camp routine as adults. The inmates' existence revolved around roll call, work, and food. The sound of a trumpet dictated the prisoners' lives. One tune woke them up; another announced the roll call, signaled the end of work, and even

accompanied the march to barracks. Roman Ferber described the camp sched-
ule: prisoners arose at five in the morning, and after roll call, they marched to
work. They toiled for twelve hours, with a one-hour break from one to two in
the afternoon, and stopped at five in the evening. At six, a general roll call tal-
lied the total prisoner count. Jews received food three times a day. "Black coffee
in the morning, a liter of soup for dinner, and coffee and a quarter of a loaf of
bread with some margarine and marmalade in the evening."[23] As these rations
were insufficient to keep the inmates alive, prisoners relied on food smuggled in
by (privileged) prisoners who worked outside the camp, who then sold the food
in the barracks. Jews also depended on goods supplied by JUS, a successor of
the Jewish Social Self-Help, which the Germans deactivated on 29 July 1942.

The Department of Population Affairs and Social Welfare (Bevölkerungswe-
sen and Fürsorge) by the Office of the Governor General reactivated JUS with
the former head of the Jewish Social Self-Help, Michał Weichert, at the helm on
13 March 1943. The Germans controlled how foreign aid (from the International
Red Cross) was channeled and allocated to Plaszow prisoners. Members of the
Council for Aid to Jews "Żegota," an arm of the Polish Underground State created specifically to help Jews, objected to the cooperation between JUS and the
Germans. The arrangement set up the Germans as protectors of Jews and posi-
tioned Weichert as their collaborator. Still, Weichert did his best to obtain food
for the needy, but little reached them. As survivor testimonies explain, the camp
elite (OD men and prisoner workers in the camp's administration), as well as
German and Ukrainian guards, and Goeth himself, grabbed most of the goods.

Notwithstanding the meager rations, according to Weichert's postwar trial
testimony against Plaszow's German and Ukrainian camp crew, "Plaszow differed from other camps in that here both the German companies and the [camp]
crew were interested in keeping Jews alive."[24] This approach highlights a split
between ideology and pragmatism. The food that JUS brought into the camp was
supposed to feed inmates who were still able to work. But the Germans did not
mean to sustain Jews' life in general. JUS activities served as a compromise
between the camp authority and German industry. The numerous specialized
workshops in the camp, as well as outside companies (such as Madritsch and
Emalia), provided ample opportunity to profit from slave labor and nestled German officers, who were responsible for running and overseeing the camp, in
their administrative positions.

From the perspective of young prisoners, there were more and less desirable
labor assignments. The "attractiveness" of the post depended on such factors as
the type of work, its location, the unit supervisor, and the frequency of German
inspections, which could expose child workers and carry punishments. Parents
and caretakers strove to find positions for children in places they considered
"safe," meaning those in which children would be inconspicuous. Marcel Grüner,
eight years old at the time, recalled, "In the Plaszow camp Daddy placed me in

a brush factory, because it was claimed that unemployed children will be shot."
He explained his tasks. "We made shoe and clothes brushes, shoe paste brushes,
shine brushes, and bottle brushes. There was a norm to be filled; one had to make
50 shoe paste brushes."[25] As a small child, Marcel was at times unable to meet
that quota; in those circumstances, an adult worker usually stepped in to help,
risking his own life in the event of discovery. The brush factory was arguably
the "safest" workplace in the camp for both boys and girls looking for anonymity. Niusia Horowitz, then twelve years old, landed a position in the same workshop as Marcel. "I became an expert in making brushes and I was quickly ready
to fulfill the quota," she explained.[26]

If the brush workshop was—in terms of life and work conditions in Plaszow—a
relatively safe workplace for children, its location across from a killing site, called
by prisoners Hujowa Górka, instilled fear in all.[27] Through his position as a central warehouse manager, Niusia Horowitz's father managed to find her work in
Oskar Schindler's Emalia factory. It was make-work that mostly involved wip-
ing pots, but it allowed her to exit the camp, if only for a few hours. Between
March and May 1943, the Germans marched daily some three hundred prisoners (Niusia among them) to the Emalia plant. When Schindler's factory became
a subcamp of Plaszow on 8 May 1943, its one thousand or so workers (including
children) were housed in barracks on the Emalia grounds. Niusia's parents and
several relatives were among them.[28] Ryszard Horowitz, Niusia's younger brother,
remembered Schindler's Emalia plant as a "haven" compared with Plaszow. Even
as a boy of four, he felt moments of danger and distress associated with being
moved back and forth between the camp and the factory.[29]

Similarly, twelve-year-old Ida Jakubowicz viewed the Emalia plant, where she
worked alongside both Jewish and Polish workers, as an improvement compared
with the camp. She performed hard work, carrying heavy dishes to the oven for
baking, but she was no longer subject to Goeth's violence, did not witness killings, and had access to food. However, as an orphan, a child, and a Jew, she had
little protection and served as an easy target. When a Polish laborer accused Ida
of stealing from the woman's pocketbook, three female German guards dragged
Ida out of the hall and flogged her. She endured assault, yet she explained, "I also
want to remember the nice things that we did for each other in our barracks,
where there were other people with some spirit, who wanted to try to keep the
other people alive."[30] Some of the coping strategies she remembered from her
time in Emalia included singing, pretending to light Shabbat candles, and saying blessings.

The Madritsch factory in Podgórze, where laborers sewed and mended German uniforms, proved another relatively benign workplace. Twelve-year-old
Celina Karp was marched back and forth from the camp to the factory each day.[31]
When workers were no longer permitted to exit Plaszow, Julius Madritsch moved
his factory into the camp (in August 1943) and Celina continued her work there.

With its two thousand workers, the Madritsch workshop became the largest private company in the camp in September 1943. Prisoners who worked for Madritsch enjoyed his protection and received larger food rations than those available to the average laborer, which allowed them to share food with their families. Yet working at the Emalia and Madritsch factories constituted a unique experience for only select children.

Children were often compelled to change their workplaces, but they usually remained within the camp proper. Roman Ferber's experience exemplifies this pattern. "I worked in the brush workshop, where we made brooms, hand brushes, shoe brushes, etc. Then I worked in a paper workshop together with my father, who made envelopes, notebooks, boxes, etc., and then [I worked] in the kitchen where my mother worked."[32] Obtaining such desirable work alongside one's parent was not easy. In Roman's case, his mother's privileged position as the sister of the OD chief, and his brother's role as a camp scribe, might have helped. Happily for Roman, his parents could keep an eye on him and he, in turn, felt somewhat protected.

However, working in the same place potentially exposed children to violence directed by the camp crew against their parents, and against the children. Rena Hocherman worked in a sewing workshop with her mother. Taking advantage of slowdowns at work, Rena read Polish books that had been smuggled into the camp. When a German officer, John, noticed her, he beat her mercilessly while her mother sat there, helpless.[33] Likewise, Ida Jakubowicz, before she was transferred to Emalia, had worked in the stone quarry alongside her mother. Beatings, kicking, and killing were widespread in that Ukrainian-guarded work squad. Ida could hardly watch as her own mother became the target of such violence.

The finding at a postwar trial against the Plaszow perpetrators concluded that "the stone quarry was inseparable from Plaszow. This was one of the methods leading to fast and thorough inanition of the prisoners."[34] Mostly women and girls were tasked with pulling carts loaded with stones. The norm was for seventy women (sometimes with the assistance of ten men) to complete thirteen to fifteen rounds in twelve hours. Assignment to the construction squad (*Barackenbau*) entailed equally difficult work. Eleven-year-old Giza Beller labored with her mother "working the wheelbarrows, rolling soil onto the road.[35] As a thirteen-year-old girl, Leah Zimmerspitz carried logs in that squad. With a look mature for her age and her mother's protection, Leah was able to survive the harrowing work.[36]

———

Parental, or even just adult, protection was vital in the attempt to ensure children's safety in the unpredictable and uncontrollable conditions of camp life. No wonder that parents and children's caretakers alike did everything in their might to assume key positions, forge the right connections, obtain timely information, and place their children in relatively safe places—all to the extent possible—in order to protect themselves and the children. It was in this context that an adult's, and by extension a child's, privileged position emerged. Status and an adult's "choiceless choices" (in the words of the literature scholar Lawrence Langer) influenced a child's trajectory in the camp, and in doing so exposed disparities in the survival strategies that were available to some Jews (especially Jews who entered the camp directly from the Kraków ghetto).[37]

"I had it good in Plaszow [*w Płaszowie było mi dobrze*]. Daddy was a warehouse manager; he had passes to exit the camp," Niusia Horowitz reflected shortly after the war.[38] Niusia assessed her experience in Plaszow in contrast to what happened after she was deported to Auschwitz-Birkenau. In retrospect, she recognized her advantageous circumstances in Plaszow in comparison with what she endured later.

Niusia's immediate and extended family remained together largely as one unit in Plaszow. That was exceptional. And Niusia was aware of it. Thanks to her father, who occupied a prominent position in the camp as a warehouse manager, the Horowitz family received extra food rations. What was key in Plaszow, they enjoyed a measure of protection by virtue of belonging to an esteemed group that Goeth found useful for his entertainment: Niusia's mother's family, the Rosners, were musicians. They were also shielded by Schindler, as they worked at Emalia. In that way, Niusia and her family acquired a more privileged position compared with other prisoners. As such, Niusia and the youngest children in her family could be openly present in the camp space. Nevertheless, Niusia's brother Ryszard was cognizant of the surrounding danger. "My initial reaction was to be frightened of all the terror and the dogs, and the shouting, and the guns, and the death," he said in a testimony many years after the events. He continued, "But after a while, being that young, you sort of tend to believe that's normal."[39]

While some children had the good fortune of being protected by their parents or caretakers who had (more or less dependable) leverage with the Germans, most other children (and their parents) in Plaszow were left to their own devices in trying to ensure their safety from incidental and organized assault. The presence of children in Plaszow posed problems from the very beginning. At first, the Germans forbade them to enter the labor camp, which, by definition, was off-limits to nonworking Jews. However, children of "prominents," meaning those who served as OD men or were otherwise useful to the Germans, were officially allowed to join their parents in the camp. Then, there were those children who entered the camp "illegally." All were an unwelcome yet obvious reality. Still, their presence allowed the camp administration to both exploit these children's slave labor and continue to deceive all Jews in the camp. Thus, on the one hand, Jews in the camp wanted to protect their children. On the other, based on what had happened in the ghetto, they understood the fragility of children's existence and the dangers of concentrating them in one place, even if that would help alleviate, to some extent, their already dire situation.

———

However greatly the Jews struggled to address the plight of children in Plaszow, the administration of the camp and control over its prisoners belonged to the realm of the Germans. A fortnight after the conversion of Plaszow into a concentration camp, Goeth ordered (15 January 1944) the creation of a special children's home (*Kinderheim*) in barrack 5.[40] Regina Nelken attributed the opening of the Kinderheim to the influx of Jews, including children, from other ghettos.[41] Stella Müller, whose father worked as a bookkeeper in the camp, stated that the prisoners bribed Goeth to open a Kinderheim. Perhaps parents hoped it would regularize children's presence in the camp.[42] It is most probable, however, that the order to establish a Kinderheim in Plaszow evolved from a combination of factors, bribery among them. First, the Kinderheim served as a response to Nazi politics. With plans to invade Hungary, the authorities needed a holding place for Hungarian Jews, and Plaszow might serve as one such destination. Unemployed children had to make room for working adults. Second, the Plaszow administration noted the excessive (by German standards) number of children in the camp, and recognized the need to fulfill anti-Jewish decrees and policies from above. Third, as Plaszow had become a concentration camp, the administration had to adhere to centrally defined rules and regulations, including those that mandated accounting for all prisoners and not allowing unemployed children on the premises.[43] All these factors necessitated the gathering and later removal of nonworking youngsters to make room for future transports of able-bodied adults.

A seemingly ad hoc German initiative, the Kinderheim was similar in scope, and eventually in its mission, to the *Tagesheim* (day care) in the ghetto. Jews were already familiar with the modus operandi from their time in the ghetto. Goeth charged the Jews with organizing the children's barrack. Compelled to comply, they relied on experience in running institutions dedicated to protecting and educating children. This undertaking was of course different. In a restricted and tightly controlled area filled with violence, lacking in food, and without the necessary structures and equipment to build and sustain child life, prisoners tasked with Goeth's project were doomed to fail. The children's barrack was nothing but a collection point for all children in the camp. Its charges included children who had one or both parents in the camp, those with only relatives there, and orphans. The determination of adult prisoners to address the acute situation of children and a glimmer of hope that these children would live motivated many of those involved in creating a semblance of childhood in Plaszow for its youngest prisoners.

Wilhelm Chilowicz, the Jewish elder of the camp, appointed Szymon Koch, an OD man, the "commandant" of the Kinderheim and its four hundred charges.[44] "I immediately called a few people to help and we began to assemble bunk beds to sleep on, we also set up a special dining hall and bathroom for children," Koch recalled in a testimony he submitted immediately after the war. He recognized the joint effort it took to establish a separate barrack amid a paucity of resources, and pointed to the fact that prisoners contributed extra time toward its development on top of their regular labor. He continued, "We bought dishes. Tables, chairs, and other equipment the carpenters built, who worked doing this at night, because during the day they had camp-related work."[45] Prisoners created a clandestine committee, which helped to feed children and finance expenses related to running a children's institution. Their efforts illuminate the extent to which Jews supported the new endeavor.[46] Koch's testimony also highlights Goeth's total disinterest in the basic needs of the new children's barrack and its inhabitants. To him, this task belonged to Jews themselves.

Strict rules applied to the functioning of the Kinderheim. The children's barrack was isolated from the rest of the camp structures and surrounded by barbed wire. Stepping beyond it carried a death penalty by shooting by the camp guards. An OD man, Salek Grüner, was responsible for overseeing the Kinderheim. Koch, called Daddy Koch by his young charges, supervised cleanliness and order in the barrack, as well as organizing food and water for the morning coffee and for cleaning. Parents could visit their children only at a set time in the evening. Despite the prohibition of the camp elder's wife, Maria Chilowicz, against parents seeing their children at any time, Koch permitted parents to visit and also to cook for and sleep next to their children. In exchange, mothers took turns cleaning the barrack and looking out for other children. Given the shortage of staff, with only two women serving as official caretakers, those mothers fulfilled an important function.[47]

Children's physical and emotional well-being assumed top priority for Koch and his crew.[48] The children's food was cooked in separate pots in the camp kitchen, and they received semolina with sugar, and groat (provided by JUS) for dinner twice a week. Adult prisoners dragged twenty pots of boiled water to the Kinderheim every day. In exchange for their service, workers received one loaf of bread for every four people. Koch explained, "This was a great expense, and we did not want to deprive children of bread, so we had to organize donations in the camp. Whoever could, contributed to making children's living conditions manageable."[49] To improve morale among his charges, Koch opened a garden in the fenced-off block in April 1944.

Yet, as Koch observed, "despite these seeming amenities, children in the *Kinderheim* were in a state of perpetual fear." Although they were cared for, and conditioned to the demands and limitations of camp existence, they were still in a hostile environment. They saw and heard what was happening around them. They were aware of their perilous circumstances. They were petrified. And not only they; the children's guardians in the Kinderheim were increasingly concerned about their safety. "We feared that Goeth would, on a whim, destroy all that in which we had put so much effort and work. We loved our children, we got attached to them, and we wanted to save them at all costs," Koch explained. Parents, too, regarded the situation with terror. Compared with else-where in the camp, children received better treatment in the Kinderheim. "Yet, mothers did not trust this 'institution' and often stole their children at night to have them close to them. They sensed that such a situation would not last long, that some terrible ill fate hung over them and their children," he recalled. Their prior experience taught them that the situation could only be temporary. "But," Koch continued, "they were powerless and had to submit [their] children to the *Kinderheim* because Goeth issued an order that every child found in the block would be instantly shot."[50]

The Kinderheim in Plaszow was a children's home in name only. It was another way to deceive Jews and lure them into thinking that their children would be saved. While not outright assaulted by the Germans, children in that barrack suffered emotional and physical deprivations, faced myriad constraints, and were subject to constant fear. A number of youngsters deliberately kept their distance from the Kinderheim. Leib Leyson, who was already fifteen years old at the time, reasoned that if Germans had no concern for able-bodied adults, they would not value a child's life either.[51] In a similar vein, Janka Warszawska refused to stay in the Kinderheim even if that meant forgoing better food. She managed to slip in occasionally before the barrack was fenced off completely. "I went there to eat because the food was better, but I didn't want to sleep there. I just didn't trust them," she said.[52] Janka and several children like her remained outside the confines of the Kinderheim despite the difficulty of keeping themselves hidden and the dangers of being discovered in the adult sector of the camp.

———

"Being a child I wanted to be invisible. Most of the time I was hiding behind people; I didn't want anyone should see me," Ida Jakubowicz recalled of her time in Plaszow.[53] Deploring the lack of support from other prisoners and suffering from her loneliness once her parents were deported, Ida tried to take her life by pouring hot water over herself and standing in the freezing winter cold. Yet she did not even get sick. After this occurrence, Ida receded into her own world. In the absence of a friend or relative whom she felt close to, she designated God as her companion. While other child survivors did not relate such intimate infor-mation as suicidal thoughts (if they had any), or, as in Ida's case, actual attempts, Ida's reflection provides a glimpse into children's psyches in Plaszow, and their innermost struggles. Her account also highlights a key aspect of children's exis-tence in the camp: the requirement to conceal themselves. Most children brought that experience from the ghetto. But finding places to hide in an environment of extreme confinement, surveillance, and terror turned out to be difficult, if not impossible for many.

Ida Jakubowicz recognized the need to hide, although she was a laborer in the camp and was considered useful. But she also knew that being a child put her at risk for incidental or deliberate disclosure, which would affect her fate in the camp, where children were disposable. Paradoxically, living in the open in the character of an adult worker also required children under the age of fourteen to employ tactics to disguise themselves. Young nonworking children, by contrast, had to fully disappear from the Germans' view, and often also from the sight of other Jews. "In Plaszow I was mostly hidden," Elsa Biller, who was between eleven and twelve at the time, explained.[54] Her use of the passive voice is deliberate. It was not she who was tasked with finding hiding places; it was her mother who pointed her daughter to them. Elsa spent her days on bunks, or generally "behind things." The fear Elsa felt was slightly assuaged by her mother, who Elsa knew would take care of everything.

Confronted with long days when everyone else departed for their work details, children (sometimes with their mothers) were left with little to do.[55] Halina Horowitz, then between ten and eleven years old, recalled that she enjoyed the company of other children (her cousins) in her barrack. They played peculiar games primarily aimed at mental escapism, such as dreaming, fantasizing, and disappearing mentally. Adults also instructed children to be inconspicuous. "What we had to do is not to show ourselves," she explained.[56] Stella Müller observed the few toddlers in her barrack. Their behavior oscillated between staying silent in mannequin-like positions and becoming panicked when they were pressed (and pushed by adults) to crawl under bunk beds to hide.[57]

The reactions of fellow barrack dwellers to the presence of children differed. Most expressed their support and participated in shielding children from the Germans, even when faced with the loss of their own children. Other responses were negative, especially immediately after the liquidation of the ghetto and the transfer to Plaszow. Renata Grünbaum Spira's three-year-old child was smuggled in by her OD brother-in-law. "In the camp, women, whose children were annihilated, could not forgive me that my child was alive. They harassed me and my child; they couldn't stand when it [sic] played or laughed," Renata recalled.[58] Mothers were devastated that their own children were either killed or left hiding without a possibility of joining them and forced to face the uncertain circumstances on their own. As a coping mechanism (psychological projection), some mothers unleashed their anger at their co-prisoners whose children were counted among the lucky few survivors and managed to slip into the camp. These children and their mothers were the objects of jealousy and loathing.

Envying and blaming parents whose children reached the camp stemmed from self-accusation about the inability to reunite with one's own children. Such feelings amplified as children continued to arrive at the camp through 1944. Eight-year-old Bernhard Kempler and his older sister Anita, with a group of other people, were brought from Montelupich prison after being discovered on the Aryan side. Thanks to the intercession of their uncle Zygmunt Grünberg, an engineer in the camp, Bernhard and Anita were placed in barracks while the other children from the group were killed. Later, a woman from that transport, whose own children were shot, went mad and followed Bernhard and Anita around. Bernhard recalled his time in Plaszow as otherwise unremarkable, perhaps because he was sheltered by his uncle, who held an important position in the camp.[59]

"A relatively large number of Kraków [Jewish] children hid in this camp. . . . These were mainly children of foremen, block supervisors, room supervisors, and Jewish policemen. It was of course easier for them to hide their own children compared to regular prisoners," Eugenia Felicja Myszkowska, a prisoner in the camp, recalled.[60] Indeed, the majority of children who entered Plaszow and were either physically camouflaged or concealed as adults belonged to what was considered the more prominent class of prisoners. These were offspring and close relatives of Jews, whom the Germans granted positions of relative (and only temporary) power. Before the creation of the Kinderheim, these children stayed in barracks with their mothers. That was public knowledge and, from the Germans' standpoint, an unacceptable reality. The OD men were in a difficult position, terrorized, and torn between loyalty to their fellow inmates and the hope of saving themselves and their loved ones if only they cooperated. While feared by the prisoners, they often warned block supervisors about planned barrack inspections. That gave parents time to conceal their children.

Hiding was not a new survival strategy for those children who had been primed to conceal themselves in the ghetto or on the Aryan side. In the camp, while the barracks served as a main hiding place, some children hid elsewhere. Roman Ferber hid in a warehouse where Jews' valuables were collected and sorted. He was lucky in that his brother Moniek warned him of incoming danger. Owing to the connections he forged with a German for whom he made boots, Zygmunt Norbert was able to take his daughter, who was about five at the time, from the Kinderheim. He hid her in a closet in the shoemaking workshop where he worked.[61] Another unlikely hiding place was the infirmary barrack. When eleven-year-old Anna Lewkowicz arrived from Montelupich prison, she was sick with typhoid fever. Despite her being visibly ill, Anna's mother persuaded the Germans that her daughter was older and able to work. Instead of being sent directly to work, Anna went straight to the infirmary. There, Leon Gross, the Jewish camp doctor, placed her in a hiding spot to avoid selection.[62]

Hiding inside the camp meant that children did not receive their own food rations. Food had to be organized by their parents. In many cases, parents shared their own meager portions. Other parents bought food that was smuggled into the camp and sold on the camp's black market. Some children, especially the older ones, realized their parents' efforts and expressed uneasiness in their postwar testimonies for having been a burden. Others accepted the food unknowingly. Still others took their own initiative. Janka Warszawska slept until noon to avoid the nagging hunger. Then, with some twenty other children in her barrack, she roamed the camp in search of food, an activity some children had practiced in the ghetto. "We were well organized. We would wander around the peeling barracks and the kitchen, and whenever there was a chance, we would immediately go and grab potatoes. Then we would go behind the barracks, make a fire, and bake them." Of course, this could not be done in the open. Children like Janka carried over their experience of stealthy behavior from their time smuggling into the ghetto. "We had to be very careful that no one noticed this. We posted guards on all sides to watch and warn us if anyone approached. In such a case, we would immediately extinguish the fire and scatter in all directions."[63] Their survival depended on finding food and remaining invisible.

The concept of survival itself acquired an extra dimension for children in Plaszow. Living in the present assumed the utmost importance. As historian Debórah Dwork has observed, the idea of survival "did not signify a long-term strategy to outlive the Nazi regime, rather it meant a more or less inchoate formulation of a number of basic precepts to help them navigate the perils of daily existence."[64] Roman Ferber quickly learned how to maneuver in the camp's realm. "You develop an interesting survival instinct; certain things that you try to avoid: the dog, the gun, the Germans. And for that matter, some of the Jewish policemen that were administering the camp."[65] Youngsters identified and reacted to warning signs to the extent possible. Their strategy consisted of circumventing rather than confronting possible danger.

For some children, staying alive implied a hope for a future that spurred some to carry on. If looking forward served as one approach to survival, reaching to the past constituted another. Whenever he was beaten while doing hard slave labor, Jan Rothbaum—who was about thirteen at the time—became numb. He dreamed about the positive things from his prewar life, like the time he learned to swim. That, he acknowledged, helped him survive.[66]

Other children employed a combination of schemes to help them make it through another day in Plaszow. Jerzy Hoffman remained in Plaszow only for a week. He remembered he was rather successful at hiding and caring for himself. He credited his survival to how he viewed himself in relation to others. "Sounds maybe selfish, but I was only interested in me at that point. I wanted to know when I would get something to eat, only made sure when shooting was going on I wasn't there, and I wanted to make sure I only somehow survived the war," he explained.[67] Jerzy did not have a plan for survival, nor could he depend on one if he had it. Circumstances forced him to focus on himself and live in the present, anticipating and responding to events as they were happening.

Dwork sums up such an approach: "To negotiate each day was the sole goal, everything else was peripheral. This was what was meant by 'survival.'"[68]

Survival through clandestine presence and covert activities was on the minds of children and their guardians alike. It was also of concern for mothers of unborn babies. Goeth required pregnant women, deemed unfit for work, to register with the OD. Eventually, they were slated to be shot. Pregnant women had two illegal choices: either give birth to the child or have an abortion. One charge against Leon Gross—introduced in a postwar trial that accused him of complying with German orders in Plaszow and thus contributing to the overall annihilation of Jews—was that of performing abortions.[69] His activities, however, point to risking his own life to rescue another person. Unable to save babies, he could help the pregnant woman live through another day. To the Germans, Gross lied that he was performing surgery for a "common female condition."

———

Notwithstanding the efforts of Jewish prisoners, German plans slated the children for death. The Kinderheim was not meant to shelter children or lead to their survival. Instead, it constituted a step in their final removal from the camp. That endeavor was connected to the Nazi anti-Jewish policy of exploitation and annihilation. Simultaneously, children's fate in Plaszow also depended on the evolving situation in German-occupied Europe and particularly on German plans for dealing with the some eight hundred thousand Hungarian Jews when Germany occupied Hungary in March 1944. In preparation for the arrival of one transport of Hungarian Jews to Plaszow, Goeth called a health roll call (Gesundheitsappel).

"One time there was a huge roll call in the camp; the date of which I don't remember," then nine-year-old Marcel Grüner began his description of the largest action in Plaszow.[70] Although he did not register the timing of the event, that action was seared into his memory precisely because of its scope and repercussions. On 7 May 1944 all prisoners had to pass naked in front of a commission led by the German camp physician, SS-Hauptsturmführer Max Blancke, brought in from the Majdanek camp in Lublin District. The estimated 1,400 prisoners who failed the selection (including the sick, those who looked weak, and children) received a red card and their data were recorded.[71] On May 10, news spread in the camp that children would be taken to Auschwitz. "Mothers, crazy with fear, rushed to the Kinderheim wanting to save their children at the last minute. Unfortunately, nothing helped," Szymon Koch recalled.[72] Ukrainian guards surrounded the barrack and its list of children was seized. For three days, children were isolated inside the barrack. On May 14, Goeth ordered all prisoners to the roll-call square.

"I remember that horrible day. . . . The heat was unbearable. We stood on the Appelplatz infinitely," Niusia Horowitz recalled.[73] Those marked off in the selection a week earlier were now called out. Giza Beller knew what that meant. "It was clear what this was all about; children were of course unnecessary, same as the elderly and the sick, and they needed to be shot."[74] But no one expected the type of suffering and death Goeth had in mind for the victims, and the pain this would inflict on their families and the prisoners in general. The OD men, tasked with assisting in the smooth progression of the action and ensuring that all those on the selection list stood separated from the rest of the prisoners, combed through the lines in search of evaders and pulled out children. Crying mightily, the children were taken out on trucks and wagons. Mothers suspected the fate the Germans had in store for their children. "There was panic on the square; mothers ran in the direction of the alleys where the children were being wheeled away; they were driven off, there was shooting, moaning and crying echoed," Niusia continued.[75] As the prisoners stood on the roll-call square, "trucks arrived in front of the *Kinderheim*. SS-men dragged children out of the block and loaded them onto the cars. Pale, frightened, crying children called desperately for their mothers' help. But the help did not come," Koch related.[76]

As the children were carted out, in a gesture of pure perfidy, Goeth ordered the prisoners to sit with their backs to the road so as not to see the children. "Perhaps he feared some spirit of resistance on our behalf as a result of desperation," Henia Wollerówna conjectured in a diary she wrote immediately after the war. "Unfortunately, we were just a bunch of helpless, desperate, and powerless prisoners." Exacerbating the despair, music started to play from loudspeakers, drowning the mothers' and children's cries. "To intensify our emotions, we heard a song of a dying child who, bidding farewell to its [sic] mother, promises her it [sic] would not forget her even in heaven. Our hearts were torn," Henia continued.[77]

Some children managed to survive primarily because of their parents' position in the camp. Wilhelm Chilowicz chose such "privileged" children. Goeth, unhappy that Chilowicz spared too many, handpicked who would be pardoned.[78] Marcel Grüner explained how a parent's or relative's "privilege" affected a child's chance for survival. Goeth "called out Romek Ferber because his brother was a camp scribe, Wilek Schnitzer because his father was the manager of the Madritsch factory, Zbyszek Gross because his father was the camp doctor, Genek Günter because his father was a supervisor at the DAW [Deutsche Ausrüstungs Werke], Rysiek Horowitz because his father was a supervisor in the Central Warehouses,[79] and two girls: Marysia Finkelstein, the step-daughter of the deputy to the camp elder; and Ewa Ratz because her mother worked for the German camp director."[80] The "saved" children were taken to the OD guardhouse, from where they observed what was happening. Other children noticed the "safe house" and wanted to hide there as well. A few managed to reach it by various means. For example, German female guards liked one girl, Halinka Mingelgrun, and allowed her to enter.[81] Marcel Grüner's father, an OD man, on the other hand, pleaded with Goeth to let his son stay with the chosen group. Eventually, Marcel joined the "saved" children. He recalled that about fifteen other children managed to enter the safe house.

Without the possibility of slipping into the OD guardhouse, other children seized the opportunity that chaos and the guards' lapse of attention on the roll-call square offered to seek refuge elsewhere within the camp. Jerzy Spira recalled, "Children ran between the barracks. The guards [ran] after them with rifles."[82] Standing still, Jerzy did not attract attention. He took advantage of the commotion and rushed to the latrine, where he saw another boy, Rysiek Nussbaum, and a cousin, Blanka Pinkusfeld. Joined by four other girls, the group sat through the action inside the latrine openings. Other children followed suit.[83] In some cases, older children assumed responsibility for younger ones. Roman Ferber took care of his younger cousin, Wilek Schnitzer (both were on the "protected list" but hid just the same). Together with three other girls, they found shelter in the latrine. They could not jump inside the opening because it was too deep for them, so they descended inside and held on to side poles.[84] For Wilek, hiding in the latrine constituted his most vivid visual memory of Plaszow. With a paucity of places to hide, the latrine became the go-to shelter. Possibly it is where children were instructed to go by adults in case of commotion. Or it was simply the only logical option at that time.[85]

Other children avoided detection with the help of their parents or other prisoners. Niusia Horowitz, whose name was on the "protected list," hid in the central warehouse in the camp, where her father was a manager. Giza Beller, on the other hand, was already standing in the children's row on the roll-call square when her mother ran for her. With the silent consent of two OD men, "Mommy caught up with me and grabbed me on my sleeve and grabbed me back into the row. This is how Mommy rescued me yet again."[86] Janka Warszawska slipped back into the workers' rows by herself. Other prisoners, including Janka's older sister Lola, protected her. "I sat down on the ground, people stood all around me, covering me, and no one noticed me," she explained.[87] Ida Jakubowicz, on the other hand, did not even appear on the square that day. She was sleeping in her barrack because she worked night shifts. Women in her barrack covered Ida, who was sleeping on the highest, third tier of the bunk bed.[88]

After several hours, the "children's action" in the camp was over. Prisoners were released from the roll-call square. Children who hid in the latrines realized when the raid ended because people began coming to that barrack. While some adults knew about children who were hiding inside the holes, some child survivors had to call for help to be noticed. After staying for hours amid feces and inhaling lethal gases, some of the children were on the verge of death. Eugenia Felicja Myszkowska led Franciszka Günter to the latrine, where she knew the latter's son was hiding. "We pulled out the boy, who was already losing consciousness from the latrine fumes. When we finally managed to revive Jerzyk, we began to scrub the child, soiled up to his eyes. We did not even have what to clean him with; we used only remnants of coffee to clean the child, who stank terribly for the next few days."[89] Once they were fetched, children were cleaned to the extent possible and placed in barracks. Not meant to exist, they had to remain in hiding.

There was yet another reason why the few child survivors of that action remained inconspicuous. Ala Dychtwald recalled that immediately after the action, "from the blocks one could hear desperate sobs of mothers and fathers, and of those whose loved ones were taken away."[90] In despair, and mourning their losses, some of those parents could not bear the sight of children who had managed to elude capture. Other parents and older children knew that. They also remembered the reactions they received when children were smuggled into Plaszow following the liquidation of the ghetto. Marcel Grüner, who belonged to the group of "saved children," explained, "The 30 of us sat in the guardhouse for two weeks. We could not enter the camp ground because people whose children were taken away could not look at us; they cried day and night."[91] Children tried to make themselves invisible. Aware of the fragile situation, Stella Müller pushed herself into a corner, feeling guilty for her own survival.[92] Parents, too, depressed, retreated into mental and physical seclusion.

The removal of children from the Kinderheim overshadowed a deportation that affected some 1,400 prisoners. Aleksander Biberstein, a Jewish doctor in the camp, recalled that 286 children were deported to Auschwitz that day.[93] Most likely, Biberstein based this number on the official register of children from the Kinderheim that Szymon Koch supplied to Goeth. The figure was probably higher as children were pulled out from the square and included in the transport. Jerzy Spira estimated that only about twenty children remained in the camp after the action, while Marcel Grüner claimed that in his own group there were thirty children.[94] Janina Ast, on the other hand, deplored that "there were now no other children left in the camp—we were the last four Jewish children of Plaszow."[95] The divergence of numbers points to an overall feeling of desolation among child survivors of that May 1944 action. It suggests that children were so well concealed they did not even know about each other's presence. This was crucial as Plaszow remained a concentration camp that formally prohibited children.

Plaszow served as a labor camp, but also as a killing site for Jews from spring 1943. In the beginning, killings took place in the area of the old Jewish cemetery. Later, executions and mass burials were transferred to what the prisoners called Hujowa/Hujarowa/Kozia Górka, or simply *górka* (the hill). There, prisoners from Plaszow, Jewish prisoners from Montelupich prison in the city (who had been discovered hiding on the Aryan side), and detainees from the OD prison in the former ghetto were killed. The second place of mass murder, called Cipowy/ Lipowy Dołek, was the killing site of the Kraków Gestapo.[96]

Prisoners, including children, quickly realized this camp function. "We entered at the moment of hanging Haubenstock and engineer Krautwirth. I was a witness of an execution."[97] This is how Niusia Horowitz recalled her introduction into Plaszow. She was smuggled into the camp with her younger brother Ryszard and their cousin Alex Rosner shortly after the liquidation of the Kraków ghetto. Their parents were already in the camp.

The day after he arrived in Plaszow, Roman Ferber witnessed the transport of corpses of elderly and children. "We later found out that these were corpses of children killed in the so-called *Kinderheim* [*Tagesheim* in the ghetto] and people who tried to hide inside the ghetto, and who were subsequently shot."[98] Their bodies were buried in mass graves in the camp. Sabina Mirowska, a former educator in the children's home in the ghetto, recalled what happened before the burial. "The children's clothes were brought to the clothing warehouse in the camp in Plaszow and more than one mother recognized a dress or a coat of their child among the clothing."[99] This left no illusions about the fate of children upon the liquidation of the ghetto.

The Germans also shot children who were smuggled into the camp and discovered at the gate. Dawid Grünwald arranged for his two children to be brought to Plaszow when a Polish manager of a mill in Podgórze refused to keep them for more than a day after the liquidation of the ghetto. One child was shot immediately upon arrival. Dawid's seven-year-old daughter, Halina, miraculously survived when the body of the person who had been killed seconds before fell on the girl.[100] Ida Jakubowicz survived to tell her own story. She was taken with a group of other inmates to a ravine that was already filled with bodies, and was ordered to undress. A bullet landed in her leg, and she fell on top of the bodies. Other Jews covered the graves with soil. She described what she felt at the time. "I am lying in the grave with all the dead people and I'm touching myself. I don't know if I'm dead or I am alive. I was lying there for a little while, but because they didn't put so much soil on the top, I don't know how long I was there." The clothes that the prisoners were ordered to submit before their execution were still scattered near the grave. "I put something on," Ida continued. Even many years after the events, she admitted, "I can't believe that I got out of that grave." Ida eventually crawled to the barrack, to the disbelief of her fellow inmates.[101]

Executions took place almost daily in the camp. Giza Beller explained, "On our way to work we passed by this 'hill' where people were shot and burned on stakes. There were constantly executions, people from the city were brought, who were caught on Aryan papers; there were many children among them."[102] Giza's recollections, as well as numerous other testimonies from Plaszow survivors, point to the frequency of such killings. What is significant is that the Germans confined their murder sprees to the camp. Niusia Horowitz described how such killings proceeded, since the brush workshop where she worked was located near the execution hill. While the Germans murdered out of non-Jews' sight, they did so in full view of the Jewish prisoners to instill terror. "I saw young people, children, and the elderly going to their death. I will not forget the macabre scenes that took place on the 'hill.' People undressed completely, laid beside each other, and the machine gun swept them into the grave dug out next to them. And then stakes were lit, on which corpses burned day and night," Niusia recalled.[103] Sometimes victims waited in the OD guardhouse for their turn to be killed. While the OD men were present at the executions, burial belonged to another prisoner unit.

The first task assigned to thirteen-year-old Eugeniusz Kamer upon entering Plaszow was to join a group of three prisoners to dig a grave and bury seven men who had tried to escape. "I was the youngest one of the group. This was the first time I had seen a dead body, let alone one bloody and riddled with bullets, and of course, this was the first time I had to dig a grave. I still relive that scene in my nightmares after more than fifty years."[104] Young people like Eugeniusz were drafted by the Germans for such labor, which intensified in the summer and fall of 1944. What they experienced served as a warning against attempts to escape from the camp and disobedience to camp rules in general.

———

In addition to its role as a labor camp, killing center, and place of mass burial, Plaszow served as a penitentiary for Jews. Two prisons operated within Plaszow. One, called Krancówka, consisted of a barrack surrounded by barbed wire and was intended for camp prisoners punished for light infractions of camp rules. The second prison, Gray House (Szary Domek), most important for this study because Jewish children passed only through this one, operated from 15 August 1943 to 14 October 1944. The Gray House consisted of five general cells, one dark room, and twenty standing bunkers. The standing bunkers were only for camp prisoners, while the regular cells in the basement were for prisoners brought on order of the Gestapo, German special police (Sonderdienst), or Criminal Police (Kriminalpolizei; Kripo). Wilhelm Kranz, a Jewish prisoner, served as the *pro-fos*, or supervisor, of the camp's internal prison system, and his postwar testimony constitutes a primary source for information about the prisons' operation and inmates.

According to Kranz, after 14 December 1943,[105] Gitla Landau Katz was brought to the prison in Plaszow with four children (her three children and niece), who ranged in age from six months to seven years old.[106] They were discovered hiding in the nearby town of Wieliczka, but they were not killed right away owing to their Hungarian citizenship. Rachel Landau, Gitla's niece, who was seven years old at the time, survived the war and submitted her testimony. Her recollections complement Kranz's version of events.

When Rachel, her two aunts, and her three cousins were brought to Plaszow, they were certain they would be killed, which suggests they already knew about Plaszow's function. But they were thrown into a big room in a cellar, with barred windows blocked with wood. Many people, both men and women, were already in that chamber. A German by the name of Karl or Karli brought them bread once a day.[107] Kranz entered the cell with the Germans twice a week. He recalled feeling a special sensitivity toward the plight of the youngest inmates. "I observed these poor children; frightened and holding their breath, stiff with fear."[108] They did not know what awaited them. Not part of the camp system, the children secretly received food from the Kinderheim. Kranz took the children on walks every day, and once a week to bathe. This special treatment resulted from the Landaus' status as relatives of Josef Nechemia Kornitzer, the prominent last pre-war chief rabbi of Kraków.

If Rachel and her cousins enjoyed a "privileged" status owing to their illustrious lineage and identification as foreign nationals, other Jews held in the prison cell with them did not possess such leverage. Similar to Rachel, these Jews, children and adults, were denounced or otherwise exposed while hiding or passing as non-Jews on the Aryan side. Once in Plaszow's prison, they refused to admit they were Jewish and continued to try to persuade their oppressors to release them. Doing so was nearly impossible to accomplish. Rachel recalled one woman with a blond-haired, blue-eyed child. The German conducting the questioning beat the mother mercilessly. When those in the cellar heard her screams and pleas, they assumed the daughter was being bludgeoned too. Thus, the prison served as a place of terror, torture, and investigation, in addition to being a holding pen for children of unconfirmed background brought from the Aryan side. Kranz recalled that at the beginning of March 1944, eight-year-old Niusia Całmińska (Bronisława Brucha Schlang) arrived in Plaszow after she was discovered hiding with her family's prewar housekeeper. Niusia was thrown into the same cell as Rachel Landau.

Youngsters such as Niusia were well versed in secrecy and adhering to their new identity and life stories in order to legitimize their presence on the Aryan side. They employed the rehearsed and ingrained practices even, and especially, upon confinement. When Niusia finally confessed to Kranz her real name, he arranged for the girl and her mother, a prisoner in the camp, to meet in the OD guardhouse in the presence of Chilowicz. Seeing Chilowicz, who was dressed in a leather coat and Tyrolean hat, waving his whip, Niusia balked at acknowledging her mother. "The girl, fearing it was a German, did not want to admit it and even in such a moment, at eight years old, knew how to control herself and behave like an adult," Kranz recalled.[109] Only when Kranz explained that Chilowicz was a Jew did Niusia embrace her mother.

Niusia remained in the prison for about two months, until May 1944. For her and most children like her, the Gray House served as a way station en route to the "hill." Thus Plaszow acted as a prison and a killing site. But as a hybrid camp, it also held another function—that of a place of transfer. For Rachel Landau and her relatives, that meant leaving Plaszow in a car on 13 July 1944. Herded onto a train, they headed west, first to the city of Breslau, and on to the Bergen-Belsen concentration camp in Germany, which served as an internment hub for Jews who held foreign passports, and who were part of exchange programs with the Nazis. However, for Jews left in Plaszow, the role of the camp as a transit place facilitated the Germans' plan to continue to exploit Jews' slave labor.

———

Following the May 1944 action, Plaszow assumed the role of a transit camp for prisoners to and from Auschwitz and to other camps in Germany, as well as for Jews from Hungary. Located in the General Government; sufficiently distant from the eastern border, where the Red Army operated in spring 1944; and close enough to Auschwitz and the western border, Plaszow constituted the ideal transit hub.[110]

"Plaszow was a horrible place," thirteen-year-old Livia Friedmann, who was deported from Auschwitz to Plaszow with her mother and aunt, recalled. She explained, "Even in Auschwitz you did not see such naked violence. Even though the gas chambers were in Auschwitz and the crematoria, you did not see the immediate violence, it was not that apparent to you as it was in Plaszow."[111] The ever-present, brutal, and unpredictable German cruelty toward Jewish prisoners is what differentiated Plaszow from other camps, including Auschwitz. It was in Plaszow that Livia discovered the German practice of decimation, the shooting of every tenth person in a line. She found herself in a new and dangerous set of camp conditions that all prisoners had to navigate, but most particularly those shipped in from elsewhere.

Transit prisoners also had to deal with the specific demography of the prisoner body in Plaszow. "We were greeted horribly in the camp," Giza Beller recalled of her transfer from the city of Tarnów to Plaszow in October 1943.[112] "I don't know why everyone was so resentful against people from Tarnów," she continued. Giza quickly realized that Plaszow mainly contained former Kraków ghetto inhabitants, who were relatives, friends, and neighbors. For this insular community, anyone from the outside—even another Polish locality—invaded their space and disturbed the relationships and structures they had preserved from the ghetto, created in the camp, and fostered throughout.[113] A particular type of power dynamic among prisoners, and between prisoners and the camp administration, ruled in Plaszow. Kinship and friendship networks determined access to food, as well as mutual aid, and often solidarity among prisoners.

Jewish prisoners from countries other than Poland had an especially hard time adapting to the conditions and demands of Plaszow. Duration of life under Nazi persecution mattered. Polish Jews, as opposed to Hungarian Jews, had experienced life under the German occupation and in the ghetto for five years. Language mattered, too. While some Hungarian Jews and Polish Jews in the camp spoke Yiddish, prisoners communicated in Polish. Mirl Rubin was thirteen years old when she was deported from Auschwitz to Plaszow with her sister. As a Hungarian Jew, Mirl sensed resentment among her fellow prisoners. For example, Krakovian Jewish "old-timers" in Plaszow would not give bread to the Hungarians. Mirl learned the importance of possessing connections in the camp. Fortunately for her, two women Mirl knew worked in the camp kitchen. They hid potato peels under the electrified barbed wire, which Mirl and her sister retrieved.[114]

Plaszow differed, too, in what inmates were allowed. When Livia Friedmann arrived in the camp and saw prisoners wearing regular clothes, women with their hair, and men wearing caps, she thought they were political prisoners, not Jews.[115] Timing mattered. After January 1944, all prisoners were required to wear camp uniforms, but the few most privileged inmates did not. The Germans, both industrial exploiters of Jews' slave labor and camp administrators, had dealt with the same Jews for a few years. Their policy was defined by constant abuse, while at the same time allowing for a few concessions. The exceptions Livia noted led to the self-positioning of old-timers higher in the camp hierarchy. The outsider status of prisoners like Livia lowered their opportunities for accessing food and decreased their chances of remaining indistinguishable from the prisoner body. And increased visibility meant heightened risk of harm.

While young transit prisoners negotiated their existence in the present realm, young old-timers in Plaszow deliberated what the camp's new function meant for the camp's and the prisoners' future. To Stella Müller, the transports from Hungary, Czechoslovakia, and the east signaled an impending end to Plaszow.[116] Chaos increased, the camp was bursting at its seams, and burnings on the hill of corpses dug out from mass graves intensified. Deportation from Plaszow loomed for the entire inmate population.

————

As the Soviet Army made its way into German-occupied Poland in late summer and early fall 1944, the Germans embarked on erasing the traces of their own crimes. They did so using the slave labor of prisoners, including children. Such work consisted of digging out mass graves, removing the corpses, and burning them to destroy the evidence of the mass murders they had committed. Moreover, the Germans ordered the barracks dismantled and loaded onto trains, and the demolition of other structures to remove physical vestiges of organized persecution.

Digging out the six mass graves began at about four in the morning on 8/9 September 1944. At first 80, and then 170, Jews (including children) were drafted for this labor. "Work consisted of digging out the graves, carrying corpses in one place (after prior removal of gold teeth), piling up wood and setting fire to it," reads a postwar report about Plaszow.[117] Prisoners who survived these assignments recalled the locations of the mass graves, the timing of killings, and the approximate number and types of victims in each grave.[118] Mirl Rubin described her work and the emotions associated with it. She was ordered to level the hill outside the camp gate. Her job was to remove the bodies with her own hands, bring them inside the camp, and burn them. Mirl admitted that she did not fully comprehend what she was doing. It was only then, in Plaszow, when she participated in the burning of corpses, that she understood the smell in Auschwitz.[119]

In conjunction with the removal of corpses, the Germans began to evacuate prisoners to camps in greater Germany beginning in August 1944. Prisoners were sent to Auschwitz, Stutthof, Flossenbürg, Mauthausen, Gross-Rosen, and Buchenwald. "In 1944, probably in the summer, I went on a transport to Gross-Rosen with my father. Some 700 people were on the train," Marcel Grüner recalled. The majority of the men went to Brünnlitz. "Everyone wanted to go there because that is where the pots factory—Emalienwerke from Zabłocie—was, and everyone was eager to go to the factory." He explained why: "A German, Schindler, was the manager of that factory; people said that he was good and helped Jews." Yet "Daddy could not get us on that transport and we stayed in Gross-Rosen."[120] Once Schindler's factory was closed in Zabłocie, "his" workers were transferred back to Plaszow. Schindler intervened through official channels in Kraków and Berlin for permission to transport the over one thousand workers and their children to his new work camp in the Sudetenland.

The deportations from Plaszow accelerated. According to a roster dated 30 September 1944, there were 4,595 prisoners (both Polish and Jewish) in Plaszow, including 16 boys and 12 girls marked as "unemployed children."[121] The final transport departed from Plaszow on 21 October 1944, and only the liquidation group remained inside the camp. The last Germans left Plaszow on 14 January 1945, and the last 646 prisoners (including 600 Jews) were marched to Auschwitz. Four days later, on January 18, the Soviets entered Kraków.[122]

A small number of Jewish children survived Plaszow thanks to extreme luck and often their parents' and caretakers' privileged position in the prisoner hierarchy. In Plaszow, where Kraków's Jews had known each other for a long time, connections to the Germans, familial and collegial networks, and valuables could translate into a chance to live another day. While no children were present in Plaszow by October 1944, a number of them continued to hide on the Aryan side of the city. They had done so throughout the existence of the ghetto, as well as during the operation of Plaszow, prompting the Germans' hunt for them. While some had been caught in the city and killed in the camp, a few survived undetected until the Soviets arrived. It is to their history that we now turn.

CHAPTER 6

Survival through Hiding
and Flight

To escape from the approaching German army, one-year-old Elżbieta Reiss, her parents, and the girl's Polish nanny, Zofia Janicka, fled from Kraków to Lwów in September 1939. By early 1942, the situation in Lwów, then occupied by the Germans and renamed Lemberg, had worsened. A personal connection saved Elżbieta: Janicka smuggled the girl back to Kraków, to the apartment that she shared with her sister, her brother-in-law, and the couple's two-year-old daughter, thereby risking the lives of several people. It was a joint effort to shelter the girl and keep her presence secret from neighbors. By the time the Germans barged into the apartment in October 1942—they had been denounced—Elżbieta was already with her parents in Warsaw. That situation did not deter Janicka from caring for Elżbieta again when the Reisses returned to Kraków in 1944 and waited to be smuggled across the Slovak border to Hungary.[1]

Elżbieta Reiss's patterns of life on the Aryan side, from flight to hiding, point to the role of mobility as a dimension of children's efforts to survive. This chapter addresses the core themes threaded throughout this book about the role of space and place and the ways in which remaining inconspicuous defined children's lives in those realms. Children passed as non-Jews, remained completely hidden, or adopted a combination of the two. Some were forced to fend for themselves. This chapter explores Jewish children's experiences in homes, in rooms, in group houses, in convents and monasteries, on the streets, and en route to perceived refuge. As life on the Aryan side was inextricably linked to the willingness of non-Jews to provide care and shelter, children often meandered between various hiding places, adapting to new conditions and people. If for some Jewish children being on the move involved operating on the Aryan side of the city until the end of the war, for others it extended to leaving Kraków, and German-occupied Poland, altogether. This time, unlike the avenues of escape pursued in September 1939 when Jewish families headed eastward, the direction led south.

———

In Kraków, children usually began their journey on the Aryan side in private homes. The sudden appearance of a child sparked questions from nosy neighbors, so aid givers used ruses to legitimize the child's presence and prove a Polish Catholic background. One way was to spread news about the arrival of an orphaned relative, or encountering a foundling. Some rescuers presented their Jewish charges as their own children, risking familial rejection and social ostracism. Katarzyna Dudzik, a twenty-six-year-old woman, took in two-year-old Isidor Poser in March 1943 on his parents' assurance of remuneration for her efforts.[2] Even when the promise of payment failed to materialize, Dudzik continued to shelter the boy, renamed Józef, claiming him as her own child. She distracted attention from herself when she married Stanisław Matusz. Isidor became the man's adopted son.[3]

Such adoptions were not as common as the more usual practice of simply taking children from orphanages. The Polish Care Committee (Polski Komitet Opiekuńczy) transferred seven-year-old Sara Warszawiak from a convent in eastern Poland to Kraków in winter 1943.[4] Given the new name of Irena Jabłońska, the girl was housed in an orphanage run by the Congregation of the Sisters of the Third Order of St. Francis (the Albertines). Polish women visited the overcrowded institution for what children themselves referred to as "market days" to pick out girls to serve as helpers in the women's homes or to select a child they could raise as their own.

Therefore, the women's actions represented either exploitation or rescue of the vulnerable children, or both simultaneously. A nun from the Congregation of the Ursulines of the Agonizing Heart of Jesus (the Ursulines) recalled the procedure. "Often, people who wanted to raise children came to the orphanage. Perhaps they looked for children who could serve as substitutes for the offspring they lost or for those they never had. Perhaps they were motivated by noble ideas to raise an abandoned, poor Polish child."[5] Sara was fortunate; she was chosen and was accepted even when she disclosed her identity to her adopted parents.[6] And the convent was relieved of a burden and had room for newcomers.

When it came to sheltering Jewish children, religious institutions, and individuals for that matter, often acted in the context of networks. Organized help emerged as non-Jews and Jews began to grasp the systematic and coordinated nature of Nazi anti-Jewish policy. That realization transpired late. In February 1943, Tadeusz "Socha" Seweryn, the Kraków delegate of the Polish Underground State and the head of the Civilian Struggle Leadership (Kierownictwo Walki Cywilnej), received an order from his superior.[7] His task was to establish a Kraków branch of the Council for Aid to Jews (Rada Pomocy Żydom "Żegota").[8] Its aim was to consolidate and coordinate help to Jews, and include in those endeavors members of different political parties, the clergy, social workers, and other individuals. The Kraków Żegota began to operate on 12 March 1943, on the eve of the liquidation of the Kraków ghetto.[9] With little time and few resources to provide effective help (arranging escape routes, recruiting escapees, and securing hiding places and money), Żegota issued a general appeal to Krakovians. Although the document originated from the Civilian Struggle Leadership in September 1942 in Warsaw, it continued to be valid in Kraków in March 1943. The Underground called on Poles to resist anti-Jewish propaganda, fight blackmailers, and help Jews. Such appeal, the activists hoped, would mold popular attitudes through education in the belief that once gentiles became aware of the Jews' plight, their prejudice would diminish.[10] That assumption, as we will see, was incorrect.

From its inception in Kraków, Żegota faced constraints. It did not have a separate children's section, and it is unclear how many of its aid recipients were children. The extant sources note that the number of Żegota's charges in the Kraków region increased in the course of seven months, between April and December 1944, from 250 to 670. These figures reflect the growing call for help, especially during winter, and against the Germans' (and their local collaborators') continued actions in the region. Żegota's expenses skyrocketed from 50,000 złoty a month in 1943 to 1,400,000 złoty a month by the end of 1944.[11] The money covered the costs of hiding places, medical care, clothing, and food. According to Miriam "Mariańska" Hochberg, the Jewish representative in Kraków's Żegota, "The main problem was how to pay, and whence to get funds to pay the hospitable Poles."[12] Many Poles had no financial means to support another person in their household.

Some members of the Underground, welfare organizations, and the church, as well as individuals not affiliated with any of these, galvanized efforts to rescue Jewish children in their homes and institutions. The activities of Aleksandra "Krysta" Mianowska, a social worker in the Main Welfare Council (Rada Główna Opiekuńcza) and a Żegota member, point to the connections that were established and how they were used to benefit children.[13] When Ewa and Janina Feldman, eleven and nine years old, respectively, and their mother, Rozalia, escaped from the ghetto after liquidation, they headed to the girls' grandparents' prewar apartment in Kazimierz.[14] The building superintendent put Rozalia in touch with Mianowska. The courier turned to the most unlikely place for a Jew to be—a convent. Seeking nuns' help was a practical decision. In theory, only Catholics stayed in Catholic institutions. The assumption was that the moral influence of the church would inhibit the Germans as well as potential denouncers from disturbing convents. Mianowska approached the Albertine nuns to arrange for one night of shelter for Rozalia and her daughters. She did not have to reveal to the mother superior that her charges were Jews. What was not clearly heard could not be confessed. In the absence of a uniform church policy on rescue, the mother superior of each convent had final discretion about admitting children.

Like all non-Jews, members of religious institutions risked the death penalty for aiding Jews. Social disapproval and intimidation also hampered their actions. In addition, they struggled with economic problems. The German authorities requisitioned their buildings, limiting the space where nuns, monks, and priests could accommodate children. They suffered, too, from food scarcity and few sources of income. And passing off Jewish children as Catholics required that they obtain proper documentation for them and teach them Catholic modes of behavior.

Despite the difficulties, some Catholic orders in Kraków either accepted Jewish children or mediated in their rescue.[15] Convents cooperated with each other, including by transferring children between their institutions. This they did for their own and the children's safety, and to cope with overcrowding in their institutions. Orphans, abandoned and neglected children, and those whose parents or guardians were unable to care for them arrived in Catholic institutions. In the conditions of war, children of various backgrounds and ages, and with different behavioral and emotional problems, were grouped together. Overseeing children meant caring for and feeding them, but also enforcing discipline and instilling Catholic beliefs. Nuns, obliged to engage in works of mercy, offered assistance in a spectrum of institutions: crèches, day care centers, kindergartens, orphanages, soup kitchens, catechism classes, and refugee centers. Often, a convent managed multiple centers in different locations.

The two Feldman girls and their mother were sheltered temporarily in one of several sites run by the Albertine convent while Mianowska contacted members of the Żegota legalizing cell, Stefan Kamiński and Edward "Felek" Marszałek, to find a new address and obtain false papers for her charges. Edmund Seyfried, the director of the Main Welfare Council, arranged for Mianowska to relocate one of the Feldman girls, Janina, to Warsaw. The transfer of children within Kraków and outside of the city was risky. A female courier always accompanied the children to their destination. Younger children had little, if any, capacity for self-censorship. The questions they asked about their parents or the Yiddish they uttered could have exposed both the courier and the child.

Hiding Jewish children called for its own language to camouflage Żegota's actions. A ciphered telegram was sent to Zofia "Weronika" Kossak-Szczucka in Warsaw that specified the day and time of a book delivery (code name for Jewish children awaiting transfer) from Stefan Kamiński's antiquarian bookshop. Żegota was known in Kraków as "the firm" (*firma*). Tissue paper (*bibuła*) signified a registry of children; subdistributors (*sieć podrozdzielców*) were caretaker networks. Mobilization of charges (*mobilizacja podopiecznych*) meant recruiting

Jews in need. Distributive emergency care (*pogotowie opiekuńcze rozdzielcze*) consisted of places where children were prepared to live on the Aryan side. Janina, her sister Ewa, and the girls' mother reached Warsaw. Only those who stitched together the Feldmans' rescue knew the coded language and the "firm's" mode of operation.

Older children had greater awareness of their and their guardians' grave circumstances. Nonetheless, they had mixed assessments of their caretakers' treatment of them. Jewish children without prior exposure to Catholic institutions, for example, were unsure of what to expect from their saviors. Halina Leiman was about eleven when she entered the boarding school run by the Congregation of Sisters of St. Felix of Cantalice (Felician nuns) in Staniątki, some eighteen miles from Kraków. She explained, "I was a bit afraid of the nuns. I had never seen them before. I had nothing to do with them before."[16] In some cases, a child's apprehension resulted from her misunderstanding; in other instances, it stemmed from harassment and mistreatment by the child's supposed protectors. The case of Rachel Verderber, who was twelve when she and her younger sister Rechavah began to hide on the Aryan side, demonstrates both scenarios. On the one hand, her negative memories and appraisal of the wartime behavior of her caretakers, Maria and Marian Gruca, as egoistic, insensitive, and violent is counterbalanced by the reality of what Maria, in particular, dealt with at the time. Maria, like many female rescuers, procured food for a larger household while making do with fewer ration cards. She received financial assistance from the sisters' parents and from Żegota for the girls' upkeep. Still, Maria's actions exposed her and her family to grave risks.[17] "She lived under constant pressure and fear because she was afraid not only of the Germans, but also of the closest neighbors, who were very much interested in the children at the house," Gruca's daughter Halina recalled.[18] Despite the difficulties, Maria tried to ensure the wellbeing of the children under her care. But Rachel, a Jew, a female, and a child, was at risk of sexual assault by Marian's drinking buddy and maltreatment by Marian. If Rachel was threatened by sexual abuse, other children in hiding endured it, even if they chose not to disclose the fact after the war. Testimonies from children living under false identities and hiding on the Aryan side routinely mention physical abuse (beatings) and mental harm inflicted by their non-Jewish guardians.

Children often blamed themselves for their guardians' discontent. They felt the need to compensate their aid givers emotionally for being sheltered. Bernhard Kempler, who was about six at the time, recalled that his and his nine-year-old sister Anita's prewar nanny and wartime rescuer, Franciszka Ziemiańska, was constantly afraid and threatened to leave them.[19] "I remember that that was frightening to me that she would leave us. And one thing that I would do in order to please her, I would be very religious as a Catholic, because she was very religious." Yet it was with her that Bernhard felt the safest. "And I began to think of her as our mother, which was helpful, actually, because that was the safest thing to do." Bernhard recognized that he had to earn his nanny's love. "I felt close to her, but, also knowing that she didn't have to be taking care of us, and that the only thing I could do for her to continue to do that was to be as good as possible, and to be as helpful as possible, to be as obedient as possible," he explained.[20] Bernhard also felt he had to redeem his sister Anita, who, in his eyes, was unruly, and whose Semitic appearance imperiled all of them.[21]

Children with stereotypically Semitic features (dark, curly hair; dark eyes; olive complexion) such as Anita Kempler's had slim, if any, chance of surviving on the Aryan side unless they remained hidden.[22] In some cases, elements of such features could be masked. As soon as Anita and her brother met their nanny after they had fled from the liquidated ghetto, Anita had a bandage wrapped around her head. The girl's cover story held that she suffered from an eye disease. In a postwar memoir written for juvenile readers, Anita recalled how her appearance affected her self-perception. "Every time I looked at myself in the mirror all I could think was: Jew, Jew. Ugly, obvious Jew girl."[23]

Masking a child's appearance was a temporary ruse. To pass as a non-Jew, children had to assume a new identity altogether. For older children, this meant observing and absorbing their caregivers' Catholicism, acquiring familiarity with religious observance, and attending church. In the prewar period, some caregivers transmitted Polish Catholic culture to Jewish children by taking them to church, teaching Catholic prayers and rituals, and exposing them to peasant culture by bringing them to their homes in the countryside.[24] This helped children during the war in their efforts to pass as non-Jews. Bernhard Kempler recalled the importance of his nanny's religious conviction in creating and sustaining his new identity. "And that part of what we did, did not feel like a masquerade. I did feel that it was safer to be a Catholic, not just appear to be a Catholic," he explained.[25] Catholicism was not the religion that led to victimization.

Ensuring that Jewish children became Catholic, or at least behaved like Catholics, posed a set of challenges, especially for nuns. Integration into the nuns' structured religious life demanded that the children become versed in Catholic tenets and rituals. Conformity was a matter of life and death. This required children to participate actively in Catholic practices, including the sacrament of communion. Children who were not baptized and could not participate in the ritual attracted attention and thus invited danger. Nuns understood this. But they were also agents of Catholicism, and their task was to proselytize. The dilemma that some faced was whether to wait for the child to mature sufficiently to make the decision to convert, to obtain a parent's consent, or to convert the child as a prerequisite for staying in the institution. For those nuns who believed that Catholicism alone offered salvation, the choice was clear.[26]

Conversion involved more than just a nun and a child.[27] Nuns and priests sent requests to the archbishop of Kraków, Cardinal Adam Sapieha, for permission to convert children. Such requests usually were granted the same day. Here, the canon law concept of conditional baptism was significant.[28] In the absence of parents, the nuns became the guardians; they were the ones who consented to baptize their charges, and they committed to raise the child Catholic. Canon law permitted, indeed required, conditional baptism for children who were in mortal danger, regardless of their parents' religion. Foundlings and children of unconfirmed background were thus eligible. The problem with the law was that it referred specifically to "infants" and "adults," with adults having to accept baptism knowingly. However, the provision that every person who had not been baptized could be baptized opened a loophole for converting Jewish children to Catholicism. Secular individuals, too, adhered to the provisions of canon law. For Aleksandra Mianowska, Żegota courier, it was insufficient that her charge, ten-year-old Felicja Seifert, held a real baptism certificate of a deceased girl. "There was nothing else to do but baptize the child at least by water," Mianowska stated in her postwar account. She recruited a priest to complete the sacrament in a private apartment so as not to endanger anyone. "Although any Christian could do that in unusual circumstances, I wanted this act to have some deeper meaning for the poor child," she explained.[29] She did it also to quell her qualms about committing potential sacrilege.

While acquiring a real or assumed religious and ethnic identity applied to both Jewish girls and boys, Jewish boys carried the additional burden of circumcision. Some parents of newborns chose not to follow this religious practice to increase the boy's chances of survival on the Aryan side. Older boys devised stratagems to conceal their circumcision. Zygmunt Weinreb, eight years old when he was denounced in summer 1943, approached the Albertine monastery for lack of other options. The brother superior suspected Zygmunt, who introduced himself as Czesław Bojdak, was Jewish. The monk instructed the boy to bathe in his underwear so that his peers would not discover his background.[30] Another option was to conceal a boy's gender. Bernhard Kempler recalled, "It was also decided that I should masquerade as a girl because that was safer."[31] Bernhard's nanny renamed the boy Bernadetta and dressed him up as a girl when they hid in a shelter run by the Albertine nuns. Since the shelter was an all-female institution, the nuns welcomed the child's disguise. Taking on a girl's identity meant dressing like a girl and learning to speak Polish using correct female forms, which Bernhard learned from his sister and their nanny. In time, Bernhard recalled, "I spoke like a girl, I looked like a girl, I braided my hair, I acted in every way like a girl from that point on until the next four, five, years." However, Bernhard never totally assumed his adopted gender. "I always knew I was a boy. I didn't fully understand why I had to do this other than it was dangerous for people to know I was a boy."[32]

Emulating a new identity by adopting another religion or imitating a different gender were two ways in which hidden children sought to pass unnoticed.

Another method was pretending to have a disability. After escaping from the ghetto following the June 1942 action, ten-year-old Maksymilian Perlmutter became Tadek Szelest. But the Germans soon assigned additional inhabitants to the Szelests' apartment. The Szelests told Maksymilian to feign deafness to avoid attention. By refraining from speaking, Maksymilian, it was believed, would have a lesser chance to reveal his origin and would not disclose his social background through his manner of speaking. The boy controlled himself not to react to voices and noises and not to talk. This tactic spared him questioning until a new tenant caught Maksymilian answering Mrs. Szelest and became suspicious. A situation like this demanded a quick and believable explanation. Mrs. Szelest clarified that the boy read lips and, out of shyness, spoke only around family.[33]

In an effort to assume another identity, Jewish hidden children learned, too, to conform to what was perceived by the majority of the Polish population as "non-Jewish" characteristics. Many Poles associated Jews with certain attributes. One was a high level of intelligence and shrewdness. Another was a preoccupation with money and skill at finances. One precaution was to feign incompetence. Before Józefa Latawiec placed Halina Leiman (who by then had assumed the identity of a deceased girl, Janina Baran) in a Felician convent, she instructed the girl how to pose as a non-Jew: she should fail math class. In addition, Mrs. Latawiec forbade Halina to cry, explaining that only Jewish children did that. Children like Halina who were separated from their families had witnessed atrocities and experienced hardships. Many were emotionally fragile. Still, to protect Halina, Mrs. Latawiec ordered the girl never to exhibit vulnerability, which might raise suspicion.[34] By learning to guard against the array of supposedly Jewish traits, hidden children often acquired a negative perception of their own Jewish identity. They came to believe, quite correctly, that any indication of their Jewishness would expose them to scrutiny and peril, for themselves and their caregivers.

Efforts to assist Jews were hindered by penalties for breaking German law, which changed over time. The decree that established the Kraków ghetto forbade non-Jews to provide shelter to Jews. Transgressing the law resulted in confiscation of one's apartment.[35] The Germans noticed that both Jews and non-Jews contravened that law even after they instituted the death penalty on 15 October 1941 for Jews who left the ghetto and remained on the Aryan side and for non-Jews who helped them. More importantly, widespread apathy as well as the heavy risks posed by blackmail and denunciation affected Jews' chances for surviving on the Aryan side. Then too, the Germans rewarded non-Jews for hunting down Jews in hiding. The German Criminal Police promised to award up to one-quarter of the value of goods that a denounced Jew carried upon being apprehended.[36] These were some reasons why assisting Jews was the exception, not the norm.

In any case, indifference to the Jews' plight prevailed. It aided Germans in pursuing their anti-Jewish policy, as the collaborators' actions went largely unchallenged by their compatriots. Collaborators were feared by some and welcomed by others. They aroused fear because their presence and modes of operation endangered the work of the Polish Underground, exposed helpers and their Jewish charges, compromised the solidarity and honor in which the Polish nation took pride, and facilitated terror. At the same time, collaborators enjoyed the social approval of many of their compatriots. Their actions offered illusive prevention of German collective reprisals against resisters. They helped expedite what a number of Poles sought: the removal of Jews as economic competitors, asset wielders, religious enemies, and the symbol of all perceived national and social ills. Complicity in the persecution and murder of Jews was thus a multilayered phenomenon.

Some Jews (sources mention a group of forty-two such informants) collaborated too, posing grave danger to other Jews. The Kraków branch of Żegota reported to the Warsaw headquarters that "the biggest plague for Jews in hiding . . . are Jewish informants who serve the Gestapo and German police."[37] If some committed out of opportunism, others were pressured by the Germans, and still others engaged in the procedure as a survival strategy. The Jewish collaborators' modus operandi was to offer hiding spots on the Aryan side, extract information from those in hiding, and then denounce them to the Gestapo. One such denouncer, Stefania Brandstaetter, focused on children who spent time with their caretakers in Planty, the city park. She fished for children with Semitic features and sought to squeeze out as much information from the child as she could.[38]

Some child survivors hiding on the Aryan side recalled dangerous encounters with Jewish women. When Emilia Heller, about ten then, and her mother escaped from the Kraków ghetto, they met a Jewish woman, whom Emilia's mother asked for tips on shelters. (The description of that woman matches Stefania Brandstaetter's profile.) Anticipating compassion and assistance from a fellow Jew, Emilia's mother agreed to meet the woman again. It turned out to be a trap. "We saw from far away that there were two men waiting." Emilia's mother retreated. "She [the Jewish woman] was known, we found out later, that she was working with the Gestapo, because she was, I think, a mistress to one of them, and [the] only way she could survive, she had to denounce so many Jews."[39]

Almost all Jewish hidden children who lived on the Aryan side of Kraków experienced at least one instance of betrayal. The few who did not either were too young to remember such an occurrence or were extremely lucky. Children who knew about their Jewish origin and understood the danger it posed to them and their rescuers feared ordinary Poles and German officials alike. The difference between dealing with the former and the latter was that Polish blackmailers were ready to negotiate. Extortion was a lucrative business. The child mattered insofar as she served as a bartering commodity. When a Polish policeman, Piotr Pawłowski, came to the house in Borek Fałęcki where Sara Melzer and her six-year-old daughter, Zofia, hid under an assumed name, it spelled their pauperization and endangered their lives.[40] Without a baptism certificate for her daughter, Sara bribed the man with two items of clothing and 1,500 złoty. Pawłowski, encouraged by the profits he reaped, returned to harass them. He used his authority as a local, low-level member of the German occupation apparatus to instill fear in his victims and exploit them. The Melzers' hiding place was "burned," and they had to flee, this time to a village outside Kraków.[41]

Rescuers and prospective helpers, as well as children and their parents and relatives with whom they hid, operated in an atmosphere of constant intimidation. Żegota warned the Delegate of the Underground State about the extent and forms of blackmail. "No day goes by without a host of instances of blackmail, robbing the victim of the last penny and belongings. There is almost no family or individual that has not fallen victim to this hideous procedure."[42] Betrayal occurred on multiple levels. A common way of denouncing Jewish children in hiding and their rescuers involved sending letters and postcards (written in German or Polish) to the Gestapo and the city commandant. Jealousy and greed were two major drivers. Some denouncers wished to remove competition or settle old scores. Frustration with and bitterness about the war, the Germans, the occupation, and deteriorating living conditions contributed to denunciations too. Writing offered a way to feel empowered. Others denounced to divert attention from themselves and their own actions that contravened German laws or from fear of collective reprisals for someone else's "wrongdoing." There were also those motivated by the duty to report instances deemed unlawful by the Germans to prove their loyalty.[43]

For example, a letter dated 10 October 1941 informed on a Jewish woman, Fryda Fuchs, who lived in the Olsza district of Kraków with her daughter. The author, referring to her- or himself as "we Catholic Poles," believed she or he spoke for all Poles by excluding Jews, and thus Fryda and her young daughter, from the Polish national community. The author complained that Fryda's daughter boasted new clothes and enjoyed bountiful food, arguing that the Jews used the war to their own advantage. The writer proposed a solution—to deport Mrs. Fuchs to a penal camp or the ghetto "in some basement so that she sleeps on the floor and the rats bite off her long nose because we can't take this Jewry anymore."[44] The informant focused on the adult, ignoring the young girl. This may have been because of the understanding that the daughter would share the fate of her mother. But it was the child who served as an illustration of how Jews in general were believed to possess wealth they did not deserve in the first place.

Some letters never reached the Germans. A unit to snatch them was organized by Józef "Rak" Baster from the Home Army (Armia Krajowa; AK), the military branch of the Polish Underground State. Stefan Faber operated the cell at the

Main Post Office.[45] At times, a Polish policeman, either out of a sense of duty as an AK member or simply out of human kindness, alerted a child's rescuer.

Denunciation grew so rampant that the Underground State instituted a judicial branch to address the problem. The Underground worried about the consequences of betrayal on resistance activities. Special courts to try oppressors, betrayers, spies, and provocateurs were created as early as May 1940. Still, the number climbed. Denouncers of Jews and their rescuers barely made the Underground's target list before their activities proved so harmful that Żegota turned to the Delegate for Occupied Poland for help in December 1942. Beginning in 1943, special civil courts put betrayers on trial.[46] A retaliation-diversion group in Kraków was tasked with executing those found guilty of denunciations. The Underground press published the sentences as a deterrent to those who considered or engaged in such activities, and to present them as examples of anti-Polish behavior.[47] With the denunciation plague spreading, the Underground issued a decree on 7 February 1944 that permitted shooting denouncers and blackmailers without trial. Estimates of the number of informants in Kraków reach up to two thousand. According to Tadeusz "Socha" Seweryn, the special civil courts issued the death penalty for two hundred denouncers, sixty-seven of whom were in Kraków between mid-1943 and October 1944.[48]

These provisions failed to stop the ever-accelerating hunt for hidden Jews. The Germans relied on tips from their informants. German officers brought betrayed children (unless they were very young, in which case they were typically killed on the spot) and their rescuers to the prison at 7 Montelupich Street, known simply as Montelupich. (Some Jews were taken first to the Gestapo prison at 2 Pomorska Street.) Montelupich served as a detention, transit, torture, and killing center for Jews caught on the Aryan side of Kraków. German officers interrogated older children and their rescuers to reveal the names of people who assisted them and of other Jews in hiding. Sophia Śpiewak was seven years old when she and her mother were discovered on the Aryan side in March 1943. A German officer attempted to lure the hungry girl with a slice of cake to extract information from her. But Sophia knew that Jewishness implied something negative that she should not admit to under any circumstances.[49] Other children were physically tortured to divulge information. Anna Lewkowicz, who was ten then, recalled, "They placed some device on my arms that squeezed the veins. It was painful in the joints. They put masks on my face, pumped out air so that I was suffocating. Then they released some air. Martinets and thin and thick whips hung on the walls. They beat me with them so badly that my back was completely black."[50] The officers offered to place Anna in a convent, but she did not trust them. Only a small number of Jewish children and their non-Jewish caretakers were released from the prison. Seven-year-old Ewa Lewi and her younger sister who were living under false identities, and the girls' guardians, the Pawlaks, were let go, not after the girls passed questioning on Catholic prayers but only after the Pawlaks' daughter clarified that her family members were brought in by mistake.[51] Ewa was lucky. Most Jews were killed in the prison courtyard or transported to Plaszow camp or Auschwitz. The Germans sent a select few prisoners who held foreign documents to the Bergen-Belsen concentration camp in Germany.

———

Despite the challenges and dangers associated with life on the Aryan side of Kraków, Jewish children continued to reach it. While some received prearranged or improvised shelter and care, others fended for themselves. Children ended up on the streets before, during, or after an action in Kraków's ghetto or another ghetto in the vicinity, following its liquidation, and after unsuccessful hiding efforts. Either a planned search or an unexpected course of events led them to a temporary place of respite. Forced to live on the streets by circumstances, they had no other options at that moment. Yet children saw their own agency in the process.

Abraham Blim decided to take care of himself when he noticed what was happening during a deportation of Jews in his hometown of Proszowice, near Kraków. "Although I was only eleven years old, I understood that women and children were the Germans' first victims. It was then and there that I decided to live on my own. I let my parents know not to worry about me; that I will take care of myself," Abraham recalled.[52] He went to Kraków and entered the ghetto, worked as a smuggler of both goods and people, and, with his friend Wilek, escaped during the liquidation of the ghetto through the sewers. The two boys banded together on the Aryan side. With no place to go, they slept at the train station. For them, Kraków offered greater anonymity than the countryside to pass undetected, and more opportunities to earn a living.

Henryk Meller also found himself on the streets. During one of his smuggling missions, on 25 August 1942, an action in the Bochnia ghetto erupted. He did not return, instead remaining in Kraków with an aunt, Helena Kuśmierczyk. She arranged (for payment) for Henryk to live in the countryside and work as farm help. When his aunt was detained on suspicion of being Jewish, the money for the child's upkeep ceased and the peasant forced Henryk to leave. Unable to shelter her nephew following her release from jail, Kuśmierczyk was forced to leave the boy to his own devices. Twelve-year-old Henryk ended up at large.[53]

Henryk's story highlights the perils of child life on Kraków's streets. Alone, hungry, homeless, exposed to the elements, and at the mercy of strangers, Henryk embarked on a life that involved wandering. He employed cunning while counting on a dose of luck to survive another day. With no place to stay or to sleep, he hopped on trains. From his time as a smuggler and regular train passenger, he knew how to stay under the radar. Avoiding the train station in Kraków, he aimed for less frequented depots in either Proszowice or Słomniki, where he slept in hay stacks in the fields and in sheds at train stations. "The worst was that I had no apartment, I had nowhere to wash, to do laundry. So, I was so infested with lice that I scooped them out by the handfuls from under my armpits and I threw them out," Henryk recalled.[54] Later he learned of a delousing center in Kraków. He also managed to secure indoor sleeping quarters. After asking around, Henryk reached an elderly woman, nicknamed "Granny." She charged 20 złoty a night to sleep in her apartment on Pawia Street near the train station. She did not demand papers, perhaps knowing that some of the boys she sheltered were Jewish.

While some children had only themselves to take care of, other street children assumed the task of looking after their loved ones. Having escaped the liquidation of the ghetto, Herman Wohlfeiler's son and Janka Warszawska became conduits for information and food for their parents, relatives, and other Jews in labor camps. When Herman was no longer able to keep his eleven-year-old son in the Czyżyny airport plant, where his son sneaked in, the boy was forced to wander the area. He slept in barns, unbeknownst to locals who offered him food but not shelter. The boy and a friend, Stefan Lieberfreund, lived on the streets and slept in bushes by the Vistula River. By day, the young Wohlfeiler served as a news messenger for prisoners in his father's camp. He also helped his father by procuring food and slipping it under the camp wires. He did the same for his mother and older brother in Plaszow.[55]

Similarly, Janka Warszawska used the business acumen that she had acquired in the Kraków ghetto as a smuggler of both goods and people to support her efforts to procure food and other items for Plaszow inmates who were marched to workshops located in Podgórze. She also served as a courier for them, delivering letters to their contacts on the Aryan side. "By doing this, I earned a good living," she admitted.[56] Jews managed to smuggle some of their remaining valuables into Plaszow, and those who left the camp in outside work details had an opportunity to renew contact with former neighbors or establish new ties on the Aryan side. That is how Janka's clients had the means to pay her. She used the money she earned to purchase food for her own family in Plaszow. When the outside work details stopped, Janka continued to supply her relatives with food until she and her sister themselves entered the camp.

Children who remained on the streets had to find some source of income. Boys typically ended up selling cigarettes or newspapers. Some, like ten-year-old Jerzy Hoffman, engaged in such business only until they found a more stable situation. Jerzy registered with the Main Welfare Council as an orphan after his aid giver stopped receiving payment from his uncle for his upkeep. He was forced to wander the streets during the day and sleep in courtyards and under benches at night. Such children had the fewest resources and needed to employ brassy ruses to acquire food. For example, Jerzy picked up old newspapers that he collected on street corners from vendors and sold them as new. His method aroused anger among those who bought the papers from him, which forced him to change locations instantly.[57]

Other children treated peddling as a more stable and profitable business, so their approach to it differed from Jerzy's. Of the 40 złoty that Henryk Meller had received from his aunt's two sisters-in-law, he had 20 at his disposal after he had spent the other 20 on his meals at a soup kitchen. He realized that the only way to earn money was by peddling. He bought one hundred issues of *Goniec Krakowski* newspaper and sold it for 50 grosz each.[58] As he wandered the streets, he noticed that boys were selling Polish and German cigarettes, buying the latter from German officers. Henryk saw a business opportunity. In time, he was doing very well financially. Without having to split it with others or support his relatives, Henryk spent the money on food, clothes, and cinema tickets. Abraham Blim, a fellow street vendor, recalled the advantages of peddling: "One earned good money from selling cigarettes, and it was easy to hide them."[59]

The ability to hide merchandise quickly and to appear inconspicuous was essential to avoid the attention of policemen and informants looking for Jews, black marketeers, and vagrant youngsters. Jewish boys on the streets of Kraków were also susceptible to threat from their non-Jewish business rivals. Jewish boys with Hebrew or Yiddish names assumed Polish-sounding names to reduce the risk of discovery. Thus Abraham became Józek. While a name could be changed, a Semitic look could not. Cornered by two Polish boys, the Jasiołek brothers, who pointed out Wilek as a Jew, Abraham and his friend paid off the young blackmailers, which left the Jewish boys without resources.

Although some of the Polish and Jewish boys shared the same occupation and fate on the street, the former often saw the latter as business competitors whom they could get rid of by disclosing their Jewish identity unless paid off. But such extortion tactics did not always work. Although one boy identified Henryk Meller as Jewish, the other boys at the train station did not act on that information. Henryk was treated as just another juvenile street seller. His nickname became "Jew boy," and the other boys called him whenever they needed German cigarettes.

Boys who experienced blackmail and product theft had to find a way to recover their losses. Desperate, Wilek arranged with other boys to mug travelers. They targeted mothers who were busy with children and luggage. Abraham Blim did not want to get involved in such activity. It was risky and against his ethical standards. All of the other boys in the gang were caught by the authorities and Abraham never saw his friend again.

Abraham, as other Jewish boys like him, devised ways to both evade capture and continue to make ends meet. Being conspicuous equaled being in danger. "I'd been in Kraków for too long, which wasn't good; too many boys knew me," Abraham explained. "And I had nowhere to sleep because it wasn't safe to sleep in stations. There were constant roundups."[60] Abraham slept on trains. He took a train that departed from Kraków at ten o'clock at night and arrived in

Warsaw at seven in the morning. Abraham relied on his impeccable Polish, proper looks, and ingenuity. Once in Warsaw, as other Jews in his situation, Abraham attempted to earn a living. He bought cigarettes and sold them at the station. The next night, he returned to Kraków to buy goods. Abraham rotated between cities because doing so allowed him to have a warm place to sleep on the train, and to avoid being recognized and caught in the marketplaces that he frequented. He also was able to establish contacts in both cities. In the course of his business endeavors, Abraham met a boy from Warsaw, Jędrek, and the two joined forces.[61]

Searches and roundups of underage cigarette dealers intensified. The German railroad police (*Bahnschutzpolizei*) maintained order at the stations and dealt with illegal trade and vagrants. Henryk Meller recalled that the police were not focused on identifying and capturing Jews among the young peddlers. Perhaps this was Henryk's perception at the time. His own non-Semitic appearance and his bravado helped boost his confidence, although he knew these would be of little avail if his identity were discovered. In some cases, pure luck saved children caught by the police. The first time Abraham Blim was nabbed, a prostitute rescued him by charming the policeman, which allowed Abraham to slip away unnoticed.

But luck and skills did not guarantee rescue. On his second encounter with the police, Abraham and his friend Jędrek were taken to a precinct on Gertrudy Street where about thirty boys were held, including the Jasiołki brothers, who had previously blackmailed Abraham and Wilek. Abraham was then transferred to a municipal arrest facility on Skawińska Street for three weeks. As a rule, boys like him stayed in the juvenile reformatory for four weeks. Their term was extended to six months in case of a second offense. Abraham was lucky; his cover story of being orphaned by nomadic parents passed muster. Henryk Meller, on the other hand, experienced a different turn of events. His story of a made-up address and name did not clear when he was caught in summer 1944 and brought to the same precinct as Abraham had been. With no other cover, he admitted that he was Jewish. However, contrary to his expectation, the Polish police officer chose to help Henryk by sending the boy to Bronowice, a district of Kraków, where the reformatory had been transferred in 1943.[62]

Abraham was already in the institution when Henryk arrived. Yet neither ever found out about the other, so well did their respective cover stories hold up. In fact, they did not even discover that another Jewish boy, Jerzy Hoffman, was among them too.[63] Perhaps there were more. Each of the three describes a different experience at the Bronowice reformatory. Henryk escaped, fearing possible disclosure. Jerzy was close to doing so. Abraham stayed.

Abraham forged a friendship with another boy, Józef Milczanowski, and became his protector. In appreciation of Abraham's efforts, Józef's parents, both black marketeers, supplied him with goods. Other children had less positive experiences, not because of the educators but because of other children. Jerzy Hoffman appreciated that he was sheltered, clothed, and fed. But he feared disclosure. Many of the sixty youths aged between six and eighteen were difficult boys whose life circumstances had taught them the tough rules of street life. Some were bullies; some were antisemites. Jerzy recalled that one boy recognized him from the time when Jerzy hid with a Polish family, and he told everyone that Jerzy was a Jew. "They began to harass me terribly, they called me names, and I didn't know what to do," Jerzy recalled.[64] A nurse in the institution urged the boys to stop and bribed them with treats, while she encouraged Jerzy to escape. He was afraid and stayed. More importantly, he had nowhere to go.

For Abraham, the institution offered stability, which his itinerant life on the city streets had lacked. He began to live the life of his alter ego, Józek. "Slowly, I began to forget who I was; I was already thinking in other categories. I did not imagine that I would ever return to Jewishness. My childhood then was the way it was supposed to be." Yet Abraham never fully forgot who he was. "Only sometimes when I lay in bed and could not fall asleep did all memories come back to me and I thought about my family," he explained.[65] If his nighttime memories reminded him of his past Jewish life, his daytime reality spurred him to embrace Catholicism. Educators prepared children of unconfirmed background such as Abraham for baptism.[66] The fact that the institution was created specifically for street children was sufficient reason for its residents not to have proper identity papers. For Abraham, attending church and sessions with a priest held no religious meaning. He did what was expected of him. And he received additional food from the priest.

Some boys, like Abraham, awaited war's end in the reformatory; others chose to continue to try to survive on the move. Jerzy Hoffman stayed in the institution until his term ended and then sought the assistance of the Main Welfare Council. He was sent to an orphanage in Kochanów. Following his escape from the institution, Henryk Meller no longer wanted to risk his life by sleeping at train stations and selling cigarettes. He went to Warsaw, to a contact his aunt had suggested. And Herman Wohlfeiler's son left Kraków and slipped out of German-occupied Poland altogether. He crossed the border to Slovakia and journeyed on to Hungary.

———

Smuggling "was the only way to run out of Poland," Emilia Heller explained. "Our aim was to reach Hungary, because at that time the Germans were not there."[67] Indeed, Germany occupied Hungary, their ally, only on 19 March 1944. Until then, Hungarian Jews endured anti-Jewish laws introduced by the Hungarian government, but they had been spared the fate of Jews in occupied Europe. With no other avenues of escape, Jews saw Hungary as a desirable destination. A number of Poles (Polish Jews among them) had already entered the country between 1939 and 1941.[68] When crossing the Hungarian border became illegal, human smuggling began.[69] In order to reach Hungary from the General Government, Jews had to cross into Slovakia. For some, Slovakia provided shelter until the end of the war. While Slovakia, an Axis-aligned country, had begun the deportation of its Jewish population to camps in March 1942, it halted its campaign in October 1942. Deportations resumed in September 1944 following the German occupation of the country on 29 August 1944.

Until then, Jews searched for ways to get to Slovakia and Hungary. Some Jews held legitimate foreign passports, so they and their immediate families were protected. An undated list compiled by the Germans provides the names and addresses of 229 Jewish foreign nationals in Kraków, with claims to the desirable Slovak (86), Hungarian (57), and Romanian (46) citizenships taking the lead.[70] But many other Jews tried to purchase false documents that identified them as foreign nationals, or forge connections with relatives and organizations that could supply such papers. Chana Kleiner, about seven years old at the time, recalled a rumor in the Kraków ghetto that Jews who held foreign papers could still live relatively freely in Slovakia, and especially in Hungary. Through an underground network composed of Jews and a German, Chana's parents procured documents stating they were Hungarian Jews.[71] While a small number of Jews, like the Kleiners, managed to obtain foreign documents to facilitate their escape from the General Government, most Jews who considered fleeing could not obtain such papers. Both those with and those without foreign passports used the services of smugglers.

Jews in the Kraków ghetto and on the Aryan side learned about smuggling channels through various routes. The father of then nine-year-old Lena Klein, separated from his wife and son, who hid in Kraków, and exhausted by the search for a hiding place for his daughter and himself, decided their only option was to flee. He casually mentioned transfer across the border to two Poles whom he had met in the south of Poland, but who turned out to be blackmailers. Father and daughter then joined the rest of the family in Kraków. Lena was placed in the care of a fortune teller's daughter, who was heavily compensated for hiding her. Worried that they would run out of money, the Kleins continued to seek a way to get to Hungary. Many people visited the fortune teller, which allowed for forging connections. Not all of them turned out to be beneficial. Quite the contrary. Lena recalled, "There Mommy met a Pole, who smuggled Jews to Hungary, and Daddy went first. . . . I never saw him again."[72] The Klein family split again, and once again a smuggler took advantage of their desperate situation. Finally, Lena's mother came across Jews preparing for escape and placed her daughter in the group with the aim of joining her later. Under the care of a woman, Lena went by train to Zakopane, a town in the Tatra Mountains. From there she trekked (with the woman) to Slovakia, and on to Hungary. There she reunited with her mother and brother, who had arrived in Hungary with another group.

Jews relied on networks composed of non-Jews, and those run jointly by Jews and non-Jews, to bring them to what were considered to be relatively safe places. One such network was organized by a Polish Jew, Ben Zion Kalb. Kalb fled to Slovakia soon after the Germans occupied Poland and settled in Kežmarok. In early 1943, he established contact with his fiancée, Clara Lieber, in the Bochnia ghetto (in Kraków District) and arranged a successful escape for her. In an effort to rescue more Jews, Kalb collaborated with a Jewish resistance organization in Slovakia, the Working Group, which points to the organized and international webs of help that Jews established, emerging as rescuers of other Jews. Money that the Working Group procured—including from international Jewish organizations in Switzerland—covered couriers, guides, and highlanders for transit from a departure point, shelter in the mountain region, and transfer across the borders and for bribes. The Kalb network smuggled some two hundred Jewish children from Poland with the help of a non-Jewish Pole, Tomasz "Tosiek" Moździerz, and his counterpart in Slovakia, Jan Melec.[73]

Kalb's network cooperated with at least two independent subgroups in Kraków alone. The link between them was a Jewish woman courier, Luba Wolf.[74] The first subgroup consisted of Zygmunt Matoga's crew;[75] the second comprised two AK soldiers (and physicians by training), Wiesław Korpal and Tadeusz "Doktorek" Dygdoń.[76] So secret were each team's activities that neither knew of the other's involvement.[77] Both subgroups used the same two smuggling modes from Kraków to the Podhale region: train and truck. As it happened, both subgroups solicited the help of Tadeusz Bielak (a body shop owner) and Stefan Syrek (an underground resister). Once the groups reached Szaflary, their first stop in Podhale, they stayed in private homes. Led by highlanders, the groups walked at night to Gronków and on to Spišské Hanušovce in Slovakia. The Korachow inn served as a transit point to Hungary.

Korpal's and Dygdoń's operations smuggling Jews from Kraków underscore the involvement of the AK. Until fall 1941, Korpal, on orders from the precursor to the AK, the Union of Armed Struggle (Związek Walki Zbrojnej; ZWZ), worked as a tram driver to smuggle underground press, parts of radios, and weapons to ZWZ fighters.[78] Korpal often operated tram number 3, which passed through the ghetto. ZWZ tasked him with delivering packages to the ghetto by dropping them in set places. When the Gestapo showed interest in Korpal, he fled to Stary Sącz. Perhaps it was then that he learned about smuggling routes. In February 1942, when ZWZ morphed into the AK, Korpal returned to Kraków. He joined the AK medical section with Dygdoń, who, in turn, organized what he referred to as the Independent Unit for the Protection of the Population Victimized and Persecuted by the Germans (Samodzielna Jednostka Ochrony Ludności Poszkodowanej i Prześladowanej przez Niemców) within the AK. Because of the secrecy that their activities required, Korpal and Dygdoń worked as a duo. Their activities fell within the Military Service for the Protection of the Uprising (Wojskowa Służba Ochrony Powstania) and were approved by the AK command.[79]

Another AK member, Adam "Cytryna" Bystroń, claimed to have operated another unit, with Stanisław Kosk, Antoni Krajewski, and their guide Ludwika "Sarenka" Porębska.[80] Between 1939 and 1943, this group acted on orders from the Home Army High Command for the District of Kraków. The transfer of people took place by trucks from the brush factory in Tarnów, as well as from Bochnia and Kraków.[81] Bearing false documentation stamped by the German Todt Organization, convoy organizers officially transported only brushes or coal.[82] Trucks headed to Piwniczna and Kosarzyska in southern Poland on the border with Slovakia, whence Porębska led escapees to Budapest.[83]

While no information exists about the contacts that allowed Bystroń's crew to operate in Podhale, postwar accounts document that both Matoga's group and Korpal and Dygdoń's unit maintained close ties with highlanders. Korpal and Dygdoń's team met on Sundays at 6 Jasna Street in Kraków to go over the details of their missions. It so happened that Adam Salomon, a Jew with Slovak papers, lived at 5 Jasna Street.[84] Salomon was active in the Kraków branch of Żegota. He hid Jews in his own apartment, then coordinated their escape by smuggling them to Slovakia. Salomon recruited his neighbor, Aleksander "Czarny Olek" Kossewski, an AK member and someone who had experience smuggling food from Slovakia to Kraków, and who was willing to extend his activities to facilitating the transfer of people from Kraków to Slovakia.

Escapees usually took the train to the border. A designated person in the group communicated with Kossewski using signals and distributed tickets to escapees. Another mode of transportation was by a truck remodeled by Zygmunt Krajewski to hold a hiding place in its undercarriage. To legitimize such "tours," Kossewski used false passes that he stole from Gestapo headquarters in Kraków, where he worked as a carpenter. Kossewski's route led through Bystra Beskidzka to Sidzina and from there to the village of Zubrzyca, and across Babia Góra to Slovakia. He recalled that the smuggling paths were difficult and involved traversing streams and slopes. Keeping silent was necessary while crossing the border because German patrols operated in the area. The Germans' activities intensified when Soviet and Polish partisan units became active on the "u Malinów" clearing near Babia Góra. Despite the difficulties, Kossewski continued his smuggling operations. In time, he learned that his cell was subordinate to Tadeusz "Socha" Seweryn of the AK and the Kraków branch of Żegota.[85]

In the wake of the liquidation of the ghetto, and as a branch of Żegota was in the process of formation in Kraków, Seweryn reissued a call to action addressed to all Poles. The same document had been published in September 1942 in Warsaw, and by March 1943 it had acquired a renewed sense of urgency. One of its eight points called for help in the transfer of Jews to Hungary.[86] By November 1943, Żegota members began cooperation with the Citizens' Committee for Care to Polish Refugees (Komitet Obywatelski do spraw Opieki nad Uchodźcami) in Hungary, headed by Henryk Sławik. Sławik, a Polish politician, fled to Hungary in September 1939. There he met József Antall, who was responsible for refugee affairs in the Hungarian government. The two cooperated in helping over one hundred thousand Polish refugees. Among them were Jews, whom Sławik supplied with false documents and money and arranged shelter for, as well as placing Jewish children in orphanages. His aide, Henryk Zvi Zimmerman, a Kraków Jew and former member of the Jewish Fighting Organization in the Kraków ghetto, served as a courier. This transnational network led by diplomats, and both Polish and Jewish resisters, encouraged Żegota to plan a robust smuggling route for Polish Jews even by July 1944 when Germans and Hungarians had deported most of Hungary's Jews to Auschwitz.[87]

Żegota established a route that led through the Nowy Sącz and Stary Sącz areas, and involved locals from these two towns. The commandant of a small sabotage unit called Ubocz, Mieczysław "Obłaz" Cholewa, was responsible for the smuggling operation. Two other AK soldiers, Adam "Teodor" Rysiewicz and Marian Bomba, traced what they called "the *sądecka* line" (to mark its geographic location in the Nowy and Stary Sącz areas). A local man, Franciszek Krzyżak, who also happened to have been born and raised in Budapest, served as a guide. He smuggled some fifty Jews across the border with Slovakia.[88]

Jewish children rarely, if ever, knew about the networks that smuggled them. They were too young to be privy to such information and they knew not to ask questions. Their journey was stressful enough, and they needed to adapt quickly to the new places. Rosa Apelzon was nine years old when she left Kraków with her mother, smuggled by the Kalb network (she referred to it as the Working Group).[89] While in her fourth hiding place in Kraków, the fear of denunciation became unbearable, and Rosa's mother searched desperately for a way out. The Apelzons took a train from Kraków to Zakopane, a risky undertaking in its own right. Controlled by the railway police and subject to the prying eyes of inquisitive informants, the train station could not serve as a contact point. All smuggling networks arranged for other meeting locations. But their guide failed to meet them and the group dispersed. Rosa and her mother returned to Kraków.

Trying more than once to flee was not uncommon. It happened for a variety of reasons. At times it was because of a child's poor health. Stefa Popowcer, around thirteen years old, fell ill after her trip from Warsaw to Kraków, made at the urging of her grandmother, who had learned about the possibility of transfer to Hungary.[90] Both her aunt and cousin had already made their way to Hungary, and Stefa, exhausted by constant hiding, wanted to do the same. However, once in Zakopane, Stefa was too weak to proceed. The guide, afraid that the Popowcers had been caught, abandoned the group.

Indefatigable, both the Apelzons and the Popowcers tried again. This time they were successful. While Rosa Apelzon and her mother continued their second attempt with a group, Stefa Popowcer, her brother Marek, and their mother followed a Polish Jewish smuggler, a Mr. Goldstein.

Because of the clandestine nature of the rescue mission, Chana Kleiner did not know the name of the network or whether it was even an organized group. All she knew was that she sneaked out of the Kraków ghetto with her family and, once outside, they went straight into an awaiting car. But she was able to recall the conditions under which her group made the passage across the border. To avoid German patrols, they walked in darkness up the hills, which was exhausting for Chana and her cousin Dora. The girls' fathers, already under emotional stress and physical strain, had to carry their daughters and calm them. Eventually, Chana's group reached their destination. A Polish guide led the group to the border and then handed it off to his Slovak counterpart.[91]

Some children were detained in a local Slovak jail. This was a step in the rescue process. Artur Spielman, his younger sister, and a cousin were among a group of ten who reached the Slovak side via Rabka and Czarny Dunajec. When the guides suddenly disappeared, panic ensued in the group. Artur, his sister, and his cousin continued walking until Slovak gendarmes stopped them. The children were surprised that the officers were friendly and gave them food. Detained in jail in Trstená, the children noticed names inscribed on the walls. They realized they were safe and added their names to mark their presence for those who came after. The children were handed over to a Jewish committee a few days later and transferred to orphanages in Prešov and Košice. From there they relocated with the Spielman children's father to Hungary.[92]

Despite the possible problems of smuggling children on foot across countries, couriers and smugglers did not exclude them from escape groups. In fact, the Kalb network focused on smuggling Jewish children, especially orphans, across the Slovak border. Bronia Bruenner was seven years old and the youngest in a group of about ten children when she left Kraków. Bronia's aunt, Rosa Berger, considered the network the last resort to save her niece. When Bronia eventually reached Bratislava, she stayed in the home of a Jewish family. After a few months, Bronia was transferred again, this time to Budapest. Once there, she was placed in an orphanage and later reunited with her aunt.[93] Some Polish Jewish (and Polish) children found shelter in places outside Budapest, like Vác, which included a boarding house and school for children ages three to seventeen. By 1943, it housed five thousand children, many of whom were Jewish.[94]

———

Jewish escapees from Kraków who reached Slovakia or Hungary considered the places relatively safe compared with their own country. As Marek Popowcer, who was around ten years old at the time, put it, "The population there [in Slovakia] was friendly as opposed to the population in Poland. And we finally breathed a sigh of relief."[95] Those conditions changed with the imposition of German authority.[96] Kraków's Jewish children were on the move again. For some of them, Slovakia and Hungary were stops on the way to refuge in Romania or Palestine. Romania was a satellite state of Nazi Germany, but Jews from certain areas were protected from deportation although they suffered state-instituted oppression. Some Jews took advantage of Romania's relative proximity to Palestine and made their way from there illegally. The attempts of others were stalled. The five-member family of Jerzy Wurzel, a boy of about seven then, escaped (with the help of Kossewski, subordinate to the AK and Żegota) first to Slovakia, then to Hungary, where they lived in a camp in Ricse. The Hungarian authorities then moved the Wurzels to a village where they passed as Catholics. Upon the Germans' entry into Hungary, Jerzy's father arranged for transit papers and train tickets to Romania, where the family had relatives. While in Arad, Jerzy's father came upon an announcement that promised illegal Jewish immigrants the opportunity to board a ship to Palestine. Desperate to save themselves, the Wurzels registered as Jews with the Romanian police. But the cattle trains with the Wurzels and other Jews headed north; the Romanians wished to get rid of illegal Jewish immigrants. Neighboring Hungary, from where the Wurzels had already once escaped, refused to let the train in. The human cargo returned to a camp in Romania. There the Wurzels awaited liberation.[97]

A small number of Jewish children managed to leave Kraków and German-occupied Poland. Flight became their strategy for survival.[98] Such escapes were possible through transnational avenues of rescue composed of Jews and non-Jews. We know about the successful stories of crossing the border from survivor testimonies. Not everyone was so fortunate. Not everyone had a connection to a competent or reputable network. Some in the smuggling webs were honest people who wanted to help and to earn a living. But some recruiters, couriers, guides, and shelter providers set traps to extort money and valuables from Jews desperate to leave Kraków and German-occupied Poland. The majority of children on the run, however, remained in the city until the war's end. They experienced cycles of separation, hiding, and adjusting their identities, while oscillating between rescue, indifference, and betrayal by the Polish population.

Epilogue

Jewish children who remained in hiding in Kraków remembered the first days of January 1945 as cold and intense. People were waiting for the war to end. Just fifty-five miles from the German-Soviet battleground, Kraków became a near-frontline city and a concentration point for Wehrmacht units. Krakovians were unsure what to expect: destruction of the city, or expulsion of the population similar to the kind the Germans executed in Warsaw.[1] Artillery sounds instilled fear and spurred descent into shelters. Doing so was not an option for six-year-old Mieczysław Arzewski and his family, who were hiding in the apartment of a German postal worker, Max Nagler.[2] It could expose them. Their rescuer, too, chose to stay. Mieczysław heard Germans pounding on the door to make sure the apartment was empty. Loud explosions followed, and the windows were blasted. People screamed.

Soviet troops entered Kraków on 18 January 1945 after three days of fighting, and the German occupation of the city ended.[3] Felicia Vogler, nearly eleven then, recalled that everyone in the apartment where she was hiding went outside to see the "Russians," as she called them. The soldiers were drunk and jovial, and to Felicia they seemed "un-German." One picked her up and kissed her; he said Felicia reminded him of his daughter, whom he missed dearly.[4] To the Jewish children, their liberators seemed different from their oppressors not only in behavior but also in appearance. Mieczysław Arzewski recalled seeing soldiers with feet wrapped in rags and carrying guns on strings. The soldiers were in a miserable state. Those assigned to Mieczysław's apartment had never used an indoor toilet. "Yet to us they were heroes, they were just wonderful," he noted.[5]

Not everyone was ecstatic. "People were afraid. Poles were afraid of the Russians," Norbert Schlang, then nearly eleven, explained. The traditional distrust that Poles harbored toward their eastern neighbors, combined with the Soviet soldiers' robberies and rapes, frightened many Poles, as did the institution of a

Soviet military regime in Poland. In this situation, "everybody was trying to keep indoors," Norbert observed.[6]

Norbert, however, wanting to find his family, ventured to Podgórze only to learn that the ghetto no longer existed and that Poles now lived there, as they did in his childhood home. "And I didn't know what to do."[7] The end of the war meant that children like Norbert had to contend with all kinds of losses. It also meant that they had a chance to continue their lives. Half a century later, Janek Weber was not reluctant to describe his feeling as an eleven-year-old boy. "The word 'liberation' is not very popular in Poland, but I still consider myself liberated." Poles and Jews in postwar Poland differed on the meaning of liberation, with the former regarding the Soviet arrival as a second occupation of their country. For Jews, including the youngest among them, the end of the German occupation spelled change. "I remember it very well; I had a moment of enormous relief," Janek declared.[8] Anna Entenberg, who was five years old when the war ended, recalled that the change was so great that "it's as though for me I came into the world really in 1945."[9] Children noticed the difference in their lives almost instantly. "I realized I did not have to be afraid anymore; no one would kill us. This was liberation," Zofia Melcer, nine years old then, explained.[10]

The Central Committee of Jews in Poland (Centralny Komitet Żydów w Polsce), the official postwar representative body of Polish Jews, reported some five thousand Jewish children in 1945 in Poland.[11] Right after liberation, Jews began to organize assistance to other Jews who emerged from their hiding places, the few who returned from camps, and those who trickled back from the Soviet Union. A branch of the Central Committee of Jews in Poland, the Voivodship Jewish Committee (Wojewódzki Komitet Żydowski; WKŻ), opened at 38 Długa Street in the northern part of Kraków, far from the prewar Jewish district. It was the sole organization to assist Jews in the city in the immediate postwar period. It offered basic help and later operated four shelters, two soup kitchens, two medical clinics, an orphanage, a boarding house, and Jewish schools. In the first weeks after liberation, 500 Jews registered with WKŻ. By 1946, that number reached 6,637, including about 2,000 prewar Kraków residents.[12] WKŻ registered 500 Jewish children in the city in May 1945, among them 40 children who lived on WKŻ premises.[13]

Jewish children ended up at WKŻ headquarters for a variety of reasons. Some wartime caretakers learned about the institution from newspapers or word of mouth. They acted out of a sense of obligation, wanting to place Jewish children in a Jewish environment, often with the hope that the children's parents or relatives would find them there. Other non-Jews had no means to provide for the children. Many others, harassed by their neighbors for keeping a Jew, were forced to place children there. Some former caregivers expected, even demanded, payment from WKŻ for returning children.[14] Some children, especially older ones, arrived at WKŻ on their own. Abraham Blim, about fifteen years old, overheard people in striped uniforms speaking Yiddish on a street in Kazimierz. "I followed them to Długa Street, where they entered a building. It was then that I learned that the Jewish Committee was located there."[15] He checked the survivors list posted outside but saw nothing about his family.

Studying lists of survivors pinned at the entrance to the WKŻ building was one way children found out about surviving family members. Some parents and relatives sent messages and emissaries to the children's known wartime guardians to inform them about their whereabouts and to arrange for their children's transfer. Such requests, especially from kin other than parents, were sometimes fulfilled unwillingly, if at all. Some caregivers did not wish to return children to family members.[16] They felt a moral duty toward the children they had harbored and the parents to whom they had promised to care for their offspring. Other rescuers, emotionally attached to their young Jewish charges, refused to part with them. Separation from foster parents was also difficult for children. Twelve-year-old Maksymilian Perlmutter, whose father arranged for him to go to Sweden, remembered the pain of leaving his caretakers and Poland. "It was a traumatic experience because they were like my family."[17]

A small number of children reunited with one parent, and even fewer with both parents. Yet some had to face loss of their loved ones soon thereafter. "I cannot describe my joy at seeing Daddy. Now we are together; Daddy, Brother, Sister and I. Mommy died this year [1947] of cardiac asthma," Halina Tydor, eight years old when the war ended, related.[18] Children's responses to the sudden appearance of parents or relatives varied, and not all family reunions were positive experiences. Anna Entenberg's mother first sent a Jewish friend to check on the girl. The girl was bribed twice—with a tomato and chocolate cake, foods she had never seen before—in advance of her mother's arrival. "I knew that I was expected soon to be going with this perfect stranger, whom I had never seen, when I had already a perfectly good mother," Anna recalled.[19] Similarly, Ewa Lewi, nine years old then, barely recognized her parents. "I couldn't say 'Mother.' Not yet." So Ewa referred to her mother as "Mrs."[20]

If dealing with the appearance of biological parents and reconstituting a family posed challenges, so did the child's self-identity. Older children faced a dilemma: Should they follow the Catholicism they had been compelled to accept in order to survive, and assimilate fully into postwar Polish society? Or should they try to embrace their Jewish identity once again? If the latter, in what form? Children who had little or no knowledge about their Jewish background and who stayed with their foster parents accepted Catholicism as a natural course of events. Felicia Vogler explained, "I didn't want to be a Jew. I was a Christian. And I wanted to be one." She internalized Christianity by observing and participating in the way of life that her then-adopted parents led. "I guess a child who is at that age [she was eleven when the war ended] is impressionable."[21] Even children whose biological parents returned did not shed their Catholic identity easily. They crossed themselves when passing by a church, attended Mass, prayed at home, and wore Catholic medallions.

Other children rejected their Jewish origins outright. Before Maria Perlberger's aunt left Poland after the war, she placed her twelve-year-old niece in the Jewish orphanage at 1 Augustiańska Boczna Street in Kraków, much to the girl's disappointment. Maria, forced to assume a Catholic identity during the war, associated Jewishness with inferiority and danger. "I looked down on the Jewish children," she recalled about her attitude while in the orphanage and the Jewish school she attended.[22] Maria went to great lengths not to appear on the street with a child who looked Jewish to her. Maria and children like her were confused about the sudden switch in their religious identity and way of life. They objected to the pressure to "be Jewish."

Educators at Jewish institutions and the orphanage tried to foster Jewish heritage in these youngsters. "I knew little about Jewishness, I did not feel Jewish," Elżbieta Schnek, six years old when the war ended, admitted. Absorbed into a Jewish environment, taught by Jewish educators, and interacting with Jewish youths, children like Elżbieta were encouraged to embrace elements of their Jewish identity, which for some meant Zionist ideals. "Suddenly in 1956, when the older boys in the orphanage revealed they were leaving Poland, that they wanted to go to Israel, a question arose for me whether to go," Elżbieta continued.[23] Her uncle, who had placed her in the orphanage because of his own living circumstances, forbade her to leave Kraków. But she, longing to live the Zionist dream of a free life, went anyway.

Jewish children in postwar Kraków were on the move once again. Children passed from their wartime guardians to their parents, relatives, or Jewish institutions. Some left Kraków for other reasons. Thirty-five-year-old Lena Kichler, a child psychologist, enlisted the support of the WKŻ to open homes for Jewish child survivors. Kichler and her aides struggled to respond to the children's needs. Many were in horrendous condition. "They were so starved, so sickly, so covered with lice, so neglected morally, physically, and intellectually, that a truly tremendous job arose before us," Kichler explained.[24] She transferred over one hundred children from Kraków to Zakopane and Rabka, two resort towns, to improve the children's health and to shelter them from the hostility of the Polish population in Kraków. But the children and staff encountered virulent antisemitism in the mountain region, too. "The children could not go on the street at all," Kichler lamented.[25] Polish children harassed them. Polish men robbed, beat, and assaulted Kichler. After three attacks in summer 1945 perpetrated by students and teachers under the leadership of a local priest, the children's home in Rabka was forced to close. In Zakopane Polish paramilitary resistance formations shelled the Jewish children's home.[26] Thanks to her brother, a government clerk, Kichler put a defense procedure in place. In addition to a Jewish self-defense crew, "a machine gun was installed on the roof, and besides that I had an alarm siren, search lights, and telephone."[27] Continued lack of funding, ongoing persecution of Jews, and Zionist fervor motivated children's activists like Kichler to leave Poland with the children in March 1946. "These children are as if they belonged to us. They belong to the entire Jewish people. I believe that their place is in Palestine," she stated.[28]

Antisemitism was a tangible threat for Jewish Krakovians and a key factor influencing the decision of some to leave Kraków, and Poland altogether. In July 1946, the number of Jews in the city grew to thirteen thousand.[29] This surge was caused by repatriation from the Soviet Union and concentration in Kraków before emigration sparked by the pogrom against Jews in Kielce (4 July 1946) prompted by a blood libel rumor that accused Jews of kidnapping a Polish boy with the aim to kill him and use his blood in perceived Jewish rituals. Poles killed forty-two Jews and injured over forty others. Kraków served as a transit place for Polish Jews before departure elsewhere. But the city was also the site of an earlier organized attack against its Jews on 11 August 1945 by the Polish population, when blood libel rumor led to the death of five Jews. Many Jewish Poles, Krakovians among them, felt they had no future in Poland as Jews.

———

Jewish child survivors who remained in Kraków focused on living in the present while also orienting themselves toward the future. Later in life, some found purpose in creating the new system, socialism, in Poland. But the Polish government's antisemitic campaign of March 1968 and the subsequent expulsion of fifteen thousand Jews from Poland reminded survivors of their volatile position.[30] For many survivors, that proved it was better to hide their Jewish roots. Still, a number of Kraków's Jews continued to participate in the city's Jewish life.

The fall of communism in 1989 brought great changes, including new curiosity about Poland's multicultural past and the need to come to terms with the history and legacy of the Holocaust and World War II. Some by then middle-aged survivors, whose families had not known about their identity and wartime experiences, "came out." Many now-adult child survivors heard from their "parents" that they had been rescued as Jews. Denied knowledge of their Jewish heritage for decades, or no longer willing to suppress it, a number of child survivors embarked on exploring this new layer of their concealed identity. Institutions and programs responded to the slow yet steady resurgence of Jewish life in Kraków. Membership in the official Jewish Religious Community (Gmina Wyznaniowa Żydowska), led since 1997 by a child survivor from Kraków, Tadeusz Jakubowicz, continues to bear importance for some child survivors. The Kraków branch of the Association of Holocaust Children was created in 1999.[31] The Ronald S. Lauder Foundation opened a branch in Kraków and introduced a range of educational programs.[32] In the Lauder summer camps for Polish Jews, many child survivors experienced a reawakening. Zofia Radzikowska (formerly Melzer) explained that, until then, "my Jewishness was dormant."[33] She decided to reclaim her Jewish heritage. Like many child survivors in contemporary Kraków, Zofia developed a double identity as a Jew and a Pole, and found both meaning and challenges in each.

No longer willing to hide, many Jewish child survivors in Kraków acquired a very visible space to fulfill their social needs—the Jewish Community Centre located in the historic Jewish district of Kazimierz. The center was opened in 2008 by the prince of Wales, following his visit to Kraków and meeting with local Jewish leaders in 2002. "This place is what I need. . . . There's nothing like it in Poland," Zofia explained.[34] Her opinion echoes that of many child survivors residing in modern Kraków, who consider the city's Jewish Community Centre to be a place where they can be Jewish on their own terms. It is a space that offers pluralistic opportunities for socializing, learning, belonging, and healing.

Not all Krakovian child survivors have recounted their wartime histories. Some never will. Still, the recollections of those who have shed light on the history of children's experiences in Kraków during the Holocaust and offer a window onto aspects of life under occupation during World War II that would otherwise have remained unknown.

Acknowledgments

My first debt of gratitude belongs to the author of the trailblazing book that set me on the path to explore Jewish children's lives during the Holocaust. Debórah Dwork became my teacher, mentor, adviser, and role model. She pushed me to see the bigger picture, to ask probing questions, and to strive to be a better writer, a better historian, and a better educator.

This project took me to archives, libraries, and homes in the United States, Poland, and Israel. I was honored to have received fellowships to pursue my research and writing. I thank the Strassler Center for Holocaust and Genocide Studies at Clark University; the Hadassah Brandeis Institute at Brandeis University; Yad Vashem; the Conference on Jewish Material Claims Against Germany (Claims Conference); the Fulbright Program; the Memorial Foundation for Jewish Culture; Proventus; the American Institute of Polish Culture; the German Historical Institute in Warsaw; the Polish and Slavic Federal Credit Union; and the Polish Student Organization. This book was made possible (in part) by funds granted to me through a David and Fela Shapell Fellowship at the Jack, Joseph and Morton Mandel Center for Advanced Holocaust Studies of the United States Holocaust Memorial Museum (USHMM). The statements made and views expressed, however, are solely my responsibility. I am also grateful to the Emerging Scholars Program at the Mandel Center for Advanced Holocaust Studies for its support in the preparation of the manuscript and of the book proposal. Scholarships at Tel Aviv University and the YIVO Institute for Jewish Research allowed me to study Yiddish.

I wish to thank the many child Holocaust survivors who relayed their histories to me. I am indebted, too, to a number of people who have helped me in various ways. In Poland: Monika Bednarek, Barbara Engelking, Nadav Eschar, Edyta Gawron, Wojciech Górny, Beata Łabno, Piotr Nawrocki, Michael Newmark, Jakub Nowakowski, Annamaria Orla-Bukowska, Jonathan Ornstein,

Tomasz Owoc, Jakub Petelewicz, Ewa Rudnik, Paweł Skorut, Anna Wencel, Michał Zajda, and Krzysztof Zamorski. I thank the nuns, monks, and priests who shared information with me: Tomasz Baluka, Paweł Flis, Antonella Gawlik, Danuta Kozieł, Lucylla Łukasik, Iwona Naglik, Maria Najowicz, Krzysztof Niewiadomski, Jerzy Rolka, Jacek Urban, Józefa Wątroba, and Paulina Wilk. In Israel: Dafna Dolinko, Lili Haber, and Eliot Nidam Orvieto. In the United States: Esther Brumberg, Judith Cohen, Ron Coleman, JoEllyn Dekel, Steven Feldman, Megan Lewis, Joanna Michlic, Misha Mitsel, Vincent Slatt, Shelly Tenenbaum, and Eleanor Yadin. I am grateful to those who have reached out to me with information and questions that left an imprint on this book: Maria Chamberlain, Alex Kerner, Alan Silberstein, Grzegorz Siwor, Magdalena Smoczyńska, Ewa Stańczyk, Marc Tannen, Marceli Wein, and Geoffrey Weisgard.

Jan T. Gross and Samuel D. Kassow offered insightful comments that have helped me to structure the book. Natalia Aleksiun, Dara Bramson, Adara Goldberg, Natalya Lazar, and Magdalena Wróbel provided feedback at various stages of this manuscript. I also benefited from suggestions from my colleagues at Clark University, the participants of the many academic seminars in which I presented my work, and from my writing group: Elizabeth (Betsy) Anthony, Sarah Cushman, and Jeffrey Koerber. I am deeply grateful to Elisabeth Maselli and the team at Rutgers University Press. My appreciation extends to Sherry Gerstein and her team at Westchester Publishing Services. I thank Daniela Blei who prepared the index. I am indebted, too, to the anonymous readers. The input of many has strengthened my work.

My friends both made sure I had a life outside of writing and cheered me on as I worked to complete the book. In particular, I shared the journey with Rachel Rothstein, my inimitable travel partner.

This book owes its inception and completion to my family. My parents inspired my interest in Poland, Jewish heritage, and the Holocaust. My brother, Lukasz, has been a generous listener, and made sure I had a steady supply of coffee. Lastly, I thank my husband, Karol Maźnicki for his unwavering support. His positive attitude and appreciation for what I do have emboldened me to finish this book.

Abbreviations Used in Notes

AAN	Archiwum Akt Nowych (Archive of New Records)
AESIP	Archive of the Embassy of the State of Israel in Poland
AIPNKr	Archiwum Instytutu Pamięci Narodowej, Oddział w Krakowie (Institute of National Remembrance Archives, Kraków Branch)
AJDC	Archives of the American Jewish Joint Distribution Committee
ANKr	Archiwum Narodowe w Krakowie (National Archive in Kraków)
ASU	Archiwum Sióstr Urszulanek (Archive of the Congregation of the Ursulines of the Agonizing Heart of Jesus)
AŻIH	Archiwum Żydowskiego Instytutu Historycznego (Archive of the Jewish Historical Institute)
FVA	Fortunoff Video Archive for Holocaust Testimonies
GFHA	Ghetto Fighters' House Archives
MJH	Museum of Jewish Heritage
USHMM	United States Holocaust Memorial Museum
VHA	Visual History Archive
YIVO	YIVO Institute for Jewish Research
YVA	Yad Vashem Archives

Notes

INTRODUCTION

1. Kraków adopted the German town rights outlined in the Magdeburg Laws in the thirteenth century. Nazi Germany strove to reclaim the city, which it believed was inherently Germanic.

2. Jacob Lestschinsky, *Crisis, Catastrophe and Survival* (New York: Institute of Jewish Affairs of the World Jewish Congress, 1948), 60.

3. The 1931 Polish census identifies nationality based on language and religion. Therefore, the census only sketches the demography and identity of Jews in Poland. "Drugi spis powszechny ludności z dn. 9 września 1931 r. Miasto Kraków," *Statystyka Polska Seria C*, zeszyt 67 (1937): 13.

4. Scholarship that employs and explores these notions is extensive. See, for example, Anne Kelly Knowles, Tim Cole, and Alberto Giordano, eds., *Geographies of the Holocaust* (Bloomington: Indiana University Press, 2014).

CHAPTER 1 — NAVIGATING SHIFTS IN THE CITY

1. Rena Finder (née Ferber), interview 21482, 1996, VHA.

2. Celina Biniaz (née Karp), interview 11133, 1996, VHA.

3. In 1935–1939, about 6,300 Jews emigrated from Poland to the United States. Palestine was a destination for some 91,100 Polish Jews in 1932–1938. Mark Tolts, "Population and Migration: Migration since World War I," *The YIVO Encyclopedia of Jews in Eastern Europe*, October 12, 2010, https://yivoencyclopedia.org/article.aspx/Population_and_Migration/Migration_since_World_War_I.

4. Ruth Gleitman (née Salomon), interview 30623, 1997, VHA.

5. Roman (Abraham) Englander, interview 16533, 1996, VHA.

6. Bernhard Kempler, interview 33193, 1997, VHA.

7. George Andrzej (Jerzy), Hoffman, interview 17554, 1996, VHA.

8. Stella Madej (née Müller), interview 670, 1995, VHA. This and other quotations from non-English sources are my own.

9. Harriet Solz (Henryka Offman), interview 1491, 1995, VHA.

10. Ruth Karan (née Eisland), interview 8046, 1996, VHA.

11. "Die jüdische Gemeinde in Krakau—in der Zeit vom 13. Sept. 1939 bis 30. Sept. 1940 und ihre Tätigkeit," undated, AŻIH 218/4a, pp. 116-117.

12. Celina Biniaz (née Karp), interview 1133, 1996, VHA.

13. Bernard Offen, interview 27135, 1997, VHA; oral history interview with Bernard Offen, 22 April and 15 December 1992, USHMM RG-50.477.0038.

14. Jack (Iziek) Geizhals, interview 7863, 1995, VHA.

15. Bernard Offen, interview 27135, 1997, VHA.

16. Stella Madej (née Müller), interview 670, 1995, VHA.

17. Rena Finder (née Ferber), interview 21482, 1996, VHA.

18. *Losy wojenne rodziny Kleinbergów i Pasterów*, undated, p. 97, private archive of Ewa Janowska-Ciońćka, née Kleinberg.

19. Account of Abraham Blim, 5 March 1961, YVA 03/221, p. 7.

20. Martin (Marcel) Baral, interview 1663, 1995, VHA.

21. Martin (Marcel) Baral, interview 1663, 1995, VHA; Jacob Baral, interview 20015, 1996, VHA; Anita Weinreich (née Baral), interview 14405, 1996, VHA.

22. An undated document lists forty-five refugee centers inhabited by 2,603 people. The number of refugees fluctuated between September 1939 and August 1940. "Ausweis der jüd: Fluchtlingsheime in Krakau," undated, AŻIH 218/14, p. 1.

23. *Der Stadthauptmann der Stadt Krakau*, or "mayor of Kraków" (in Polish: *Starosta*), exercised power over Kraków's population, and to mark his role I use the term "Kraków city commandant." The position of *Stadthauptmann* existed from 23 December 1939 to the end of March 1941. On 1 April 1941, the post was renamed plenipotentiary of the governor of the Kraków District for the City of Kraków (*der Beaufträgte des Distriktschefs für die Stadt Krakau*). The last change was made on 30 September 1941, when the title *der Stadhauptmann der Stadt Krakau* was reinstalled. The position was held by Karl Schmidt (21 February 1940–31 March 1941), Rudolf Pavlu (1 April 1941–April 1943), and Josef Kramer (April 1943–January 1945).

24. The Jewish Affairs unit was headed by SS-Oberscharführer Paul Siebert, followed by Oscar Brandt, Wilhelm Kunde, and Hermann Heinrich.

25. "Verzeichnis der Angehörigen des jüdischen Altestenrates in Krakau," 1940, AŻIH 288/7, p. 41.

26. "Des Distriktchef von Krakau, Wächter; Rozporządzenie: znamionowanie żydów w okręgu Krakowa," 18 November 1939, ANK SMKr J13922, p. 5.

27. The census counted Jews in Kraków proper and in its nineteen suburban communities: Borek Fałęcki, Bronowice Małe, Czernichów, Jurczyce, Liszki, Mogiła, Ochojno, Piaski Wielkie, Prądnik Czerwony, Prokocim, Radziszów, Ruszcza, Rzeszotary, Skawina, Świątniki Górne, Tyniec, Wola Duchacka, Zabierzów, and Zielonki. "Die jüdische Gemeinde in Krakau—in der Zeit vom 13. Sept. 1939 bis 30. Sept. 1940 und ihre Tätigkeit," undated, AŻIH 218/4a, p. 89.

28. Report of the Jewish Community in Kraków, 20 May 1940, AŻIH 228/11, p. 22.

29. Katarzyna Zimmerer, "Życie codzienne niemieckich urzędników w Krakowie," in *Kraków—czas okupacji 1939–1945*, ed. Monika Bednarek et al. (Kraków: Muzeum Historyczne Miasta Krakowa, 2010), 150.

30. Account of Alicja Langer, 1945, YVA M-49/3863, p. 1.

31. Michael (Mieczysław) Arzewski, interview 41930, 1998, VHA; Relacje: Stanisław Arzewski, undated, AŻIH 301/4216.

32. Ruth Gleitman (née Salomon), interview 30623, 1997, VHA.

33. Mark (Maurycy) Sternlicht, interview 42790, 1998, VHA.

34. Frances Gelbart (Francis Immergluck), interview 12003, 1996, VHA.

35. Rena Finder (née Ferber), interview 21482, 1996, VHA.

36. Frances Gelbart (Francis Immergluck), interview 12003, 1996, VHA.

37. Eva Wald (Ewa Heublum), interview 28166, 1997, VHA.

38. Renate Schondorf (née Leinkram), interview 35582, 1997, VHA.

39. Relacje: Eugeniusz Redlich, 1945, AŻIH 301/779.

40. Roman (Abraham) Englander, interview 16533, 1996, VHA.

41. Ester Friedman (née Spagatner), *Daleka droga do domu* (Kraków: Ambrozja, 1997).

42. Celina Biniaz (née Karp), interview 11133, 1996, VHA.

43. Tadeusz Wroński and Ewa Zachwieja, *Szkolnictwo podstawowe Miasta Krakowa w czasie okupacji hitlerowskiej 1939–1945 (Wybór dokumentów)* (Warsaw: Ministerstwo Sprawiedliwości Główna Komisja Badania Zbrodni Hitlerowskich w Polsce, 1977), 7, 8, 22–23.

44. Renate Schondorf (née Leinkram), interview 35582, 1997, VHA.

45. Rena Finder (née Ferber), interview 21482, 1996, VHA.

46. After the expulsion of Jews from Kraków in 1940, Jews who possessed residence permits wore celluloid armbands to distinguish them from those who did not possess such permits.

47. Jack Kleiner (Jakiw Klajner), interview 24467, 1997, VHA.

48. Leon (Leib) Leyson, interview 8916, 1995, VHA.

49. The reports collected between September 1940 and February 1941 specify how many Jews were apprehended by the Polish (255) and the German (51) police. Reports, ANK SMKr J 13942, pp. 3, 7, 8, 15, 49, 55, 61; Reports, ANK SMKr J 13942, pp. 65, 71; Reports, ANK SMKr J 13942, pp. 29, 35, 43.

50. Frances Gelbart (Francis Immergluck), interview 12003, 1996, VHA.

51. George Andrzej (Jerzy) Hoffman, interview 17554, 1996, VHA.

52. Order of Hans Frank to governors of the four districts regarding the resettlement of Jews, May 1940, USHMM 1999 A 0055 reel 27, p. 142.

53. "Wytyczne dla ewakuacji Żydów z Krakowa: Jednostki dla ogółu pożyteczne, starcy, ciężko chorzy, mogą pozostać: Węzły rodzinne nie zostaną rozerwane," *Gazeta Żydowska*, 6 August 1940, 3.

54. Symche Spira headed the Jewish Order Service as of 23 November 1940. The unit included 122 members. Its headquarters was at 6 Estery Street, and from 1 February until March 1941 at 41 Krakowska Street, both in Kazimierz.

55. Rena Finder (née Ferber), interview 21482, 1996, VHA.

56. Those forced to resettle went to Biała Podlaska, Bobowa, Bochnia, Bogumiłowice, Brzesko, Brzesko Nowe, Chełm, Cienżkowice, Dąbrowa, Dębica, Gromnik, Jasło, Kielce, Krosno, Lublin, Mielec, Międzyrzec Podlaski, Myślenice, Niepołomice, Nowy Sącz, Opole Lubelskie, Pilzno, Radom, Ropczyce, Rzeszów, Sanok, Sędziszów, Szczecin, Tarnów, Tuchów, Trzynica, or Warsaw. Listy transportów z Krakowa, 1940–1941, AŻIH 228/70-80.

57. Jews in other districts numbered 310,000 in Radom (10.4 percent), 540,000 in Warsaw (5.3 percent), and 250,000 in Lublin (9.6 percent). "Zarządzenie niemieckie w stosunku do Żydów: Bericht über den Aufbau im Generalgouvernement bis 1 Juli 1940," undated, AŻIH 233/31, p. 30.

58. Undated report of the Kraków Jewish Council, AŻIH 218/32; "Poważne chwile dla Żydostwa Krakowa: Przesiedlenie faktem nieuniknionym—Zamiast złudzeń—gotowość!," *Gazeta Żydowska*, 30 July 1940, 2.

59. Undated report of the Kraków Jewish Council, AŻIH 218/32, p. 2.

60. "Mój dom jest również i twoim domem," *Gazeta Żydowska*, 9 December 1940, 2.

61. Roman Ferber, interview 43707, 1998, VHA.

62. Jerzy Biernacki, 8 August 1940, AAN, Dzienniki Kroniki Pamiętniki, p. 15.

63. "Starosta—korespondencja wpływająca: Anonimy i doniesienia na Żydów, 1940–1942," undated, AŻIH 228/5, pp. 7–10.

64. "Do ludności żydowskiej m. Krakowa!," *Gazeta Żydowska*, 6 August 1940, 4.

65. Jewish Council report for August 1940, undated, AŻIH 228/10, pp. 39–40.

66. Germans from the Reich (*Reichsdeutsche*) numbered 7,000 and accounted for 2.8 percent of Kraków residents; ethnic Germans (*Volksdeutsche*) 1,700 (0.7 percent); and Ukrainians 3,200 (1.2 percent). Poles dominated with 191,800 people, representing 80 percent of the population. Josef Bühler, "Dot. Wysiedlenia w Krakowie," preface to "Ein Jahr Sufbauarbeit im Distrikt Krakau," 26 October 1940, AŻIH 233/66, p. 1.

67. "Zarządzenie o wysiedleniu Żydów z terenu miasta Krakowa: Wächter," 25 November 1940, AŻIH 241/81.

68. The Jewish Council bribed a representative of the city commandant's resettlement commission, a *Volksdeutsch*, Reichert. Reichert agreed to issue ten thousand permits for 100,000 złoty. The Gestapo, however, discovered the deal and arrested six Jewish Council members and Reichert. Aleksander Biberstein, *Zagłada Żydów w Krakowie* (Kraków: Wydawnictwo Literackie, 1985), 37.

69. Beila Stoger Matzner to the city commandant, letter, 20 November 1940, ANK 29/208/o/GDKr, p. 78.

70. Lea Sonnabend to the city commandant, letter, 23 November 1940, ANK SMKr 680, p. 617.

71. Louise Gans (Luiza Grüner), interview 40851, 1998, VHA.

72. "Die jüdische Gemeinde in Krakau—in der Zeit vom 13. Sept. 1939 bis 30. Sept. 1940 und ihre Tätigkeit," undated, AŻIH 218/4a, p. 30.

73. Account of Helena Anifeld-Dobrowolska, undated, YVA 0.3/583, p. 1; "Die jüdische Gemeinde in Krakau—in der Zeit vom 13. Sept. 1939 bis 30. Sept. 1940 und ihre Tätigkeit," undated, AŻIH 218/4a, pp. 41, 69.

74. "Sprawozdanie z działalności 'Punktu Dożywiania biednych dzieci' za czas od 12/XI.1940 do 2.II.1941," 5 February 1941, USHMM RG 37–97.0072.

75. "Sprawozdanie Towarzystwa Opieki nad Dziećmi i Sierotami 'Centos' w Krakowie obecnie Żydowska Samopomoc Społeczna Żydowski Komitet Opiekuńczy Miejski w Krakowie Wydział Opieki nad Dziećmi i Sierotami 'Centos' [thereafter Sprawozdanie Centos] za czas od 1.VI.1940 do 31.XII.1940," undated, AŻIH 211/16, p. 18.

76. A report prepared by Józef Steinberg of Centos listed twenty refugee centers in Kraków and counted 597 children below the age of fourteen who lived in them. "Wykaz ośrodków dla uchodźców w Krakowie," 10 May 1940, JDC Archives, Warsaw Collection, 1939–1941, item 2627168. A detailed report written by Dr. Gizela Thon provides information about the refugee and local children who received assistance. "Sprawozdanie z Krakowa z dnia 26 maja 1940 r," 26 May 1940, JDC Archives, Warsaw Collection, 1939–1941, item 2627175.

77. "Sprawozdanie Centos za czas od 1.VI.1940 do 31.XII.1940," undated, AŻIH 211/16, p. 20.

78. Jakub Silberman served as director of both day care centers. Two educators worked in the day care on Dajwór Street, and four educators (all women) in the day care on Meiselsa Street. "Notatka w sprawie opieki nad dzieckiem," 26 December 1940, USHMM RG 37-97.0067, 0068.

79. "Sprawozdanie Centos za czas od 1.VI.1940 do 31.XII.1940," undated, AŻIH 211/16, p. 21.

80. "Sprawozdanie Centos za czas od 1.VI.1940 do 31.XII.1940," undated, AŻIH 211/16, pp 23-25; Jewish Council report for October 1940, undated, AŻIH 218/7, pp. 23-24.

81. "Sprawozdanie Centos za czas od 1.VI.1940 do 31.XII.1940," undated, AŻIH 211/16, p. 25; Jewish Council report for October 1940, undated, AIH 218/7, p. 22.

82. "Wiadomości z Krakowa: Sieroty wołają o pomoc," Gazeta Żydowska, 8 November 1940, 3.

83. "Wiadomości z Krakowa: Impreza w Zakładzie Sierot Żydowskich w Krakowie," Gazeta Żydowska, 21 January 1941, 4.

84. The German law stipulated that confiscated real estate that had served educational purposes before the decree could continue to so serve with the permission of the appropriate German offices.

85. "Wiadomości z Krakowa: Szkoły żydowskie w Krakowie," Gazeta Żydowska, 24 September 1940, 3; Jewish Council report for October 1940, undated, AŻIH 218/7, pp. 25-26. Dawid Bulwa and Hersch Ohringer supervised the Jewish Council's Education Department. The Jewish Council also wanted to open separate trade schools for boys and girls.

CHAPTER 2 — ADAPTING TO LIFE INSIDE THE GHETTO

This chapter is derived, in part, from "Coping with Distorted Reality: Children in the Kraków Ghetto," Holocaust Studies 16, no. 1-2 (Summer/Autumn 2010): 177-202.

1. Untitled German report dated 20 September 1941, ANK SMKr reel J8187, p. 81. The city commandant assumed authority over that policy. While the Jewish Council was tasked with organizing and maintaining the ghetto, the director of the Labor Department in the city commandant's office was responsible for enforcing the law. "Wiadomości z Krakowa: Przydział mieszkań w dzielnicy żydowskiej," Gazeta Żydowska, 11 March 1941.

2. The concept of the "Aryan side" emerged with the establishment of the ghetto that divided spaces into Jewish and non-Jewish. German law delineated the boundaries of Jewish-gentile relations in a geographic, physical, and mental sense.

3. These numbers derive from the pioneering research done for The United States Holocaust Memorial Museum Encyclopedia of Camps and Ghettos.

4. Rodler was referred to as chief officer (Amtsleiter) in correspondence of the Jewish Social Self-Help ("Notatka do wiadomości Prezydium ŻSS," 2 December 1941, AŻIH 211/593) and as administrator of the Resettlement Office by the governor of Kraków District ("Sprawozdanie z konferencji z p. Rodlerem Kierownikiem Wydziału Umsiedlung Szefa Dystryktu dnia 8 marca 1941," undated, USHMM 1997 A 0124, reel 31, p. 33). He is even called commissar of the Jewish Residential District in Aleksander Biberstein, Zagłada Żydów w Krakowie (Kraków: Wydawnictwo Literackie, 1985), 59.

5. Kazimierz was established as a town in 1335. In 1800, it was incorporated as a district of Kraków. It was considered a "Jewish district" because of the size of its Jewish

population and the Jewish character of businesses, sacral buildings, and communal institutions.

6. Formerly a town, Podgórze was incorporated into Kraków in 1915. A separate Jewish Community existed in Podgórze until 1937, when it joined the main Kraków Jewish Community.

7. The Nazis associated a ghetto with the image of East European Jews (Ostjuden) and their language, Yiddish. To complicate life for Jews who were unfamiliar with Yiddish, the Germans ordered (4 April 1941) that all signs in the ghetto be written in Yiddish.

8. "Karty Żydów ubiegających się o pozostanie w getcie krakowskim, 1941," AŻIH 218.III.

9. The Germans issued the first decree about eligibility for acquiring identity papers on 26 October 1939. In order to receive such a card, one had to be at least fifteen years old and a resident of Kraków. (At the same time, German labor laws considered Jews who reached the age of fourteen as adults, which points to the inconsistencies in German policy regarding "the Jewish child.") As of 25 April 1941, the Germans stopped issuing identity cards for Jews in Kraków altogether, thereby making it illegal for them to remain in the city. "Obwieszczenie Stadthauptmanna dotyczy: Kart rozpoznawczych dla nie niemieckiej ludności," 25 April 1941, ANK SMKr reel J13913, p. 599.

10. "Wiadomości z Krakowa: Ważne dla osób nie posiadających Kart Rozpoznawczych," Gazeta Żydowska, 6 May 1941, 3; "Obwieszczenie Stadthauptmanna dotyczy: Kart rozpoznawczych dla nie niemieckiej ludności," 25 April 1941, ANK SMKr reel J13913, p. 599.

11. "Obwieszczenie o cenach najwyższych za owoce, warzywa i drób na targach tygodniowych i w sklepach w mieście Krakowie za czas od 24 marzec 1941 do 6 kwiecień 1941," 21 March 1941, ANK PNN 42, p. 1559.

12. Biberstein, Zagłada Żydów w Krakowie, 45–46; Tadeusz Pankiewicz, The Cracow Ghetto Pharmacy, trans. Henry Tilles (Washington, DC: U.S. Holocaust Memorial Museum, 2000), 2. It is unclear whether Christian Poles opposed the creation of a ghetto altogether and expressed their stance indirectly through complaints, or whether they were dissatisfied with the measures the Germans imposed on them.

13. Martin (Marcel) Baral, interview 1663, 1995, VHA.

14. "Wiadomości z Krakowa: Zakończenie akcji przesiedleńczej," Gazeta Żydowska, 21 March 1941, 4.

15. Martin (Marcel) Baral, interview 1663, 1995, VHA.

16. Rena Finder (née Ferber), interview 21482, 1996, VHA.

17. Ephroim Jablon (Jan Rothbaum), interview 43451, 1998, VHA.

18. Paul Faynwachs (Pinkus Fajnwaks), interview 14951, 1996, VHA.

19. "Vermerk I: Betr.: Wohnungs- und Gesundheitsverhaeltnisse im Abschnitt 'A' des juedischen Wohnbezirkes in Krakau," 20 September 1941, USHMM RG 15–245, pp. 39–97.0148–0150; "Wiadomości z Krakowa: Zarządzenie. Przedmiot: Utworzenie dzielnicy mieszkaniowej dla żydów w Krakowie," Gazeta Żydowska, 7 March 1941, 4; "Wiadomości z Krakowa: Przydział mieszkań w dzielnicy żydowskiej," Gazeta Żydowska, 11 March 1941, 3.

20. "Ludność Dzielnicy Żydowskiej w Krakowie według płci i wieku. Stan z 1.V.1941," 1 May 1941, Gmina Żydowska Kraków, Biuro Ewidencji Ludności, ANK J13871, p. 1.

21. These included Bielany, Przegorzały, Czyżyny, Łęg, Bodzów, Pychowice, Kostrze, Rybitwy, Bronowice Małe, Bronowice Wielkie, Chełm, Tonie, Wola Justowska, Prądnik Czerwony, Olsza, Prądnik Biały, Rakowice, Witkowice, Górka Narodowa, Wola Duch-

acka, Bieżanów, Piaski Wielkie, Prokocim, Rżąka, Borek Fałęcki, Jugowice, Kobierzyn, Kurdwanów, Łagiewniki, and Skotniki.

22. Werner Prag and Wolfgang Jacobmeyer, eds., *Das Diensttagebuch des deutschen Generalgouverneur in Polen, 1939–1945* (Stuttgart: Deutsche Verlags-Anstalt, 1975), 386, 436; Dan Michman, *The Emergence of Jewish Ghettos during the Holocaust* (New York: Cambridge University Press, 2011), 124.

23. "Perzentuelles Verhaltniss der Wohnstubenzahl zur Einwohnerzahl im Judenwohnbezirk," 13 October 1941, ANKr reel J13871, p. 19; "Die Belegung von Wohnstatten im Judenwohnbezirk: Stand vom 14 Oktober 1941," 14 October 1941, ANK, reel J13871, p. 21.

24. "Vermerk II: Betr.: Auffullung des Abschnittes 'A' des judischen Wohnbezirk in Krakau," 13 October 1941, USHMM RG 15–245, pp. 39–97.0157–0158.

25. Janina Fischler-Martinho, *Have You Seen My Little Sister?* (London: Vallentine Mitchell, 1997), 133–135.

26. Celina Biniaz (née Karp), interview 11133, 1996, VHA.

27. Lucie Brent (née Stern), interview 396, 1994, VHA.

28. Aneta Weinreich (née Baral), interview 14405, 1996, VHA.

29. Ester Friedman (née Spagatner), *Daleka droga do domu* (Kraków: Ambrozja, 1997), 31.

30. Bronisława (Niusia) Horowitz-Karakulska, interview 647, 1995, VHA; Ryszard Horowitz, interview 8402, 1995 VHA; Alexander Rosner, interview 1017, 1995, VHA.

31. Norbert Schlang (Szlang), interview 27127, 1997, VHA.

32. Tosia Gringer (née Sztahl), interview 28313, 1997, VHA.

33. Tosia Gringer (née Sztahl), interview 28313, 1997, VHA.

34. Bronisława (Niusia) Horowitz-Karakulska, interview 647, 1995, VHA.

35. A "postal depot" (*Sammelstelle für Brief, Geld und Paket Drepen*) existed in the ghetto from March 1941 to July 1942. Letters, money orders, and packages (and in them tea, coffee, cocoa, almonds, and sardines) flowed into the depot. Account of N. N., undated, YVA M.49.E/5093, pp. 3–4.

36. Biberstein, *Zagłada Żydów w Krakowie*, 58.

37. Michael (Mieczysław) Arzewski, interview 41930, 1998, VHA.

38. Anna Balaban (née Blatt), interview 26141, 1997, VHA.

39. Hanna Wechsler (Chana Kleiner), interview 43550, 1998, VHA.

40. Felicia Liban (née Vogler), interview 1451, 1995, VHA.

41. Before the war, it was customary to bring formed dough to bakeries for baking because not every household had a separate kitchen or an oven. In the ghetto, where not everyone had access to a kitchen (and if they did, they often feared that the baked goods would be taken by other inhabitants), some Jews brought items to a bakery and received a stub, which they later presented to receive their baked goods.

42. Mark (Marek) Goldfinger, interview 44971, 1998, VHA.

43. Aneta Weinreich (née Baral), interview 14405, 1996, VHA.

44. "Kochana dziatwo i młodzieży żydowskiej!," *Gazeta Żydowska*, 23 July 1940, 12.

45. Martin (Marcel) Baral, interview 1663, 1995, VHA. His activity might also have been a child's way of venting frustration on other creatures and projecting his own condition.

46. George (Jerzy) Hoffman, interview 17554, 1996, VHA.

47. In "Children in the Holocaust: Dealing with Affects and Memory Images in Trauma and Generational Linking" (PhD diss., Uppsala University, 2002), Suzanne Kaplan introduces the concept of "space creating" by children in response to destruction. Their

thinking/fantasizing and thinking/taking action lead to creating distance to ongoing threats. Kaplan also notes that creating excitement and devising games constitutes part of children's coping mechanisms.

48. "Wiadomości z Krakowa: Szanujcie przyrodę!," *Gazeta Żydowska*, 13 June 1941, 4. See also "Wiadomości z Krakowa: Ławki w Dzielnicy," *Gazeta Żydowska*, 17 May 1942, 3.

49. "Wiadomości z Krakowa: Tragiczny wypadek na Krzemionkach," *Gazeta Żydowska*, 29 May 1942, 6.

50. "Wiadomości z Krakowa: Szanujcie przyrodę!," *Gazeta Żydowska*, 13 June 1941, 4.

51. Frances Gelbart (Francis Immergluck), interview 12003, 1996, VHA.

52. Roman Polanski (Raymond/Roman Liebling), *Roman* (New York: William Morrow, 1984), 25–26.

53. Polanski, 30.

54. George Eisen, *Children and Play in the Holocaust: Games among the Shadows* (Amherst: University of Massachusetts Press, 1988), 84.

55. Miriam Bruck (Emilia Heller), interview 21495, 1996, VHA.

56. Polanski, *Roman*, 21.

57. Marian Keren (Kwaśniewski), interview 42453, 1998, VHA.

58. Miriam Akavia (Matylda Weinfeld), *Jesień młodości* (Kraków: Wydawnictwo Literackie, 1989), 53.

59. Renée Stern (Rena Hocherman), interview 22644, 1996, VHA.

60. Elsa Chandler (née Biller), interview 7744, 1995, VHA.

61. Fischler-Martinho, *Have You Seen?*, p. 164.

62. Halina Nelken, *And Yet, I Am Here!* (Amherst: University of Massachusetts Press, 1999), 84.

63. Stella Müller-Madej, *Oczami dziecka: Wspomnienia z dzieciństwa w getcie i obozach koncentracyjnych* (Kraków: Nakład Autora, 1991), 24.

64. Jewish children in Kraków were multilingual. In some Jewish families in which a parent originated from Germany or Austria or attended university there, children spoke German at home. At times, parents employed German-speaking nannies for their children. Hence, for a number of Jewish children in prewar Kraków, German was either their first language or one of the languages they knew. On the other hand, some children spoke Yiddish with their family members. Jewish children who attended the Hebrew School used both Hebrew and Polish. Most Jewish children in prewar Kraków, however, knew Polish.

65. "Kwestia językowa," *Gazeta Żydowska*, 17 June 1941, 2.

66. "Z Warszawy: Posyłajcie dzieci do szkół," *Gazeta Żydowska*, 1 March 1942, 2.

67. "Kwestia szkolna także problemem społecznym," *Gazeta Żydowska*, 8 May 1942, 1.

68. "Wiadomości z Krakowa: Z żydowskiej szkoły," *Gazeta Żydowska*, 25 July 1941, 2.

69. Ruta Sakowska, "O szkolnictwie i tajnym nauczaniu w getcie warszawskim," *Biuletyn Żydowskiego Instytutu Historycznego*, no. 55 (July–September 1965): 64.

70. "Szkolnictwo żydowskie w Generalnym Gubernatorstwie," *Gazeta Żydowska*, 3 May 1942, 1. The basis for this order was Hans Frank's decree of 31 August 1940, which went into force a day later. "Rozporządzenie o szkolnictwie żydowskim w Generalnym Gubernatorstwie z dnia 31 sierpnia 1940 r," *Verordnungsblatt für das Generalgouvernement* 51 (11 September 1940): 258.

71. Frances Gelbart (Francis Immergluck), interview 12003, 1996, VHA.

72. Sakowska, "O szkolnictwie (. . .)," 83.

73. Menasche Lewertow, "Z życia religijnego Żydów w Krakowie w okresie okupacji," in *W 3-cią rocznicę zagłady ghetta w Krakowie (13.III.1943–13.III.1946)*, ed. Michał M. Borwicz, Nella Rost, and Józef Wulf (Kraków: Centralny Komitet Żydów Polskich, 1946, reprinted 2013), 85–87.

74. Mark (Maurycy) Sternlicht, interview 42790, 1998, VHA.

75. In April 1942, the Germans allowed Jews to hold religious services on the second day of Passover in the Zucker Synagogue at 5 Węgierska Street. "Wiadomości z Krakowa: Nabożeństwa w bożnicy," *Gazeta Żydowska*, 8 April 1942, 3.

76. Roman Ferber, interview 43707, 1998, VHA.

77. Anita Lobel (née Kempler), *No Pretty Pictures: A Child of War* (New York: Harper-Collins, 1998), 45.

78. Müller-Madej, *Oczami dziecka*, p. 47.

CHAPTER 3 — CLANDESTINE ACTIVITIES

1. Janka Warszawska (after the war Jeannette Geizhals), "Janka Warshavska's Story," a translation from the Hebrew version of Lena Küchler, *My Hundred Children*, 1959, 12–13. I thank Professor Shelly Tenenbaum for bringing her aunt's written testimony to my attention and for providing a copy of it. See also Janka Warszawska, 1945, GFHA 22817.

2. Warszawska, 15.

3. Adalbert Schepessy headed the Labor Office until the June 1942 action in the ghetto. Afterward, Otto Klingbeil presided over the office until the October 1942 action. Then the SS took over labor matters. Aleksander Biberstein, *Zagłada Żydów w Krakowie* (Kraków: Wydawnictwo Literackie, 1985, reprinted 2001), 188.

4. Survivors often credit their lives to luck. As the personal histories throughout this book show, and as the literature on the phenomenon underscores, luck was the result of a convergence of factors.

5. Oskar Schindler, a German businessman, took over a plant at 4 Lipowa Street in Zabłocie, specializing in the production of enameled dishes and bullet shells. The biography and legacy of Schindler and the one thousand Jews whom he rescued have prompted a rich literature.

Together with his factory manager, Raimund Titsch, Madritsch, an Austrian businessman, employed about eight hundred Jews in the factory at 2 Rynek Podgórski. They offered bearable conditions for their Jewish laborers and accepted the use of fake birth certificates to enable child labor.

6. Testimony of Bernard Offen, 22 April and 15 December 1992, USHMM RG-50.477.0038.

7. Jane Schein (Janina Ast), interview 415, 1994, VHA. Janina's story can also be found in Azriel Eisenberg, *The Lost Generation: Children in the Holocaust* (New York: Pilgrim, 1982), 216, and Isaiah Trunk, *Jewish Responses to Nazi Rule* (New York: Stein and Day, 1978), 117–122.

8. Members of the Jewish Association of Artisans (Żydowski Związek Rzemieślników) created cooperatives in the ghetto, which took orders from both German and Polish industrialists. Biberstein, *Zagłada Żydów w Krakowie*, 61–62.

9. Celina Biniaz (née Karp), interview 11133, 1996, VHA.

10. Louise Gans (Luiza Grüner), interview 40851, 1998, VHA; Relacje: Luiza Grüner, 1945, AŻIH 301/837, p. 2.

11. Celina Biniaz (née Karp), interview 11133, 1996, VHA.

12. Mark (Maurycy) Sternlicht, interview 42790, 1998, VHA.

13. Tosia Gringer (née Sztahl), interview 28313, 1997, VHA.

14. The action was led by SS-Hauptscharführer Wilhelm Kunde.

15. Biberstein, *Zagłada Żydów w Krakowie*, 64–75. Because of his position as a physician, Biberstein moved around the ghetto, which allowed him to witness many scenes.

16. The Germans deported the former Jewish Council president, Dr. Artur Rosenzweig, and his family during the June 1942 action. Its new leader, Dawid Gutter, held the title "commissar."

17. As in the previous action, only members of the Jewish administration of the ghetto and their immediate families received exemption from selections. SS-Sturmbannführer Willi Haase and SS-Hauptscharführer Kunde led the second major action in the ghetto.

18. Biberstein, *Zagłada Żydów w Krakowie*, 82.

19. Bibestein, 89. After the October 1942 action, Jews in the ghetto came under the purview of the chief of SS and police in the General Government, Friedrich Wilhelm Krüger.

20. The chief of SS and police ordered the creation of five remnant ghettos in Kraków District (in Kraków, Bochnia, Tarnów, Rzeszów, and Przemyśl) on 10 November 1942 to serve as holding pens for Jews who had not yet been deported. In December 1942, all of those ghettos were divided into sections A and B, and Jews were placed in them according to their work capabilities. By September 1943, all five remnant ghettos were liquidated.

21. Biberstein, 87–93.

22. SS-Sturmführer Amon Goeth, the commandant of the Plaszow camp, spearheaded the action.

23. Renate Schondorf (née Leinkram), interview 35582, 1997, VHA.

24. Miriam Bruck (Emilia Heller), interview 21495, 1996, VHA.

25. Louise Gans (Luiza Grüner), interview 40851, 1998, VHA.

26. Richard (Henryk) Haber, interview 6517, 1995, VHA.

27. When the Kraków ghetto was created, the Jewish police (Jüdischer Ordnungsdienst) headquarters moved to 39 Józefińska Street, where it also included a jail for Jews brought in from the Aryan side, and those who were punished for various offenses. Until September 1942, Jewish policemen and their families had lived together with other Jews in the quarters they were assigned by the Housing Office. Symche Spira, the commandant of the Jewish police, then commandeered the Jewish Orphanage building at 31 Józefińska Street as the living quarters for his men and their families.

28. Account of Jerzy Aleksandrowicz, 1946, YVA M.49/2060, p. 1.

29. Account of Aleksandrowicz, 2.

30. Wiktoria Śliwowska, ed., *The Last Eyewitnesses: Children of the Holocaust Speak*, trans. Julian Bussgang and Fay Bussgang (Evanston: Northwestern University Press, 1998), 6.

31. Jane Schein (Janina Ast), interview 415, 1994, VHA.

32. Relacje: Marcel Grüner, 11 May 1945. AŻIH 301/410, p. 2.

33. Account of Aron Geldwert, undated, YVA M.49/3366, p. 1.

34. The OD found all but five boys who had managed to escape. Members of Aron's group were once again jailed. In all, he counted 234 prisoners, which suggests the extent of hiding efforts during the final liquidation of the ghetto.

35. Roma Ligocka (Roma Liebling), *The Girl in the Red Coat* (New York: St. Martin's, 2002), 15–16, 19.

36. Aneta Weinreich (née Baral), interview 14405, 1996, VHA.

37. Louise Gans (Luiza Grüner), interview 40851, 1998, VHA.

38. Relacje: Irena Joachimson, undated, AŻIH 301/4120, p. 3.

39. Janina Fischler-Martinho, *Have You Seen My Little Sister?* (London: Vallentine Mitchell, 1997), 159–186.

40. Ida Turner (née Jakubowicz), interview 7712, 1995, VHA.

41. Jacob Baral, interview 20015, 1996, VHA.

42. Relacje: Zygmunt Gelband, 7 September 1945, AŻIH 301/776.

43. Michael (Mieczysław) Arzewski, interview 41930, 1998, VHA.

44. Elsa Chandler (née Biller), interview 7744, 1995, VHA.

45. The Polish (Navy) Blue police (called so because of the color of their uniforms) was composed of prewar gentile Polish policemen. Their task was to maintain law and order and guard the external perimeter of the ghetto. Some of its members joined the Polish resistance and some helped Jews. However, as new research has uncovered, the role of the Polish policemen extended to cooperation with the Germans and to murdering Jews..

46. Relacje: Mendel Feichtal, 1945, AŻIH 301/609.

47. Relacje: Bronisława (Niusia) Horowitz, undated, AŻIH 301/4041.

48. Mark (Maurycy) Sternlicht, interview 42790, 1998, VHA.

49. Roman Polanski (Raymond/Roman Liebling), *Roman* (New York: William Morrow, 1984), 75.

50. Polanski, 76.

51. Fischler-Martinho, *Have You Seen?*, 27, 36.

52. David Zauder, interview 22599, 1996, VHA.

53. According to German reports, between 3 March and 8 September 1941, German patrols stopped 827 Jews and Polish police stopped 374 Jews for lack of proper identity papers and for not wearing an armband. Since the reports do not contain a breakdown by age, it is unknown how many children were detained, if any. The lower number of Jews stopped by the Polish police may indicate three things: the Polish police did not pursue anti-Jewish policy as fiercely in the first months of the ghetto's existence; Jews managed to pass undetected; extortions freed individual Jews from being reported. ANK, J13942, pp. 75, 79, 83, 87, 91, 95, 99, 103, 107, 111, 117, 127.

54. Fischler-Martinho, *Have You Seen?*, 56.

55. Bernard Offen, interview 27135, 1997, VHA.

56. Oral history of Janina Stefaniak, 2 October 2004, USHMM RG-50.488.0212.

57. David Zauder, interview 22599, 1996, VHA.

58. Kerry Bluglass, ed., *Hidden from the Holocaust: Stories of Resilient Children Who Survived and Thrived* (Westport, CT: Praeger, 2003), 88–89; Fischler-Martinho, *Have You Seen?*, 56.

59. The Kraków branch of ŻOB was established in September 1942 from an earlier merger of Akiba (an organization of Zionist youths), led by Adolf Liebeskind and Szymon Draenger, with Dror-Frayhayt (an organization of Zionist-socialist youths), led by Abraham Lejbowicz. Headquartered at 13 Józefińska Street in the Kraków ghetto, ŻOB extended its network to outside localities. Its members refused to comply with German orders, engaged in sabotage and the execution of death sentences, and supplied its members with false documents and weapons. Until the October 1942 action in the ghetto, ŻOB focused on creating a unit in the forest. Afterward, it staged a number of diversion actions outside the ghetto.

60. Account of Abraham Blim, 5 March 1961, YVA 0.3/2221, p. 13.

61. Sophia Aferiat (née Śpiewak), interview 19545, 1996, VHA.

62. Paul Faynwachs (Pinkus Fajnwaks), interview 14951, 1996, VHA.

63. Fischler-Martinho, *Have You Seen?* 78.

64. Louise Gans (Luiza Grüner), interview 40851, 1998, VHA.

65. Max Pelton (Maksymilian Perlmutter), interview 38075, 1998, VHA.

66. Pelton, interview.

67. "Trzecie rozporządzenie o ograniczeniach pobytu w Generalnym Gubernatorst-wie," *Verordnungsblatt für das Generalgovernement* 99 (15 October 1941), p. 593.

68. "Zarządzenie Stadthauptmanna w sprawie zakazu czynienia zakupów przez żydów w sklepach poza żydowską dzielnicą mieszkaniową z dnia 28.VII.1942.," 28 July 1942, ANK J13915, p. 985.

69. The term *szmalcownicy* stems from the Polish word *smalec* (lard) and implies greas-ing one's hand.

70. Bernard Offen, interview 27135, 1997, VHA.

71. Historian Joanna Michlic raises the need to explore the phenomenon of young "sud-den protectors," or older children who saved the lives of younger children, to gain a refined understanding of the extent of rescue activities. Joanna Beata Michlic, "An Untold Story of Rescue: Jewish Children and Youth in German-Occupied Poland," in *Jewish Resistance against the Nazis*, ed. Patrick Henry (Washington, DC: Catholic University of America Press, 2014), 300–318.

72. Pursuing their policy to Germanize Kraków and to solidify its role as the capital of the General Government, the Germans began to change street names in August 1941. This affected Jews. Not knowing the new street and place-names put them at risk. With limited access to information regarding policies that affected gentiles, Jewish child smugglers were compelled to rely on observation and their memory of the city's prewar landscape.

73. Warszawska, "Janka Warshavska's Story," 15.

74. Account of Abraham Blim. YVA 0.3/2221, 5 March 1961, pp. 15–16.

75. Bluglass, *Hidden from the Holocaust*, 70.

76. Letters from Eda and Salek to the Zendler family, 1943, Anita Epstein Papers, USHMM 2001.321.1, items 2001.321.1_001_001_001-004. See also "Sendler, Mr., and Send-ler, Zofia," in *The Encyclopedia of the Righteous among the Nations: Rescuers of Jews during the Holocaust: Poland*, ed. Israel Gutman, Sara Bender, and Shmuel Krakowski (Jerusalem: Yad Vashem, 2004), 2:702; "Sendler Zofia; Husband: First Name Unknown," Righteous among the Nations Database, Yad Vashem, accessed May 24, 2019, http://db .yadvashem.org/righteous/family.html?language=en&itemId=4035266; "Sendler Mr. and Sendler Zofia," Righteous among the Nations Database, Yad Vashem, accessed May 24, 2019, http://db.yadvashem.org/righteous/righteousName.html?language=en&itemId =4038010; Eda Kaminski, interview 8985, 1995, VHA; Anita Epstein and Noel Epstein, *Miracle Child: The Journey of a Young Holocaust Survivor* (Boston: Academic Studies Press, 2018); and Joanna Sliwa, "Rescue and Parenting through Correspondence," 2 November 2020, EHRI Document Blog, accessed February 7, 2021, https://blog.ehri -project.eu/2020/11/02/rescue-and-parenting-through-correspondence/.

77. Eva Wald (Ewa Heublum), interview 28166, 1997, VHA. Ewa then took a train to the man's sister, who lived outside the city.

78. Pankiewicz's assistants, Helena Krywaniuk, Aurelia Danek-Czortowa, and Irena Droździkowska, helped him in his efforts to assist Jews. They facilitated contact between

the ghetto and the Aryan side of the city, dispensed medicine (paid for by wealthy Jews) free of charge, offered emotional support, hid Jews during actions, and used Pankiewicz's connections to release Jews from prison.

79. "Skrzynski, Tadeusz; Skrzynska, Paulina," in Gutman, Bender, and Krakowski, *Encyclopedia of the Righteous*, 2:718–719.

80. "Zabierzowska-Krystian, Katarzyna," in Gutman, Bender, and Krakowski, 2:911.

81. Some of those Jews then fled to Tarnów, where Madritsch ran another factory. From there, a number of families continued their escape to Hungary via Slovakia. Poles employed in the plant also helped by arranging hiding places, making connections, and smuggling in food. See "Mazur Helena, Mazur Jan," in Michał Grynberg, *Księga Sprawiedliwych* (Warsaw: Państwowe Wydawnictwo Naukowe, 1993), 337.

82. The deputy commandant of the German police in Podgórze, Bousko has been credited with saving the lives of a number of Jews from the Kraków ghetto by warning them of impending actions, ignoring their exits from and entrance into the ghetto, and bringing food for Jews inside the ghetto. He was, in the eyes of survivors, someone both the Jews and Poles could count on. "Karol or Oswald Bousko, known as Bosko: Akta w sprawie: Karol Bosko," 1948, AIPNKr 502/3315; account of Eugenia Felicja Myszkowska, YVA 0.3/1353, 1959, p. 34; "Madritsch, Julius; Titsch, Raimund" and "Bosko, Oswald," in Main Commission for the Investigation of Crimes against the Polish Nation, Institute of National Memory, and Polish Society for the Righteous among the Nations, *Those Who Helped: Polish Rescuers of Jews during the Holocaust*, pt. 3 (Warsaw: n.p., 1997), 19; Relacje: Helena Brinfeld, undated, AŻIH 301/3428, p. 1; and statement of Adolf Żabner, 22 December 2008, AESIP, Folder: "Sprawiedliwy: Stanisław Śliżewski." In 1964, Yad Vashem recognized Oswald Bousko as a Righteous among the Nations.

83. Relacje: Lewi Ewa, undated, AŻIH 301/3868; Chava Mandelbaum (Cyla Chava Lewi), 1986, MJH 1986.T.47. Other sources provide a different account of events: Malvina Graf, *The Kraków Ghetto and the Płaszów Camp Remembered* (Tallahassee: Florida State University Press, 1989), 47; David Crowe, *Oskar Schindler: The Untold Account of His Life, Wartime Activities, and the True Story behind the List* (Cambridge, MA: Westview, 2004), 199–201; and Tadeusz Pankiewicz, *The Cracow Ghetto Pharmacy*, trans. Henry Tilles (Washington: U.S. Holocaust Memorial Museum, 2000), 51–53.

84. Ligocka, *The Girl*, 19.

85. Warszawska, "Janka Warshavska's Story," 20.

86. Polanski, *Roman*, 34.

87. Polanski, 34–35.

88. Account of Abraham Blim, 5 March 1961, YVA 0.3/2221, p. 15.

89. Śliwowska, *Last Eyewitnesses*, 6–7.

90. Bluglass, *Hidden from the Holocaust*, 71.

91. Janina Pietrasiak (née Feldman), interview 22050, 1996, VHA; Jakub Gutenbaum and Agnieszka Latała, eds., *The Last Eyewitnesses: Children of the Holocaust Speak*, trans. Julian Bussgang, Fay Bussgang, and Simon Cygielski (Evanston, IL: Northwestern University Press, 2005), 2:197–207.

92. Ligocka, *The Girl*, 27.

CHAPTER 4 — CHILD WELFARE

1. Also known by its German name, Jüdische Soziale Selbsthilfe, and its Yiddish term, Aleynhilf.

2. "Wiadomości z Krakowa: Z komisji sanitarnej," *Gazeta Żydowska*, 15 April 1941, 3.

3. ŻKOM, "Protokół z odbytego dnia 20 maja 1941 posiedzenia Żydowskiego Komitetu Opiekuńczego Miejskiego w Krakowie," 20 May 1941, USHMM RG 15.245, 38-97.0110–38-97.0121; ŻSS, "Sprawozdanie z działalności Wydziału Opieki nad Dziećmi i Sierotami / dawniej 'Centos' / w Krakowie Żydowskiej Samopomocy Społecznej—Żydowskiego Komitetu Opiekuńczego Miejskiego za czas od 1 stycznia 1941 do 1 maja 1941," undated, AŻIH 211/14, p. 42; "Wiadomości z Krakowa: Królestwo dzieci," *Gazeta Żydowska*, 9 May 1941, 4.

The day care sites had to be changed four times as a result of German orders. ŻSS, "Dot: Ich listu z dnia 19 maja 1942 w sprawie dożywialni dla dzieci przy ul. Węgierskiej," 25 May 1942, USHMM 1997.A.0124, reel 31, p. 52.

4. Sabina Hochberger-Mirowska, a secretary in the orphanage, dates the relocation on 1 April 1941 in her testimony. Account of Sabina Hochberger-Mirowska, 1946, YVA M-49/2048, p. 2. Other sources, however, mention the end of May 1941.

5. "Abschrift: An die Bewirtschaftungsstelle für Spinnstoffe durch die Jüdische Soziale Selbsthilhe," 12 May 1941, USHMM RG 15.245, 37-97.0055.

6. "Sprawozdanie z rozmowy w sprawie fuzjowania sierocińców i skoordynowania akcji opieki nad sierotami z dnia 7 kwietnia 1941," 8 April 1941, USHMM RG-15-245, 37-97.0089, p. 1.

The Vocational Hostel for Jewish Orphaned Boys (Stowarzyszenie i Bursa Żydowskich Sierot Rękodzielników) housed and cared for about fifty boys aged fourteen to eighteen. In the ghetto, the two hostels previously located at 53 Krakowska Street and 6 Podbrzezie Street merged into one institution located at 35 Józefińska Street. It then moved to 39 Józefińska Street. The institution was directed by Matylda Schenkerowa and managed by Chaskel Entenberg. All boys worked and contributed from their pay to the upkeep of their hostel.

7. "Sprawozdanie z rozmowy w sprawie fuzjowania sierocińców i skoordynowania akcji opieki nad sierotami z dnia 7 kwietnia 1941," 8 April 1941, USHMM RG-15-245, 37-97.0092, p. 4.

8. "Sprawozdanie z rozmowy," 2–4.

9. "Notatka z rozmowy odbytej dnia 26 sierpnia br. między członkami KOM-u pp. Sternbergiem, Lowenherzem, Schmelkesem a przybyłymi na zapowiedzianą konferencję przedstawicielami Domu Sierot pp. Drem Biebersteinem, Kurzmannem, Mgrem Salpetrem i Drem Zimmerspitzem w sprawie sytuacji Domu Sierot," 27 August 1941, USHMM RG 15.245, 37-97.0141. This statement could be read as an attempt by the Jewish Welfare Committee to evade financial responsibility for the orphanage, or as a statement of fact. On the one hand, the orphanage was always a private institution, supported by members of Kraków's Jewish community. On the other, in a situation of tightening resources, it was convenient for the Jewish Welfare Committee to cede an additional responsibility.

10. "Bł. P. Matylda Karmelowa w Szloszim . . . ," *Gazeta Żydowska*, 8 May 1942, 4.

11. Eva Wald (Ewa Heublum), interview 28166, 1997, VHA.

12. "Die Belegung von Wohnstätten im Judenwohnbezirk," 14 October 1941," ANKr, reel J13871, p. 21.

13. ŻKOM, "Protokół z odbytego dnia 4 września 1941 posiedzenia Żydowskiego Komitetu Opiekuńczego Miejskiego w Krakowie," 5 September 1941, USHMM RG 15.245, 38-97.0133.

14. ŻSS on behalf of the Jewish Orphanage to the Kraków city commandant [in German], 26 October 1941, USHMM RG 15.245, 37-97.0046-49.

15. Aleksander Biberstein, *Zagłada Żydów w Krakowie* (Kraków: Wydawnictwo Literackie, 1985, reprinted 2001), 242; Miriam Hochberg-Mariańska and Noe Grüs, eds., *The Children Accuse*, trans. Bill Johnston (Portland, OR: Valentine Mitchell, 1996), 240–246; Relacje: Sabina Mirowska-Hochberger, 1 December 1946, AŻIH 301/2048, p. 3. Possibly, those ten children had previously lived in the building of the Krakovian Charitable Society (Krakowskie Towarzystwo Dobroczynności), located at 12 Koletek Street in Kazimierz. The building had belonged to the Koletki nuns, who had donated their premises to the society and moved to the nearby convent of the Bernardine Sisters at 21 Poselska Street.

16. Some of these factors have been listed by Martyna Grądzka in *Przerwane dzieciństwo: Losy dzieci Żydowskiego Domu Sierot przy ul. Dietla 64 w Krakowie podczas okupacji niemieckiej / A Broken Childhood: The Fate of the Children from the Jewish Orphanage at 64 Dietla Street in Cracow during the German Occupation* (Kraków: Wysoki Zamek, 2012), 108, 341–342.

17. Relacje: Mirowska Sabina, AŻIH 301/4693, 17 October 1945, pp. 1–2. Sabina Mirowska and Sabina Mirowska-Hochberger were the same person. She submitted two testimonies, one under her family name and one under her married name. Citations refer to the name under which she submitted her testimony.

18. ŻKOM, "Protokół z odbytego dnia 12 czerwca 1941 posiedzenia Żydowskiego Komitetu Opiekuńczego Miejskiego w Krakowie," undated, USHMM RG 15.245, 38-97.0122.

19. ŻKOM, "Protokół z odbytego dnia 4 sierpnia 1941 posiedzenia Żydowskiego Komitetu Opiekuńczego Miejskiego w Krakowie," undated, USHMM RG 15.245, 38-97.0130.

20. ŻSS, "Miesiąc Dziecka," undated, AŻIH 211/17, p. 3.

21. ŻSS, "Dla Dziecka," 2 November 1941, USHMM RG 15.245, 37-97.0038.

22. ŻSS–ŻKOM, "Miesiąc Dziecka w Krakowie,"undated, AŻIH 211/17, p. 5.

23. ŻSS–ŻKOM, "Program przedstawienia 'Dzieci dla Dzieci' z okazji 'Miesiąca Dla Dziecka' w Krakowie," November 1941, AŻIH 211/17, p. 6.

24. ŻKOM, "Protokół posiedzenia Żyd. Komitetu Opiekuńczego Miejskiego w Krakowie, odbytego w dniu 12 stycznia 1942," 14 January 1942, USHMM 1997 A 0124, reel 31, p. 23. Similar sums were allocated to the Infectious Disease Hospital, the infirmary, the Home for the Elderly, and soup kitchens.

25. ŻSS, "Ogólny bilans wydatków na opiekę w pierwszym półroczu 1942 r.," undated, YIVO 335.1, folder 91.

26. ŻKOM, "Protokół posiedzenia Żyd. Komitetu Opiekuńczego Miejskiego w Krakowie, odbytego w dniu 12 stycznia 1942," 14 January 1942, USHMM 1997 A 0124, reel 31, p. 24.

27. ŻKOM, "Protokół posiedzenia Żyd. Komitetu Opiekuńczego Miejskiego w Krakowie odbytego w dniu 17 grudnia 1941," 18 December 1941, AŻIH 211/593, p. 21.

28. Dr. Maurycy Haber, a member of the Jewish Council, assumed responsibility for the Sanitary Commission, directly subject to the German sanitary chief of Kraków (Drs. Reichel, Burmann, and Ohrloff in order). The Sanitary Commission was tasked with checking the hygienic condition of apartments in the ghetto and with the medical care of the ghetto inhabitants. When the ghetto in Kraków was opened, the commission transferred the Disinfection-Delousing Station from 17 Gertrudy Street to 3 Józefińska Street. Biberstein, *Zagłada Żydów w Krakowie*, 201–203.

29. "Wiadomości z Krakowa: Z działalności Komisji Sanitarnej w styczniu 1942," *Gazeta Żydowska*, 18 February 1942, 3.

30. The Infectious Disease Hospital, directed by Dr. Aleksander Biberstein, was created in response to the increasing number of infectious diseases among Jews in Kraków and the German order against treating Jews in "Aryan" hospitals. The hospital admitted its first patient on 28 April 1940. After the first action in the ghetto on 8 June 1942, the hospital moved from 30 Rękawka Street into a building at 3 Plac Zgody. Biberstein, *Zagłada Żydów w Krakowie*, 212–225.

31. Halina Nelken, *And Yet, I Am Here!* (Amherst: University of Massachusetts Press, 1999), 84.

32. Nelken, 80.

33. "Apel Wydziału Opieki nad Dzieckiem pod auspicjami dawnego Centosu na Józefińskiej 37," 15 July 1941, YIVO 335.1, folder 91; AJDC, AR 1933/44, Poland, folders 821–826.

34. Testimony of Helena Anifeld-Dobrowolska, undated, YVA 0.3/583, p. 1.

35. "Protokół z konferencji z kierowniczkami Poradni Higienicznych w dniu 15 kwietnia 1942 r.," 15 April 1942, AŻIH 211/595.

36. In 1938–1942, 487 babies were born (including 151 in 1941 and 38 in 1942). Korespondencja ŻSS z ŻKOM, "Zestawienie liczbowe dzieci, przebywających w Dzielnicy Żydowskiej w Krakowie, urodzonych w latach 1938–1942, według płci i roku urodzenia," undated, AŻIH 211/596, p. 6.

37. "Wiadomości z Krakowa: Uruchomienie ambulatorium Szpitala w dzielnicy żydowskiej," *Gazeta Żydowska*, 6 May 1941, 3; "Wiadomości z Krakowa: Przeniesienie Poradni Przeciwgruźliczej TOZ-u," *Gazeta Żydowska*, 13 May 1941, 3. The Jewish Hospital was initially located at 8 Skawińska Street in Kazimierz. The Jewish Council managed to secure an extension until 31 October 1941 for the hospital to move into the ghetto, where it relocated to 14 Józefińska Street. The hospital included a pediatric and an OB-GYN section. Biberstein, *Zagłada Żydów w Krakowie*, 204–211.

38. In *American Jewry and the Holocaust: The American Jewish Joint Distribution Committee, 1939–1945* (Detroit: Wayne State University Press, 1981), Yehuda Bauer observes that "JDC went underground in December 1941, but in fact nothing much changed" (322). JDC channeled funds into the General Government through the International Red Cross using fictitious addresses in Lisbon (the location of the wartime JDC Europe Office) and the federation of Jewish Communities in Switzerland (Schweizerische Israelitischer Gemeinde; SIG) run by Saly Mayer (321). While JDC's sphere of influence in the General Government focused on Warsaw, its activities had wider impact.

39. ŻSS, "Sprawozdanie z wizytacji dożywialni dla dzieci świetlic przy ul. Wegierskiej 5 i Rekawka 22 /dawny 'Centos'/ i z konferencji z kierowniczką tych placówek w dniu 10 marca 1942," undated, USHMM 1997 A.0124, reel 31, p. 56.

40. "Wiadomości z Krakowa: Nowy azyl w dzielnicy," *Gazeta Żydowska*, 1 May 1942, 3; "Wiadomości z Krakowa: Z działalności azylu przy ul. Limanowskiego 36," *Gazeta Żydowska*, 3 May 1942, 3.

41. ŻKOM, "Protokół posiedzenia Żyd. Komitetu Opiekuńczego Miejskiego w Krakowie odbytego w dniu 17 grudnia 1941," 18 December 1941, AŻIH 211/593, p. 21; ŻKOM, "Protokół posiedzenia Żyd. Komitetu Opiekuńczego Miejskiego w Krakowie, odbytego w dniu 12 stycznia 1942," 14 January 1942, USHMM 1997 A 0124, reel 31, p. 24.

42. "Wiadomości z Krakowa: Kobieta-matka, to nasza świętość," *Gazeta Żydowska*, 10 May 1942, 1.

43. ŻSS, "Protokół posiedzenia Żydowskiego Komitetu Opiekuńczego Miejskiego w Krakowie odbytego w dniu 12 maja 1942," 14 May 1942, USHMM 1997 A.0124, reel 31, pp. 50–51.

44. ŻSS, "Dot: Ich listu z dnia 19 maja 1942 w sprawie dożywialni dla dzieci przy ul. Węgierskiej," 25 May 1942, USHMM 1997.A.0124, reel 31, p. 52.

45. Relacje: Sabina Mirowska-Hochberger, 1 December 1946, AŻIH 301/2048, p. 3; Biberstein, *Zagłada Żydów w Krakowie*, 246.

46. Cover article, *Gazeta Żydowska*, 19 June 1942, 1.

47. Korespondencja ŻSS z Prezydium ŻKOM, "Notatka: W sprawie opieki wychowawczej nad dziećmi w Dzielnicy Żydowskiej w Krakowie," 10 July 1942, AŻIH 211/596, p. 5.

48. Korespondencja ŻSS z Prezydium ŻKOM, 5.

49. ŻSS, "Uwagi do sprawozdania Wydziału Opieki Sanitarnej i Higienicznej za miesiąc lipiec 1942," 3 August 1942, AŻIH 211/596, pp. 11, 12.

50. ŻSS, 12.

51. ŻSS, "Okólnik Nr. 64 dotyczy: Dodatkowego dożywiania dzieci," 15 July 1942, AŻIH 211/15, p. 49.

52. "Wiadomości z Krakowa: O lokal dla świetlicy ŻSS (dawniej Centos)," *Gazeta Żydowska*, 12 July 1942, 2. Another article expounded on the day care: "Kraków: Opieka nad dzieckiem," *Gazeta Żydowska*, 12 August 1942, 2.

53. "Wiadomości z Krakowa: Zakład Sierot w nowym budynku," *Gazeta Żydowska*, 3 July 1942, 3; Relacje: Sabina Mirowska, 1 December 1946, AŻIH 301/2048, p. 4; Hochberg-Mariańska and Grüss, *Children Accuse*, 240–246.

54. Biberstein, *Zagłada Żydów w Krakowie*, 244.

55. Wydział Opieki nad Dziećmi i Młodzieżą (dawniej "Centos"), "Wykaz proponowanych subwencji na rzecz opieki nad dzieckiem z uwzględnieniem jedynie ośrodków najbardziej skazanych na pomoc," 22 June 1942, AŻIH 211/15, p. 43.

56. In fall 1942, the Germans reactivated the organization under the name Jewish Aid Agency in the General Government (Jüdische Unterstützungstelle für das GG [JUS]), but it only lasted for a month. In March 1943, JUS was reestablished under full German control. Headquartered in Kraków, it was led by Michał Weichert, the former president of ŻSS. The Jewish National Committee warned against channeling funds and donations through the International Red Cross, fearing this would undermine reports on German crimes and provide an aura of humanitarianism to the Nazis. Barbara Engelking and Jacek Leociak, *The Warsaw Ghetto: A Guide to the Perished City*, trans. Emma Harris (New Haven, CT: Yale University Press, 2009), 295, 299–300.

57. No sources about Centos could be found after that date.

58. Cover article, *Gazeta Żydowska*, 19 June 1942, 1.

59. Biberstein, *Zagłada Żydów w Krakowie*, 242, 244; Katarzyna Zimmerer, *Zamordowany świat: Losy Żydów w Krakowie 1939–1945* (Kraków: Wydawnictwo Literackie, 2004), 88, 90.

60. Biberstein, *Zagłada Żydów w Krakowie*, 244–245. As of April 1942, there were officially forty-two boys at the hostel, ages fourteen to eighteen. "Sprawozdanie z wizytacji Bursy Młodzieży Rękodzielniczej w Krakowie przy ul. Józefińskiej L. 39 w dniu 19 kwietnia 1942," undated, AŻIH 211/595, p. 10.

61. Relacje: Sabina Mirowska-Hochberger, 1 December 1946, AŻIH 301/2048, p. 6.

62. Regina Nelken, "Dzieci w krakowskim ghetcie," undated, YVA, M.49.E/2047, pp. 1–2.

63. Relacje: Sabina Mirowska, 17 October 1945, AŻIH 301/4693, p. 2; Regina Nelken, "Dzieci w krakowskim ghetcie," undated, YVA, M.49.E/2047, p. 2; Nelken, *And Yet, I Am Here!*, 174; Biberstein, *Zagłada Żydów w Krakowie*, 246.

64. Relacje: Sabina Mirowska, 17 October 1945, AŻIH 301/4693, p. 2.

65. Relacje: Sabina Mirowska-Hochberger, 1 December 1946, AŻIH 301/2048, p. 4.

66. Account of Eugenia Felicja Myszkowska, 1959, YVA 0.3 file 1353, pp. 35–44; Biberstein, *Zagłada Żydów w Krakowie*, 83, 210, 220, 226. The Germans brutally killed patients in the third hospital, the Hospital for the Chronically Ill, which was directed by Dr. Jakub Kranz, and located at 15 Limanowskiego Street.

67. Hochberg-Mariańska and Grüss, *Children Accuse*, 240–246; Relacje: Heinz Pieterkowski, undated, AŻIH 301/5331, p. 1; Biberstein, *Zagłada Żydów w Krakowie*, 84, 245.

68. Relacje: Sabina Mirowska, 17 October 1945, AŻIH 301/4693, p. 2. The children were most likely killed and buried in the Plaszow camp, which was being built at the time of the October 1942 action.

69. Relacje: Sabina Mirowska Sabina, 17 October 1945, AŻIH 301/4693, p. 2; Biberstein, *Zagłada Żydów w Krakowie*, 84.

70. Relacje: Sabina Mirowska-Hochberger, 1 December 1946, AŻIH 301/2048, p. 5.

71. Biberstein, *Zagłada Żydów w Krakowie*, 85. This is not to dismiss Biberstein's account of the events. Clearly, his comparison was influenced by the international stature of Korczak.

72. Engelking and Leociak, *Warsaw Ghetto*, 716.

73. Relacje: Sabina Mirowska-Hochberger, 1 December 1946, AŻIH 301/2048, p. 5.

74. Relacje: Sabina Mirowska, 1 December 1945, AŻIH 301/4693, p. 3.

75. Biberstein, *Zagłada Żydów w Krakowie*, 246.

76. Regina Nelken, "Dzieci w krakowskim ghetcie," undated, YVA M.49/2047, p. 2.

77. Relacje: Regina Nelken, undated, AŻIH 301/2047, pp. 2–3; Relacje: Sabina Mirowska-Hochberger, 1 December 1946, AŻIH 301/2048, p. 5.

78. Grądzka, *Przerwane dzieciństwo*, 122, 355.

79. Relacje: Sabina Mirowska, 17 October 1945, AŻIH 301/4693, p. 3.

80. In her postwar account, Regina Nelken mentions a section for babies at the Tagesheim, which points to the fact that babies continued to be born in the ghetto and were hidden during actions. Relacje: Regina Nelken, undated, AŻIH 301/2047, p. 3.

81. Henryk Zvi Zimmerman, *Przeżyłem, pamiętam, świadczę* (Kraków: Baran i Suszczyński, 1997), 139–140.

82. The two accounts submitted by educators who worked at the institution refer to it as a Tagesheim: Relacje: Regina Nelken, undated, AŻIH 301/2047; and Relacje: Sabina Mirowska-Hochberger, 1 December 1946, 17 October 1945, AŻIH 301/2048, 4693.

83. Relacje: Sabina Mirowska-Hochberger, 1 December 1946, AŻIH 301/2048, p. 6.

84. Biberstein, *Zagłada Żydów w Krakowie*, 250–251.

85. Relacje: Regina Nelken, undated, AŻIH 301/2047, p. 3.

86. Blanche Fixler (Bronia Bruenner), interview 33934, 1997, VHA.

87. Relacje: Regina Nelken, undated, AŻIH 301/2047, p. 5.

88. Pearl Benisch, *To Vanquish the Dragon* (Jerusalem: Feldheim, 1991), 177. See also testimony of Pearl Benisch, 29 October 2013, USHMM RG-50.677.0011.

89. Relacje: Regina Nelken, undated, AŻIH 301/2047, p. 4.

90. Roman Polanski (Raymond/Roman Liebling), *Roman* (New York: William Morrow, 1984), 34.

91. Regina Nelken, "Dzieci w krakowskim ghetcie," undated, YVA M.49/2047, p. 5.

CHAPTER 5 — CONCEALED PRESENCE IN THE CAMP

1. Eva Lavi (Ewa Ratz), oral history recorded by author, Israel, 8 May 2013.

2. Account of Regina Nelken, undated, YVA M-49/2047, pp. 5–6.

3. See Debórah Dwork and Robert Jan van Pelt, *Holocaust: A History* (New York: W. W. Norton, 2002), 280–282.

4. The labor installation for 1,800 Jewish workers in Płaszów called Julag I, located on Jerozolimska Street (hence the camp's other name, Jerozolimska), was announced in *Gazeta Żydowska* on 29 July 1942. Its construction began on the initiative of the German railway that paid the chief of SS and police in Kraków District per day for each worker.

5. When created in summer/fall 1942, the three *Julags* were independent camps subject to the chief of SS and police in Kraków District. They joined the Plaszow camp in 1943 as its branches. Despite official prohibition, women and children stayed in those camps. Apart from *Julags*, branches of German companies became subcamps of ZAL Plaszow in 1943. The three *Julags* were dissolved and their prisoners were transferred to Plaszow after two interconnected events. The first one occurred on 14 October 1943 when Jewish prisoners in the Sobibór death camp rebelled, leading the Germans to close the camp. They feared similar uprisings in other camps. The second event, a killing spree code-named Harvest Festival (Erntefest), approved by Himmler, ensued on 3 November 1943 in Lublin District, claiming the lives of forty-two thousand Jews.

6. On 9 July 1943, a section, called a correctional camp (*Arbeitsziehungslager*), for about one thousand adult Polish prisoners was created in Plaszow, overseen by SS-Unterscharführer Lorenz Landsdorfer. During mass roundups in Kraków on 6 August 1944 ("Black Sunday"), in response to the outbreak of the Warsaw Uprising, the number of Polish prisoners increased to a few thousand.

7. Effective 1 May 1943, Jewish labor became subject to the Inspectorate for Jewish Labor by the Office of the Chief of SS and Police in Kraków District. "Betreff: Richtlinien über den Einsatz jüdischer Arbeitskrafte," 30 April 1943, AŻIH 228/44, pp. 16, 19–20.

8. Ryszard Kotarba, *Niemiecki obóz w Płaszowie 1942–1945* (Warsaw-Kraków: Instytut Pamięci Narodowej, 2009), 35.

9. The cemetery at 3 Abrahama Street belonged to the Kraków Jewish Community. The old cemetery at 25 Jerozolimska Street had been the property of the Podgórze Jewish Community. Survivors of the Plaszow camp recalled the gruesome feeling of being concentrated on a burial ground. To them, that environment symbolized the Jews' fate, as had previously the ghetto wall shaped as tombstones.

10. Although they were formally called *Feuermanner* (firemen) after Plaszow became a concentration camp in 1944, prisoners continued to refer to them as OD. Finkelstein's first name also appears as Maurycy in sources.

11. In neighboring District Galicia, the Janowska camp in Lwów served a similar purpose. See Waitman Wade Beorn, "Last Stop in Lwów: Janowska as a Hybrid Camp," *Holocaust and Genocide Studies* 32, no. 3 (Winter 2018): 445–471.

12. Marcel Haber to sister Tusienka, 21 March 1943, GFHA 2022, p. 1.

13. Relacje: Jerzy Andrzej Hoffman, undated, AŻIH 301/1520, p. 1.

14. Relacje: Roman Ferber, 25 April 1945, AŻIH 301/5401, p. 1; Roman Ferber, interview 43707, 1998, VHA.

15. Relacje: Ignacy Markiewicz, 31 July 1946, AŻIH 301/1919, p. 1.

16. Janka Warszawska (Jeannette Geizhals), "Janka Warshavska's Story," a translation from the Hebrew version of Lena Küchler, My Hundred Children, 1959, 32; Azriel Eisenberg, *The Lost Generation: Children in the Holocaust* (New York: Pilgrim, 1982), 120.

17. Renée Stern (Rena Hocherman), interview 22644, 1996, VHA.

18. Marian Keren (Kwaśniewski), interview 42453, 1998, VHA.

19. Paul Faynwachs (Pinkus Fajnwaks), interview 14951, 1996, VHA.

20. Helen Finkelstein (née Ungar), interview 27485, 1997, VHA.

21. The Jewish Council's administrative building was located at 25 Józefińska Street (Pankiewicz gives the address as Józefińska 2A). Kotarba, *Niemiecki obóz w Płaszowie*, 32; Tadeusz Pankiewicz, *The Cracow Ghetto Pharmacy*, trans. Henry Tilles (Washington, DC: U.S. Holocaust Memorial Museum, 2000), 125, 138.

22. Stella Müller-Madej, *A Girl from Schindler's List*, trans. William R. Brand (London: Polish Cultural Foundation, 1997), 93, 94. See also Stella Madej (née Müller), interview 670, 1995, VHA.

23. Relacje: Roman Ferber, 25 April 1945, AŻIH 301/5401, p. 2.

24. Proces w Krakowie, 16 członków załogi KL Płaszów (1947), AIPNKr 1/22, p. 87.

25. Relacje: Marcel Grüner, 11 May 1945, AŻIH 301/410, p. 2.

26. Relacje: Bronisława (Niusia) Horowitz, 1945, AŻIH 301/4041, p. 1.

27. Hujowa Górka has a vulgar connotation in Polish. Its name derived from the last name of a German guard, SS-Oberscharführer Albert Hujar, who was responsible for executions there.

28. Bronisława (Niusia) Horowitz-Karakulska, interview 647, 1995, VHA.

29. Ryszard Horowitz, interview 8402, 1995, VHA.

30. Ida Turner (née Jakubowicz), interview 7712, 1995, VHA.

31. Celina Biniaz (née Karp), interview 11133, 1996, VHA.

32. Relacje: Roman Ferber, 25 April 1945, AŻIH 301/5401, pp. 1-2.

33. Renee Stern (Rena Hocherman), interview 22644, 1996, VHA.

34. Proces w Krakowie, 16 członków załogi KL Płaszów (1947), AIPNKr 1/22, p. 60.

35. Relacje: Giza Beller, 20 October 1945, AŻIH 310/2040, p. 5.

36. Leah Lichtiger (née Zimmerspitz), interview 23429, 1996, VHA.

37. Lawrence Langer, *Versions of Survival: The Holocaust and the Human Spirit* (Albany: State University of New York, 1982), 72.

38. Relacje: Bronisława (Niusia) Horowitz, 1945, AŻIH 301/4041, p. 1.

39. Ryszard Horowitz, interview 8402, 1995, VHA.

40. Relacje: Szymon Koch, 14 April 1947, AŻIH 301/3205, p. 1.

41. Account of Regina Nelken, undated, YVA M-49/2047, p. 6.

42. Stella observed that children in the Kinderheim were trained to become invisible when Nazi commissions visited the camp. For camouflage, the windows of their barrack were marked with the sign Attention: Typhus. This maneuver meant that Goeth felt he had to keep the children's presence secret in the camp, especially from higher German officials based in Berlin.

43. The shift from a labor to a concentration camp affected Plaszow prisoners. Random violence was forbidden. Prisoners' names were recorded in a registry, and Polish and Jewish prisoners were counted together. Poles and Jews wore the same uniform, and

their numbers were sewn onto the left side of their chest, left arm, and right leg. In addition to the red triangles, Jews had yellow triangles sewn on top of them. A new category of prisoners arrived—German asocials, who oversaw blocks and workshops. Proces w Krakowie, 16 członków załogi KL Płaszów (1947), AIPNKr 1/22, pp. 58–60; Kotarba, *Niemiecki obóz w Płaszowie*, 37–38.

44. The exact number of children in the barrack, or in the camp for that matter, remains unknown. If the barrack's capacity was planned for four hundred children, that was perhaps the maximum estimate of children in the camp at that time. A number of children were registered as older and thus worked and remained in the camp as adults. It appears that children were not registered until they were placed in the Kinderheim and a detailed roster was submitted daily at roll call. Relacje: Szymon Koch, 24 April 1947, AŻIH 301/3205, p. 4.

45. Relacje: Szymon Koch, 1.

46. All workers at the Madritsch workshop were committee members.

47. One mother claimed that Mala Hofstater-Mandelbaumowa, a staff member at the Kinderheim and manager of its food pantry, harassed mothers who were not "prominent" prisoners. Such mothers were allowed to see their children only if they scrubbed floors in the Kinderheim. Other mothers, especially those whose husbands were in the OD, were allowed to visit their children at any time. Relacje: Renata Grünbaum, undated, AŻIH 301/4215, p. 4.

48. Koch also arranged for a doctor to examine children. Described as an ill-tempered man by Koch, Dr. Spira was willing to examine children for money.

49. Relacje: Szymon Koch, 24 April 1947, AŻIH 301/3205, p. 2.

50. Relacje: Szymon Koch, 3, 4.

51. Leon (Leib) Leyson, interview 8916, 1995, VHA.

52. Warszawska, "Janka Warshavska's Story," 36.

53. Ida Turner (née Jakubowicz), interview 7712, 1995, VHA.

54. Elsa Chandler (née Biller), interview 7744, 1995, VHA.

55. Some workshops introduced two shifts, so some prisoners stayed in their barracks during the day and worked at night.

56. Halina Balfour (née Horowitz), interview 3346, 1995, VHA.

57. Müller-Madej, *A Girl from Schindler's List*, 80.

58. Relacje: Renata Grünbaum, undated, AŻIH 301/4215, p. 4.

59. Bernhard Kempler, interview 33193, 1997, VHA.

60. Account of Eugenia Felicja Myszkowska, 1959, YVA 0.3/1353, p. 57.

61. Proces w Krakowie, 16 członków załogi KL Płaszów (1947), AIPNKr 1/22, p. 102.

62. Relacje: Anna Lewkowicz, 13 July 1945, AŻIH 301/1558, pp. 5, 6. Some Jewish prisoners saw Gross as cooperating with the Germans. However, he reportedly refused to apply lethal injections to three hundred children, for which he was imprisoned in the camp. Akta: Majer Kerner, dr. Leon Gross. AIPNKr 502/565, 1945–1946, p. 136.

63. Warszawska, "Janka Warshavska's Story," 35.

64. Debórah Dwork, *Children with a Star: Jewish Youth in Nazi Europe* (New Haven, CT: Yale University Press, 1991), 224.

65. Roman Ferber, interview 43707, 1998, VHA.

66. Ephroim Jablon (Jan Rothbaum), interview 43451, 1998, VHA. See also Sam Weisberg, *Carry the Torch*, and Johnny Jablon, *A Lasting Legacy* (Toronto: Azrieli Foundation, 2018), 87–152.

67. George Andrzej (Jerzy) Hoffman, interview 17554, 1996, VHA.

68. Dwork, *Children with a Star*, 247.

69. According to one witness, Felicja Sandberg, four to five women were admitted every night for abortion. This seems like an exaggerated number. Still, such testimonies highlight Gross's efforts to save pregnant women and underscore the fate of unborn babies. Akta: Majer Kerner, dr. Leon Gross, AIPNKr 502/565, 1945–1946, p. 316.

70. Relacje: Marcel Grüner, 11 May 1945, AŻIH 301/410, p. 2.

71. Kotarba, *Niemiecki obóz w Płaszowie*, 145; Proces w Krakowie, 16 członków załogi KL Płaszów (1947), AIPNKr 1/22, p. 60.

72. Relacje: Szymon Koch, 24 April 1947, AŻIH 301/3205, p. 5.

73. Relacje: Bronisława (Niusia) Horowitz, 1945, AŻIH 301/4041, p. 2.

74. Relacje: Giza Beller, 20 October 1945, AŻIH 310/2040, p. 5.

75. Relacje: Bronisława (Niusia) Horowitz, 1945, AŻIH 301/4041, p. 2.

76. Relacje: Szymon Koch, 24 April 1947, AŻIH 301/3205, p. 4.

77. Pamiętniki Żydów: Henia Wollerówna, 1943–1945, AŻIH 302/74, p. 11.

78. Niusia Horowitz claimed seven children were saved this way, and Jerzy Spira remembered the group consisted of sixteen. While it is impossible to establish the exact number of officially "saved children," the fact that a few were saved thanks to their caretakers' prominent status remains evident. Relacje: Bronisława (Niusia) Horowitz, 1945, AŻIH 301/4041, p. 2; Relacje: Jerzy Spira, 1945, AŻIH 301/238, p. 2.

79. Ryszard Horowitz went so far as to assume that his father, owing to his position and the "special relationship" his family had with Goeth and Schindler, was tipped off about the action, which allowed him to act accordingly. It is more probable, however, that Ryszard and Niusia's father was quick to evaluate the situation and respond to the events as they were happening without having been warned about the upcoming action. Still, his position in the camp facilitated the protection of his two children. Ryszard Horowitz, interview 8402, 1995, VHA. Ryszard's sister, Niusia, counted in this group. Relacje: Bronisława (Niusia) Horowitz, 1945, AŻIH 301/4041, p. 2.

80. Relacje: Marcel Grüner, 11 May 1945, AŻIH 301/410, pp. 2–3.

81. Relacje: Jerzy Spira, 1945, AŻIH 301/238, p. 2.

82. Relacje: Jerzy Spira, 2.

83. Janina Ast recalled that six other children jumped into the latrine after her. Account of Janina Ast, 7 October 1945, YVA M.1.E/1158, p. 2. In a later testimony, she said it was three children. Jane Schein (Janina Ast), interview 415, 1994, VHA. Alexander Rosner also mentioned hiding there. Alexander Rosner, interview 1017, 1995, VHA.

84. Roman Ferber, interview 43707, 1998, VHA; William Shnycer (Wilhelm/Wilek Zeev Schnitzer), interview 33837, 1997, VHA.

85. Eugenia Felicja Myszkowska encouraged children to hide there (the stench kept out the Germans). She said it was possible because the latrines had been cleared out before the action. Account of Eugenia Felicja Myszkowska, 1959, YVA o.3/1353, p. 59.

86. Relacje: Giza Beller, 20 October 1945, AŻIH 310/2040, pp. 5–6.

87. Warszawska, "Janka Warshavska's Story," 38. Her sister Halina and two other girls (Sarenka Kleiner and Henia Ziedler) managed to escape to the latrine.

88. Ida Turner (née Jakubowicz), interview 7712, 1995, VHA.

89. Account of Eugenia Felicja Myszkowska, 1959, YVA o.3/1353, p. 59.

90. Relacje: Ala Dychtwald, 1945, AŻIH 301/330, p. 15.

91. Relacje: Marcel Grüner, 11 May 1945, AŻIH 301/410, p. 3.

92. Stella Madej, (née Müller), interview 670, 2013, VHA; Müller-Madej, *A Girl from Schindler's List*, 123–126.

93. Aleksander Biberstein, *Zagłada Żydów w Krakowie* (Kraków: Wydawnictwo Literackie, 1985, reprinted 2001), 161.

94. Relacje: Jerzy Spira, 1945, AŻIH 301/238, p. 3; Relacje: Marcel Grüner, 11 May 1945, AŻIH 301/410, p. 3.

95. Testimony of anonymous girl (Janka Avram), interview by Icek Shmulewitz, New York, 1955, in *Jewish Responses to Nazi Persecution: Collective and Individual Behavior in Extremis*, ed. Isaiah Trunk (New York: Stein and Day, 1982), 117–119; Patricia Heberer, ed., *Documenting Life and Destruction: Holocaust Sources in Context: Children during the Holocaust* (Lanham, MA: AltaMira in association with the United States Holocaust Memorial Museum, 2011), 179. Both refer to the story of Janina Ast (Jane Schein).

96. The site name (Cipowy Dołek) carries a vulgar connotation in Polish.

97. Relacje: Bronisława (Niusia) Horowitz, 1945, AŻIH 301/4041, p. 1.

98. Relacje: Roman Ferber, 25 April 1945, AŻIH 301/5401, p. 2.

99. Relacje: Sabina Mirowska-Hochberger, 1 December 1946, AŻIH 301/2048, p. 6.

100. Relacje: Dawid Grünwald, 2 September 1945, AŻIH 301/815, pp. 1–2. Dawid's daughter Halina was taken away in the children's action in 1944. These events were also told by Eva Lavi, Dawid's niece. Eva Lavi (Ewa Ratz), oral history recorded by author, Israel, 8 May 2013.

101. Ida Turner (née Jakubowicz), interview 7712, 1995, VHA.

102. Relacje: Giza Beller, 20 October 1945, AŻIH 310/2040, p. 5.

103. Relacje: Bronisława (Niusia) Horowitz, 1945, AŻIH 301/4041, p. 2.

104. Eugene (Eugeniusz) Kamer, "Memoir of Eugene Kamer as Told to Silvia Kamer," unpublished, 2008, 15. I thank Jo-Ellyn Decker from the Mandel Center at the USHMM for providing me with a copy of the unpublished memoir.

105. Until 14 December 1943, holders of foreign passports were held in the OD prison in the remnant ghetto in Podgórze.

106. Kranz did not account for another adult woman who arrived with Gitla Landau Katz.

107. Rachel Gosstein [Gottstein] (née Landau), interview 24137, 1996, VHA.

108. Relacje: Wilhelm Kranz, 25 April 1947, AŻIH 301/3209, p. 1.

109. Relacje: Wilhelm Kranz, 3.

110. Already in 1942–1943, Plaszow supplied Jewish workers to other labor camps in the General Government, such as Skarżysko-Kamienna.

111. Livia Bitton-Jackson (née Friedmann), interview 2916, 1995, VHA.

112. Relacje: Giza Beller, 20 October 1945, AŻIH 310/2040, p. 5.

113. Ala Dychtwald, who arrived from Majdanek in 1943, was amazed at how the situation of Jews in Plaszow reminded her of life in the ghetto. Jewish prisoners still wore their own clothes, they moved around the camp, the black market thrived, there was family life, and the camp had a hospital. What struck her was that, "in general, connections [protekcja] and money held unlimited power." Relacje: Ala Dychtwald, 1945, AŻIH 301/330, p. 14.

114. Mirl Meisels (née Rubin), interview 16359, 1996, VHA.

115. Livia Bitton-Jackson (née Friedmann), interview 2916, 1995, VHA.

116. Müller-Madej, *A Girl from Schindler's List*, 129.

117. "Płaszów," undated, AŻIH 209/28, p. 1.

118. Grave 1 held 2,500 Jews, including children killed in March 1943 in the ghetto. In grave 2 were buried 50 Jews from the *Sauberungskolonne*, killed in March and April 1944. In grave 3 were the corpses of 250 Jews from the action in May and June 1943. Grave 4 was located on Hujowa Górka, the killing site of Jews who were discovered with Aryan papers and prisoners from Montelupich prison, killed between June and July 1943. In grave 5 were the corpses of 50 OD men killed in April 1943. And in grave 6 were Poles and Jews with Aryan papers, including prisoners from Montelupich. The time of their executions was not established. "Płaszów," undated, AŻIH 209/28, pp. 1–2.

119. Mirl Meisels (née Rubin), interview 16359, 1996, VHA.

120. Relacje: Marcel Grüner, 11 May 1945, AŻIH 301/410, p. 3.

121. "Arbeitskommando—Bericht KL Plaszow, 30.X.1944," AŻIH 209/21, p. 3. Another count is provided in the document "Verpflegskarte des KL Plaszow," AŻIH 209/22: 1,924 Jews as of 15 September 1944 (p. 3), 4,089 prisoners (4,024 Jews and 65 Aryans) as of 12 October 1944 (p. 2a), and 2,424 prisoners (2,370 Jews and 54 Aryans) as of 20 November 1944 (p. 2).

122. Kotarba, *Niemiecki obóz w Płaszowie*, 151–154. At that time, SS-Hauptscharführer Kurt Schupke served as commandant.

CHAPTER 6 — SURVIVAL THROUGH HIDING AND FLIGHT

1. Maj Zofia z d. Janicka, 1989–1990, AŻIH 349/1466.

2. Matusz Stanisław i Katarzyna, 1988–1992, AŻIH 349/1338; "Matusz, Stanislaw, Matusz-Dudzik, Katarzyna," in *The Encyclopedia of the Righteous among the Nations: Rescuers of Jews during the Holocaust: Poland*, ed. Israel Gutman, Sara Bender, and Shmuel Krakowski (Jerusalem: Yad Vashem, 2004), 1:498; Ruchelle Poser, interview 6614, 1995, VHA.

3. A prewar Polish ruling regulated the adoption of minors. "416 Ustawa z dnia 13 lipca 1939 r. o ułatwieniu przysposobienia małoletnich," *Dziennik Ustaw Rok 1939 Nr .63*, 967–969.

4. Branches of the Polish Care Committee were subject to the Main Welfare Council (Rada Główna Opiekuńcza).

5. M. Bernadeta Dzieniakowska, Placówki Wojenne SS. Urszulanek w Krakowie (Rokiciny Podhalańskie, 1955), ASU 211/C-III-24, p. 48.

6. Sara Avinun, *Rising from the Abyss: An Adult's Struggle with Her Trauma as a Child in the Holocaust* (Hod Hasharon, Israel: Astrolog, 2005), 100–106; Relacje: Sala [Sara] Warszawiak (Irena Jabłońska), 26 June 1945, AŻIH 301/431, p. 1.

7. The Polish Government-in-Exile (Rząd Rzeczpospolitej Polskiej na Uchodźstwie), legitimized by the Western powers, served as a representation of the Polish government abroad after the German and Soviet invasions of Poland and the escape of Polish leaders from Poland. Initially based in France, it moved to the United Kingdom in 1940. In German-occupied Poland, the Polish Government-in-Exile created, supported, and oversaw the Polish Underground State.

8. Following the deportations of Jews from the Warsaw ghetto on 27 September 1942, Zofia Kossak-Szczucka and Wanda Krahelska led the creation of a Temporary Committee named for Konrad Żegota, attached to the Delegate of the Underground State in German-occupied Poland (Delegatura Rządu na Kraj). On 4 December 1942, the committee was transformed into the Council for Aid to Jews Żegota.

9. Stanisław Wincenty "Staniewski" Dobrowolski served as Kraków Żegota president, Władysław "Żegociński" or "Czerski" Wójcik as secretary, Anna "Michalska" Dobro-

wolska as treasurer, Tadeusz "Socha" Seweryn as controller, and Maria "Mariańska" Hochberg as Jewish emissary.

10. Władysław Bartoszewski and Zofia Lewinówna, *Ten jest z Ojczyzny mojej: Braterstwo w czasach pogardy*, 3rd ed. (Warsaw: Świat Książki, 2007), 130; Marek Arczyński and Wiesław Balcerak, *Żegota: Konspiracyjna Rada Pomocy Żydom 1942–1945* (Toronto: Aga, 2009), 117.

11. This meant that monthly subsidies per rescuee swelled from 300–500 złoty per month to 1,000–1,500 złoty. Maria Hochberg-Mariańska, undated, YVA M-49/3422, p. 1.

12. M. M. Mariańscy, *Wśród przyjaciół i wrogów: Poza gettem w okupowanym Krakowie* (Kraków: Wydawnictwo Literackie, 1988), 141.

13. Róża Łubieńska from the Main Welfare Council, which oversaw all child care institutions in the city, cooperated with convents in Kraków in placing Jewish children in religious institutions.

14. Stefan Kamiński and Aleksandra Mianowska, "Wspomnienia: Żołnierze Żydzi w szpitalach jenieckich w Krakowie," *Przegląd Lekarski* 47, no. 1 (1990): 156, 157. See also Mianowska Aleksandra, 1993–1994, AŻIH 349/2440; Relacje: Ewa Feldman-Kwiatkowska, 2 September 1965, AŻIH 301/6125; Jakub Gutenbaum and Agnieszka Latała, eds., *The Last Eyewitnesses: Children of the Holocaust Speak*, trans. Julian Bussgang, Fay Bussgang, and Simon Cygielski (Evanston, Northwestern University Press, 2005), 2:199; and Janina Pietrasiak (née Feldman), interview 22050, 1996, VHA.

15. Out of the twenty-two female Catholic orders in Kraków in 1939, half have a documented history of helping Jewish children during the occupation.

16. Janina Ecker (Halina Leiman), oral history recorded by author, Israel, 5 May 2013.

17. Gruca also cared for the girls' cousins, Edek and Zygmunt. File of Rachel Verderber-Garfunkel, 1961–1985, GFHA 28606; Gruca Maria, 1966–1985, AŻIH 349/650; Maria i Marian Gruca, AESIP, Folder: Kraków 16.III.2008; "Black Snow: Survivor Stories of the Holocaust," dir. Laurie Long and Terra Jean Long, 2006, USHMM DVD-0143; Rachel Garfunkel (née Verderber), 1980, MJH 1980.T20; Rachel Garfunkel (née Verderber), interview 55341, 2007, VHA. See also Bertha Ferderber-Salz, *And the Sun Kept Shining...* (New York: Holocaust Library, 1980).

18. "Letter from Halina Czerwieniec," undated, File of Rachel Verderber-Garfunkel, GFHA 28606, p. 3.

19. Natkaniec Rozalia, 1976–1986, AŻIH 349/707; "Ziemianska, Franciszka," in Gutman, Bender, and Krakowski, *Encyclopedia of the Righteous*, 2: 939.

20. Bernhard Kempler, interview 33193, 1997, VHA.

21. Hiding with a brother or sister affected sibling relations. The preference showered on one sibling, usually the younger, obedient, or less Jewish-looking, aroused anxiety in the other child. The fear that the caretaker would keep the one he or she liked better and let go the other sometimes turned into reality.

22. Miriam "Mariańska" Hochberg claimed she could recognize a Jew posing as an Aryan through sad eyes, Semitic features, perceptible fear, dress, and behavior. Mariańscy, *Wśród przyjaciół i wrogów*, 156.

23. Anita Lobel, *No Pretty Pictures: A Child of War* (New York: HarperCollins, 1998), 55.

24. Jennifer Lynn Marlow explores this topic in "Polish Catholic Maids and Nannies: Female Aid and the Domestic Realm in Nazi-Occupied Poland" (PhD diss., Michigan State University, 2014).

25. Bernhard Kempler, interview 33193, 1997, VHA.

26. In her study *Hidden Children of the Holocaust: Belgian Nuns and Their Daring Rescue of Young Jews from the Nazis* (New York: Oxford University Press, 2008), Suzanne Vromen observes that baptism did not automatically mean conversion. Many children were baptized to blend in. Some were pressured into it, while others chose it as a sign of gratitude to the nuns and for emotional safety.

27. The Germans forbade such practice in October 1942, but the clergy found ways to bypass the law. Priests penciled names of newly baptized Jewish children into parish registries for fast removal in case of German control.

28. Code of Canon Law, cc. 864–871, *The Code of Canon Law: Latin-English Edition* (Washington, DC: Canon Law Society of America, 1983).

29. Kamiński and Mianowska, "Wspomnienia," 158; See also Elah Manor (Felicja Seifert), interview 44239, 1998, VHA.

30. The other boys discovered that Zygmunt was Jewish and the boy spent the rest of the war hidden in his teacher's home. Relacje: Zygmunt Weinreb, 8 May 1945, AŻIH 301/406; Bartoszewski and Lewinówna, *Ten jest z Ojczyzny mojej*, 139.

31. Bernhard Kempler, interview 33193, 1997, VHA. See also Michał Grynberg, *Księga Sprawiedliwych* (Warsaw: Państwowe Wydawnictwo Naukowe, 1993), 371.

32. Bernhard Kempler, interview 33193, 1997, VHA.

33. Max Pelton (Maksymilian Perlmutter), interview 38075, 1998, VHA.

34. Janina Ecker (Halina Leiman), oral history recorded by author, Israel, 5 May 2013.

35. "Zarządzenie: utworzenie dzielnicy mieszkaniowej dla żydów w Krakowie," 3 March 1941, ANK J13922, SMKr 63, p. 33.

36. "Sprawozdanie K Z [Komitetu Żydowskiego] Kraków za okres VII i VIII 1943 r.," 17 September 1943," AŻIH 230/136, p. 17.

37. "Sprawozdanie K Z [Komitetu Żydowskiego] Kraków," 17.

38. Witold Mędykowski, "Przeciw swoim: Wzorce kolaboracji żydowskiej w Krakowie i okolicy," *Zagłada Żydów: Studia i Materiały* 2 (2006): 207; Alicja Jarkowska-Natkaniec, *Wymuszona współpraca czy zdrada? Wokół przypadków kolaboracji Żydów w okupowanym Krakowie* (Kraków: Universitas, 2018), 324–335.

39. Miriam Bruck (Emilia Heller), interview 21495, 1996, VHA.

40. Before June 1941 when the Germans incorporated the village into Kraków, many Jews settled in Borek Fałęcki after the expulsion from the city between May and August 1940 and the subsequent establishment of the ghetto in March 1941. Jewish families rented housing from Poles. Interactions occurred and relationships were forged. Some of them yielded subsequent assistance.

41. Relacje: Sara Melzer, 3 July 1947, AŻIH 301/3277; Zofia Radzikowska (née Melzer), interview by author, Poland, 21 December 2011.

42. Rada Pomocy Żydom przy Delegacie Rządu na Kraj do Pana Pełnomocnika Rządu na Kraj, Warszawa, 6 April 1943, YVA 06/83, p. 27.

43. Barbara Engelking studied denunciation notes in Warsaw and discusses the motivations for writing them in *"Szanowny panie gistapo": Donosy do władz niemieckich w Warszawie i okolicach w latach 1940–1941* (Warsaw: Instytut Filozofii i Socjologii Polskiej Akademii Nauk, 2003).

44. "Starosta—korespondencja wpływająca: Anonimy i doniesienia na Żydów, 1940–1942," undated, AŻIH 228/5, p. 15.

45. Jacek Chrobaczyński, *Postawy, zachowania, nastroje: Społeczeństwo Krakowa wobec wojny i okupacji, 1939–1945* (Kraków: Wydawnictwo Literackie, 1993), 115. Chrobaczyński refers to a collection of such notes held in private hands. See also Ryszard Nuszkiewicz, *Uparci* (Warsaw: PAX, 1983), 153.

46. Bartoszewski and Lewinówna, *Ten jest z Ojczyzny mojej*, 137–139; Józef Bratko, *Gestapowcy: Kontrwywiad, konfidenci, konspiratorzy* (Kraków: Krajowa Agencja Wydawnicza, 1990), 164–165. Podgórze, the district where the ghetto was located, was known as "informants' central" *(centrala konfidentów)*. Stanisław Strzelichowski, *Dwa lata: Grudzień 1942–październik 1944* (Wrocław, Poland: Ossolineum, 1972), 303.

47. Norms of behavior during the German occupation promoted by the Underground were published as "Code of a Pole" (Kodeks Polaka) in September 1940. In 1941, a "Code of Civic Morality" (Kodeks moralności obywatelskiej) was issued that regulated the types of attitudes and behaviors acceptable during the war. Tadeusz "Socha" Seweryn authored and ordered brochures for the Bureau of Information and Propaganda. The five thousand flyers issued by the bureau in 1943 specified the death penalty for anyone whose actions contributed to the persecution, imprisonment, exile, or death of Polish citizens, and for those who blackmailed or partook in murdering a Polish citizen. Bartoszewski and Lewinówna, *Ten jest z Ojczyzny mojej*, 78, 140–141. Żegota appealed to the Delegate for Occupied Poland to publicize fake death penalties to deter potential offenders. Rada Pomocy Żydom przy Delegacie Rządu na Kraj do Pana Pełnomocnika Rządu na Kraj, Warszawa, 6 April 1943, YVA 06/83, p. 27.

48. Bartoszewski and Lewinówna, *Ten jest z Ojczyzny mojej*, 140–141.

49. Sophia Aferiat (née Śpiewak), interview 19545, 1996, VHA.

50. Relacje: Anna Lewkowicz, 13 July 1945, AŻIH 301/1558, p. 4.

51. Chava Mandelbaum (Cyla Chava / Ewa Lewi), 1986, MJH 1986.T.47. See also Relacje: Ewa Lewi, undated, AŻIH 301/3868.

52. Account of Abraham Blim, 5 March 1961, YVA 03/2221, p. 9.

53. Relacje: Henryk Meller, 1945, AŻIH 301/830, p. 1; Henryk Meller, oral history recorded by author, Poland, 15 February 2012.

54. Meller, oral history.

55. Relacje: Herman Wohlfeiler, 1945, AŻIH 301/769. The son survived.

56. Janka Warszawska, (Jeannette Geizhals), "Janka Warshavska's Story," a translation from the Hebrew version of Lena Küchler, My Hundred Children, 1959, 31.

57. Relacje: Jerzy Andrzej Hoffman, undated, AŻIH 301/1520; George Andrzej (Jerzy) Hoffman, interview 17554, 1996, VHA.

58. Relacje: Henryk Meller, 1945, AŻIH 301/830, p. 1.

59. Account of Abraham Blim, 5 March 1961, YVA 03/2221, p. 13.

60. Account of Abraham Blim, 17.

61. Perhaps unaware of the killing center there, the boys went to the village of Bełżec upon learning that this was where rich peasants lived. Abraham felt uneasy when they reached the area. He explained, "They talked a lot about Jews, how they were caught, deported, murdered, etc. I didn't like this; I felt bad listening to these stories." Account of Abraham Blim, 18.

62. The reformatory (*Knabenerziehungsanstalt*) was opened specifically for juvenile street peddlers. It was moved from the city to the Rydlówka estate in Bronowice Małe. Parafia św. Antoniego, "Historia," undated, accessed January 21, 2021, http://

antonibronowice.org/index.php?p=5. After the Warsaw Uprising, the authorities suspended their roundups of street children and instead brought to the reformatory children from Warsaw and Roma children whose parents had been deported to the Plaszow camp. Account of Abraham Blim, 5 March 1961, YVA 03/2221, p. 24.

63. Relacje: Jerzy Andrzej Hoffman, undated, AŻIH 301/1520, p. 2.

64. Relacje: Jerzy Andrzej Hoffman, 3.

65. Account of Abraham Blim, 5 March 1961, YVA 03/2221, p. 22.

66. On 15 October 1943, the priest Antoni Gigoń moved into the Rydlówka estate and held daily prayers at the chapel. Perhaps it was he with whom Abraham studied. Parafia św. Antoniego, "Historia." The Red Army entered Kraków before Abraham underwent baptism.

67. Miriam Bruck (Emilia Heller), interview 21495, 1996, VHA.

68. A traditional ally of Poland, Hungary clandestinely supported the transfer of Polish soldiers and civilians (over one hundred thousand) into the country following the German and Soviet invasions of Poland.

69. A Polish legation operated legally in Budapest until June 1941. With the help of Hungarians, its members and couriers transferred persecuted Poles from German-occupied Poland to Hungary.

70. Undated list of 229 foreign Jews residing in Kraków, AŻIH 218/21, pp. 1–5. The list was probably compiled before the liquidation of the ghetto in 1943. It includes a breakdown of Jews who possessed documents that identified them as foreigners, and the countries of their nationality: Belgium: three; Bolivia: three; Guatemala: two; Haiti: two; Hungary: fifty-seven; Lithuania: one; the Netherlands: three; Paraguay: two; Portugal: two; Romania: forty-six; Russia: one; Slovakia: eighty-six; stateless: five; Turkey: twelve; United States: three.

71. Hanna Wechsler (Chana Kleiner), interview 43550, 1998, VHA.

72. Relacje: Lena Klein, 28 February 1949, AŻIH 301/4271, p. 3.

73. For more information, see Family of Ben Zion and Clara Colb Collection, USHMM 2014.406.1; Relacje: Tomasz Moździerz, ps. Tosiek, 1945, AŻIH 301/246, p. 1; Clara Calb, interview 9261, 1995, VHA; Clara C., interview 2084, 1992, FVA.

74. Wolf held a Hungarian passport under the last name Tőmeri. Korpal Wiesław, AŻIH 349/1829, undated, p. 3.

75. Binder: Medale '98, "Matoga Zygmunt," 1998, AESIP.

76. Korpal's pseudonym was either Gaduła or Lis. "Sylwetka: Wiesław Korpal—lekarz artysta," Gazeta Myślenicka, no. 17/2015 (7 May 2015). See also Korpal Wiesław, 1992–1996, AŻIH 349/1829; Binder: Korespondencja z Yad Vashem December 1995, AESIP; "Relacja Wiesław Korpal," undated, AESIP; "Oświadczenie: Chilek Schusterman" 1993; and "List Wiesław Korpiel [sic]," 15 July 1996, AESIP. Among the two hundred people Korpal claimed to have rescued, some of the names he listed matched those rescued by the Kalb group. He did not mention Kalb, which underscores the secrecy of the endeavors.

77. Neither Matoga nor Korpal mentioned the other's name in their postwar accounts. However, both men lived in the same building at 3 Filipa Street. They both remarked on sheltering a ten-year-old Jewish girl in the building, and both discussed the same smuggling path from Kraków to Hungary, and the same names of people involved in the process.

78. ZWZ (derived from Służba Zwycięstwu Polski [Poland's Victory Service]) served as the military force of the Polish Underground State from 13 November 1939 to 14 Feb-

ruary 1942, when ZWZ morphed into the AK to raise its rank and increase its membership.

79. "Sylwetka: Wiesław Korpal—lekarz artysta." In July 1941, General Stefan "Grot" Rowecki, the commandant of ZWZ, a precursor to the AK, created the Service for the Protection of the Uprising (Służba Ochrony Powstania). Its aim was to protect military plants and the infrastructure in preparation for the Germans' retreat from Poland. At the beginning of 1943, the service became the Military Service for the Protection of the Uprising (Wojskowa Służba Ochrony Powstania).

80. Bystroń Adam, 1985–1986, AŻIH 349/676.

81. Eliezer Landau, a Jewish Krakovian entrepreneur who served as director of a Jewish labor office in the Bochnia ghetto, was instrumental in facilitating Jews' transfer to Slovakia. He cooperated with and survived thanks to the Kalb rescue network. I thank Marc Tannen for providing me with information about the activities of his great-grandfather.

82. The Todt Organization (Organisation Todt) grew out of a German engineering company to become part of Nazi Germany's Ministry for Armaments and War Production. The organization used slave laborers from German-occupied territories to produce items for the German war effort.

83. Bystroń estimated he rescued 43 people, while he attributed 861 rescue cases to Porębska.

84. Undated list of 229 foreign Jews residing in Kraków, AŻIH 218/21, p. 1. In a postwar account, Adam Salomon claimed he was a Hungarian national. Relacje: Adam Salomon, undated, AŻIH 301/3426, p. 1.

85. Kossewski Aleksander, 1968–1980, AŻIH 349/69; Relacje: Abraham Singer, undated, AŻIH 301/3425. Kossewski claimed to have smuggled 246 individuals from Dębica, Kraków, Tarnów, Bochnia, and Warsaw.

86. The seven other points of the call to action were providing shelter; making contact with prisoners in camps; ensuring food, medicine, and money; forging documents; protecting Jews by the law maintained by the Polish Underground State; disabling informants; and countering Nazi anti-Jewish propaganda. Bartoszewski and Lewinówna, *Ten jest z Ojczyzny mojej*, 130.

87. "Sprawozdanie okresowe za II-gi kwartał 1944r. RPŻ Kraków," 24 July 1944, AŻIH 230/136, pp. 25, 28. When Germany occupied Hungary, General Kołłątaj-Srzednicki, a member of the Citizens' Committee who issued false documents to Jews, destroyed all registry books. See transcript of an oral history of Rafał Kołłątaj-Srzednicki ("Rafał"), Warsaw Rising Museum, Archiwum Historii Mówionej, 5 March 2005, p. 2; and Maj Zofia z d. Janicka, 6 November 1990, AŻIH 349/1466, pp. 13–15.

88. Bartoszewski and Lewinówna, *Ten jest z Ojczyzny mojej*, 29, 129–143.

89. Lea Goodman (Rosa Apelzon), interview 21677, 1996, VHA. See also Leah G., interview 2492, 1991, FVA.

90. Relacje: Stefa Popowcer, undated, AŻIH 301/4033, p. 8.

91. Hanna Wechsler (Chana Kleiner), interview 43550, 1998, VHA.

92. Oral history of Barbara Firestone (Bronisława Spielman), 2 March 2010, USHMM, RG-50.030.0570; Arthur (Artur) Spielman, interview 35001, 1997, VHA.

93. Blanche Fixler (Bronia Bruenner), interview 33934, 1997, VHA; Photograph #75475, circa 1945–1947, Blanche and Benzion Fixler Collection, USHMM.

94. Helena Csorba, "Dzieci uratowane od Zagłady," *Biuletyn Żydowskiego Instytutu Historycznego*, no. 35 (July–September 1960): 100–105; Grzegorz Łubczyk, *Polski*

Wallenberg: Rzecz o Henryku Sławiku (Warsaw: Rytm, 2004). Another institution, a Polish school in Balatonboglár, also sheltered Polish Jewish children.

95. Relacje: Marek Popowcer, 29 January 1949, AŻIH 301/4228, p. 3.

96. When Germany occupied Hungary, Sławik and Zimmerman began preparations for escape, mindful of the speed with which the Germans pursued their policy of the annihilation of Jews in Poland. They conferred with Rezsö Kasztner and Joel Brand of the Jewish Rescue Committee in Budapest. Henryk Zvi Zimmerman, *Przeżyłem, pamiętam, świadczę* (Kraków: Baran i Suszczyński, 1997), 251–255, 257–258.

97. Jeremy Keidar (Jerzy Wurzel), oral history recorded by author, Israel, 1 May 2013; Anat Keidar, *On the Road: The Story of Jeremy Keidar* [in Hebrew] (Kiryat Ono, Israel: Shanie Story, 2011). I thank Jeremy Keidar for providing me with the book.

98. This concept is explored by Debórah Dwork and Robert Jan van Pelt in *Flight from the Reich: Refugee Jews, 1933–1946* (New York: W. W. Norton, 2009).

EPILOGUE

1. After the Poles' defeat in the Warsaw Uprising (1 August–2 October 1944), the Germans leveled over 30 percent of the city (in total, the Germans destroyed over 80 percent of the city throughout the war), killed two hundred thousand civilians, and expelled six hundred thousand to camps outside Warsaw.

2. Michael (Mieczysław) Arzewski, interview 41930, 1998, VHA.

3. To prepare their troops for defending Upper Silesia, the Germans retreated from Kraków. Still, a myth of Soviet liberation of Kraków was born. The legend holds that the Soviet Army intentionally protected the city by employing a special military tactic to outmaneuver the Germans. In fact, the Germans' near-complete evacuation from Kraków on the eve of the Soviet attack prevented the destruction of the city. Contrary to the myth, the Soviet military command planned to proceed with Kraków as with any other city in the path of the Red Army advance. Grzegorz Jeżowski, "Ostatnie miesiące okupacji (czerwiec 1944-styczeń 1945)," in *Kraków—czas okupacji 1939-1945*, ed. Monika Bednarek et al. (Kraków: Muzeum Historyczne Miasta Krakowa, 2010), 441, 447–449.

4. Felicia Liban (née Vogler), interview 1451, 1995, VHA.

5. Michael (Mieczysław) Arzewski, interview 41930, 1998, VHA.

6. Norbert Schlang, interview 27127, 1997, VHA.

7. Schlang, interview.

8. "Janek Weber," in *Hidden from the Holocaust: Stories of Resilient Children Who Survived and Thrived*, ed. Kerry Bluglass (Westport, CT: Praeger, 2003), 73.

9. Anna Gouttman (née Entenberg), interview 44141, 1998, VHA.

10. Zofia Radzikowska (née Melcer), oral history recorded by author, Kraków, 21 December 2011.

11. Helena Datner- Śpiewak, "Instytucje opieki nad dzieckiem i szkoły powszechne Centralnego Komitetu Żydów Polskich w latach 1945–1946," *Biuletyn Żydowskiego Instytutu Historycznego* 3 (1981): 37.

12. Małgorzata Kostecka, "Z dziejów ludności żydowskiej Krakowa w latach 1945–1947" (MA thesis, Jagiellonian University, 1997), 30, 31, 33, 35, 37, 63, quoted in Anna Cichopek, *Pogrom Żydów w Krakowie 11 sierpnia 1945* (Warsaw: Żydowski Instytut Historyczny, 2000), 54, 55. In addition to the Central Committee of Jews in Poland, other Jewish religious and political organizations established child care institutions.

13. Noemi Bażanowska, *To był mój dom: Żydowski Dom Dziecka w Krakowie w latach 1945–1957* (Warsaw: Żydowski Instytut Historyczny im. Emanuela Ringelbluma, 2011), 29. See 49–54 for a discussion of the numbers of children in postwar Kraków in various time periods.

14. One rescuer of a Jewish girl in Kraków reasoned that children's wartime protectors had the right to request compensation for a child's upkeep from the child's parents, or from Jewish organizations. "The risk of caring for the child, feeding, and keeping it [*sic*] during the German occupation cannot be estimated in financial terms because of the death penalty that a few or even several people were subjected to," Jan Tomaszkiewicz explained. Relacje: Jan Tomaszkiewicz, 25 February 1945, AŻIH 301/4672, p. 6.

15. Account of Abraham Blim, 5 March 1961, YVA 03/2221, p. 25.

16. The retrieval of Jewish children from foster parents and convents in Poland by Jewish organizations (especially the Zionist Coordination for the Redemption of Jewish Children) and individuals was an ideological project to transform child survivors into a Jewish national asset and secure the future of the Jewish people, particularly in Palestine (later Israel).

17. Max Pelton (Maksymilian Perlmutter), interview 38075, 1998, VHA.

18. Account of Halina Tydor, undated, YVA M-49/3744, p. 2.

19. Anna Gouttman (née Entenberg), interview 44141, 1998, VHA.

20. Account of Chava Mandelbaum (Cyla Chava / Ewa Lewi), 1985, MJH 1986.T.47.

21. Felicia Liban (née Vogler), interview 1451, 1995, VHA.

22. Miriam Shmuel (Maria Perlberger), oral history recorded by author, Israel, 30 April 2013. See also Maria Perlberger-Schmuel, "W chowanego ze śmiercią," *Więź*, no. 7–8 (July–August 1988): 185–224; and Miriam Perlberg-Shmuel, *This Girl Is Jewish!* [in Hebrew] (Haifa, Israel: Shurot, 1997).

23. Account of Ela Łuczkiewicz (Elżbieta Schnek), 8 July 1960, YVA 03/1874, p. 3.

24. "The Story of Miss Lena Kuechler" (spools 114, 115), 1956, YVA 0.36/61, p. 27. Kichler (also spelled Kuechler and Küchler) recounted her experiences in an audio account that she gave to David Boder (an American Jewish psychologist who first recorded survivor testimonies) on 8 September 1946 in Paris, where she awaited transfer to Palestine. See also Lena Küchler-Silberman, *My Hundred Children*, trans. David C. Gross (New York: Dell, 1987).

25. "The Story of Miss Lena Kuechler" (spools 114, 115), 1956, YVA 0.36/61, p. 29.

26. See, for example, Karolina Panz, "Testimonies of Survivors of Post-War Anti-Jewish Violence: Deconstructing a Myth of Polish Collective Memory," *Societas/Communitas* 25.1a (2018): 151–164.

27. "Story of Miss Lena Kuechler," 30.

28. "Story of Miss Lena Kuechler," 40.

29. Józef Adelson, "W Polsce zwanej Ludową," in *Najnowsze dzieje Żydów w Polsce*, ed. Jerzy Tomaszewski (Warsaw: Państwowe Wydawnictwo Naukowe, 1993), 389, 399.

30. The campaign, which the Polish communist government termed "anti-Zionist," was caused by antisemitism (especially after Poland had condemned Israel as an aggressor in the Six-Day War of 1967) and competition for power within the Communist Party. It culminated in protests organized by university students in Warsaw against the government's censorship, and subsequent arrests of students, some of whom were of Jewish descent. The political narration blamed Polish Jews for disloyalty to Poland.

31. The Association of Children of the Holocaust in Poland was created in September 1991.

32. The American Jewish Joint Distribution Committee also has held an important role for promoting Jewish life in Poland.

33. Zofia Radzikowska (née Melcer), oral history recorded by author, Kraków, 21 December 2011.

34. Radzikowska, oral history.

Bibliography

BOOKS

Arad, Yitzhak, Israel Gutman, and Abraham Margaliot, eds. *Documents on the Holocaust: Selected Sources on the Destruction of the Jews of Germany and Austria, Poland, and the Soviet Union.* 8th ed. Jerusalem: Yad Vashem, 1999.

Arczyński, Marek, and Wiesław Balcerak. *Żegota: Konspiracyjna Rada Pomocy Żydom 1942–1945.* Toronto: Aga, 2009.

Banaś, Beatrix. *Dzieje Urszulanek w Polsce.* Vols. 1 and 2. Lublin, Poland: Zgromadzenie Sióst Urszulanek, 2000.

Baran, Marcin, ed. *Płaszów—odkrywanie.* Kraków: Muzeum Historyczne Miasta Krakowa, 2016.

Baranowski, Daniel, ed. *Ich bin die Stimme der sechs Millionen: Das Videoarchiv im Ort der Information.* Berlin: Stiftung Denkmal für die Ermordeten Juden Europas, 2009.

Bartoszewski, Władysław, and Zofia Lewinówna. *Ten jest z Ojczyzny mojej: Braterstwo w czasach pogardy.* 3rd ed. Warsaw: Świat Książki, 2007.

Bauer, Yehuda. *American Jewry and the Holocaust: The American Jewish Joint Distribution Committee, 1939–1945.* Detroit: Wayne State University Press, 1981.

———. *Rethinking the Holocaust.* New Haven, CT: Yale University Press, 2001.

Bażanowska, Noemi. *To był mój dom: Żydowski Dom Dziecka w Krakowie w latach 1945–1957.* Warsaw: Żydowski Instytut Historyczny im. Emanuela Ringelbluma, 2011.

Bednarek, Monika, Edyta Gawron, Grzegorz Jeżowski, Barbara Zbroja, and Katarzyna Zimmerer, eds. *Kraków—czas okupacji 1939–1945.* Kraków: Muzeum Historyczne Miasta Krakowa, 2010.

Belda, Maciej W., Piotr Figiela, and Justyna Kozioł-Marzec, eds. *To była hebrajska szkoła w Krakowie: Gimnazjum Hebrajskie 1918–1939.* Kraków: Muzeum Historyczne Miasta Krakowa, 2011.

Berenstein, Tatiana, and Adam Rutkowski. *Pomoc Żydom w Polsce 1939–1945.* Warsaw: Polonia, 1963.

Berglass, Itzhok, and Shlomo Yahalomi-Diamand, eds. *The Book of Stryzow and Vicinity.* Translated by Harry Langsam. Israel: Natives of Stryzow Societies in Israel and the Diaspora, 1990.

Biberstein, Aleksander. *Zagłada Żydów w Krakowie.* Kraków: Wydawnictwo Literackie, 1985. Reprint, 2001.

Bieniarzówna, Janina, and Jan M. Małecki. *Dzieje Krakowa: Kraków w latach 1918–1939.* Vol. 4. Kraków: Wydawnictwo Literackie, 1998.

Bluglass, Kerry, ed. *Hidden from the Holocaust: Stories of Resilient Children Who Survived and Thrived.* Westport, CT: Praeger, 2003.

Bogner, Nahum. *At the Mercy of Strangers: The Rescue of Jewish Children with Assumed Identities in Poland.* Translated by Ralph Mandel. Jerusalem: Yad Vashem, 2009.

Borwicz, Michał M., Nella Rost, and Józef Wulf, eds. *W 3-cią rocznicę zagłady ghetta w Krakowie (13.III.1943–13.III.1946).* 1946. Kraków: Austeria, 2013.

Bratko, Józef. *Gestapowcy: Kontrwywiad, konfidenci, konspiratorzy.* Kraków: Krajowa Agencja Wydawnicza, 1990.

Brosterman, Norman. *Inventing Kindergarten.* New York: Harry N. Abrams, 1997.

Bukowski, William M., Andrew F. Newcomb, and Willard W. Hartup, eds. *The Company They Keep: Friendship in Childhood and Adolescence.* Cambridge: Cambridge University Press, 1996.

Brzoza, Czesław. *Kraków między wojnami: kalendarium 28 X 1918–6 IX 1939.* Kraków: Towarzystwo Sympatyków Historii, 1998.

———. *Żydzi krakowscy w okresie międzywojennym: Wybór dokumentów.* Kraków: Polska Akademia Umiejętności, 2015.

Chrobaczyński, Jacek. *Postawy, zachowania, nastroje: Społeczeństwo Krakowa wobec wojny i okupacji, 1939–1945.* Kraków: Wydawnictwo Literackie, 1993.

Chruszczewski, Adam, Krystyna Dębowska, Piotr Paweł Gach, Jerzy Kłoczowski, and Anna Siewierska, eds. *Żeńskie Zgromadzenia Zakonne w Polsce 1939–1947.* Vol. 7. Lublin, Poland: KUL, 1994.

Chwalba, Andrzej. *Dzieje Krakowa: Kraków w latach 1939–1945.* Vol. 5. Kraków: Wydawnictwo Literackie, 2002.

———. *Dzieje Krakowa: Kraków w latach 1945–1989.* Vol. 6. Kraków: Wydawnictwo Literackie, 2004.

Cichopek, Anna. *Pogrom Żydów w Krakowie 11 sierpnia 1945.* Warsaw: Żydowski Instytut Historyczny, 2000.

Cichopek-Gajraj, Anna. *Beyond Violence: Jewish Survivors in Poland and Slovakia, 1944–48.* Cambridge: Cambridge University Press, 2014.

Cobel-Tokarska, Marta. *Bezludna wyspa, nora, grób: Wojenne kryjówki Żydów w okupowanej Polsce.* Warsaw: Instytut Pamięci Narodowej, 2012.

Crowe, David. *Oskar Schindler: The Untold Account of His Life, Wartime Activities, and the True Story behind the List.* Cambridge, MA: Westview, 2004.

Csorba, Helena, and Tibor Csorba. *Losy młodzieży polskiej na Węgrzech w latach II wojny światowej.* Warsaw: Państwowe Wydawnictwo Naukowe, 1981.

Cunningham, Hugh. *Children and Childhood in Western Society since 1500.* 2nd ed. New York: Routledge, 2014.

Czerepak, Stanisław, and Tadeusz Wroński. *Ulica Pomorska 2: O krakowskim Gestapo i jego siedzibie w latach 1939–1945.* Kraków: Muzeum Historyczne Miasta Krakowa, 1972.

Czocher, Anna. *W okupowanym Krakowie: Codzienność polskich mieszkańców miasta 1939–1945.* Gdańsk, Poland: Oskar, 2011.

Datner, Szymon. *Las sprawiedliwych—karta z dziejów ratownictwa Żydów w okupowanej Polsce.* Warsaw: Książka i Wiedza, 1968.

Dieckmann, Christoph, Babette Quinkert, and Tatjana Tönsmeyer, eds. *Kooperation und Verbrechen: Formen der Kollaboration im östlichen Europa 1939–1941*. Göttingen, Germany: Wallstein, 2003.

Dobroszycki, Lucjan. *Survivors of the Holocaust in Poland: A Portrait Based on Jewish Community Records, 1944–1947*. New York: YIVO Institute for Jewish Research, 1994.

Duch-Dyngosz, Marta. *Odrodzenie życia żydowskiego w Krakowie?* Kraków: Muzeum Historyczne Miasta Krakowa, 2015.

Dwork, Debórah. *Children with a Star: Jewish Youth in Nazi Europe*. New Haven, CT: Yale University Press, 1991.

Dwork, Debórah, and Robert Jan van Pelt. *Flight from the Reich: Refugee Jews, 1933–1946*. New York: W. W. Norton, 2009.

———. *Holocaust: A History*. New York: W. W. Norton, 2002.

Dzierżak Adolfina, Stanisława Motyka, Władysław Bomba, and Jan Dukała, eds. *Zgromadzenie Sióstr Miłosierdzia św. Wincentego a Paulo w Polsce (1652–2002)*. Vol. 2. Kraków: Instytut Wydawniczy Księży Misjonarzy "Nasza Przeszłość," 2002.

Eisen, George. *Children and Play in the Holocaust: Games among the Shadows*. Amherst: University of Massachusetts Press, 1988.

Eisenberg, Azriel. *The Lost Generation: Children in the Holocaust*. New York: Pilgrim, 1982.

Engel, David. *In the Shadow of Auschwitz: The Polish Government-in-Exile and the Jews, 1939–1942*. Chapel Hill: University of North Carolina Press, 2012.

Engelking, Barbara. *Holocaust and Memory: The Experience of the Holocaust and Its Consequences: An Investigation Based on Personal Narratives*. Edited by Gunnar S. Paulsson. Translated by Emma Harris. London: Leicester University Press in association with the European Jewish Publication Society, 2001.

———. *"Szanowny panie gistapo": Donosy do władz niemieckich w Warszawie i okolicach w latach 1940–1941*. Warsaw: Instytut Filozofii i Socjologii Polskiej Akademii Nauk, 2003.

Engelking, Barbara, and Jacek Leociak. *The Warsaw Ghetto: A Guide to the Perished City*. Translated by Emma Harris. New Haven, CT: Yale University Press, 2009.

Fass, Paula S., and Michael Grossberg, eds. *Reinventing Childhood after World War II*. Philadelphia: University of Pennsylvania Press, 2013.

Felman, Shoshana, and Dori Laub. *Testimony: Crises of Witnessing in Literature, Psychoanalysis, and History*. New York: Routledge, 1991.

Finder, Gabriel N., Natalia Aleksiun, Antony Polonsky, and Jan Schwarz, eds. *Polin: Studies in Polish Jewry*. Vol. 20, *Making Holocaust Memory*. Portland, OR: Littman Library of Jewish Civilization, 2007.

Finkel, Evgeny. *Ordinary Jews: Choice and Survival during the Holocaust*. Princeton, NJ: Princeton University Press, 2017.

Fogelman, Eva. *Conscience and Courage: Rescuers of Jews during the Holocaust*. New York: Doubleday, 1994.

Frącek, Teresa. *Zgromadzenie Sióstr Franciszkanek Rodziny Marii w latach 1939–1945*. Warsaw: Akademia Teologii Katolickiej, 1981.

Gadacz, Jan Ludwik. *Słownik polskich kapucynów*. Wrocław, Poland: Wydawnictwo oo. kapucynów, 1985.

Galas, Michał, and Antony Polonsky, eds. *Polin: Studies in Polish Jewry*. Vol. 23, *Jews in Kraków*. Portland, OR: Littman Library of Jewish Civilization, 2011.

Galicia Jewish Museum. *Fighting for Dignity: Jewish Resistance in Kraków / Walka o godność: Żydowski ruch oporu w Krakowie*. Kraków: Galicia Jewish Museum, 2008.

———. *Polscy Bohaterowie: Ci, ktorzy ratowali Żydów / Polish Heroes: Those Who Rescued Jews*. Kraków: Galicia Jewish Museum, in cooperation with Centrum Żydowskie w Oświęcimiu, Polish American Jewish Youth Alliance for Youth Action, 2006.

Garmezy, Norman, and Michael Rutter, eds. *Stress, Coping, and Development in Children*. Baltimore: Johns Hopkins University Press, 1988.

Głowiński, Tomasz. *O nowy porządek europejski: Ewolucja hitlerowskiej propagandy politycznej wobec Polaków w Generalnym Gubernatorstwie, 1939–1945*. Wrocław, Poland: Wydawnictwo Uniwersytetu Wrocławskiego, 2000.

Gondek, Leszek. *W imieniu Rzeczypospolitej: Wymiar Sprawiedliwości w Polsce w czasie II wojny światowej*. Warsaw: Państwowe Wydawnictwo Naukowe, 2011.

Grabowski, Jan. *Ja tego Żyda znam! Szantażowanie Żydów w Warszawie, 1939–1943*. Warsaw: Centrum Badań nad Zagładą Żydów, 2004.

———. *Na posterunku. Udział polskiej policji granatowej i kryminalnej w zagładzie Żydów*. Wołowiec, Poland: Czarne, 2020.

Grabowski, Jan, and Dariusz Libionka, eds. *Klucze i Kasa: O mieniu żydowskim w Polsce pod okupacją niemiecką i we wczesnych latach powojennych, 1939–1950*. Warsaw: Stowarzyszenie Centrum Badań nad Zagładą, 2014.

Grądzka, Martyna. *Kobieta żydowska w okupowanym Krakowie (1939–1945)*. Kraków: Wysoki Zamek, 2016.

———. *Przerwane dzieciństwo: Losy dzieci Żydowskiego Domu Sierot przy ul. Dietla 64 w Krakowie podczas okupacji niemieckiej / A Broken Childhood: The Fate of the Children from the Jewish Orphanage at 64 Dietla Street in Cracow during the German Occupation*. Kraków: Wysoki Zamek, 2012.

Greenspan, Henry. *On Listening to Holocaust Survivors: Beyond Testimony*. 2nd ed. Saint Paul, MN: Paragon House, 2010.

Gross, Jan Tomasz. *Polish Society under German Occupation: The Generalgouvernement, 1939–1944*. Princeton, NJ: Princeton University Press, 1979.

———. *Upiorna dekada: Eseje o stereotypach na temat Żydów, Polaków, Niemców, komunistów i kolaboracji 1939–1948*. Kraków: Austeria, 2007.

Grudzińska-Gross, Irena, and Jan Tomasz Gross, eds. *War through Children's Eyes: The Soviet Occupation of Poland and the Deportations, 1939–1941*. Translated by Ronald Strom and Dan Rivers. Stanford, CA: Hoover Institution Press, 1981.

Grynberg, Michał. *Księga Sprawiedliwych*. Warsaw: Państwowe Wydawnictwo Naukowe, 1993.

Gutenbaum, Jakub, and Agnieszka Latała, eds. *The Last Eyewitnesses: Children of the Holocaust Speak*. Vol. 2. Translated by Julian Bussgang, Fay Bussgang, and Simon Cygielski. Evanston, IL: Northwestern University Press, 2005.

Heberer, Patricia, ed. *Documenting Life and Destruction: Holocaust Sources in Context: Children during the Holocaust*. Lanham, MA: AltaMira in association with the United States Holocaust Memorial Museum, 2011.

Hein, Wincenty, and Czesława Jakubiec. *Montelupich*. Kraków: Wydawnictwo Literackie, 1985.

Heksel, Bartosz, and Katarzyna Kocik. *Żegota: Ukryta Pomoc*. Kraków: Muzeum Historyczne Miasta Krakowa, 2017.

Heller, Celia S. *On the Edge of Destruction: Jews of Poland between the Two World Wars.* Detroit: Wayne State University Press, 1977.

Helphand, Kenneth. "Ghetto Gardens: Life in the Midst of Death." In *Jewish Topographies: Visions of Space, Traditions of Place,* edited by Julia Brauch, Anna Lipphardt, and Alexandra Nocke, 83–99. Aldershot, UK: Ashgate, 2008.

Hembera, Melanie. "Die Stadt Krakau müsse die judenreinste Stadt des Generalgouvernements werden: Die Umsiedlung der jüdischen Bevölkerung aus Krakau." In *Narrative im Dialog: Deutsch-polnische Erinnerungsdiskurse,* edited by Wolfgang Form, Kerstin von Lingen, and Krzysztof Ruchniewicz, 311–334. Dresden: Neisse Verlag, 2013.

Henry, Patrick, ed. *Jewish Resistance against the Nazis.* Washington, DC: Catholic University of America Press, 2014.

Hochberg-Mariańska, Miriam, and Noe Grüs, eds. *The Children Accuse.* Translated by Bill Johnston. Portland, OR: Valentine Mitchell, 1996.

Horowitz, Sara R., ed. *Lessons and Legacies.* Vol. X, *Back to the Sources: Reexamining Perpetrators, Victims, and Bystanders.* Evanston, IL: Northwestern University Press, 2012.

Jarkowska-Natkaniec, Alicja. *Wymuszona współpraca czy zdrada? Wokół przypadków kolaboracji Żydów w okupowanym Krakowie.* Kraków: Universitas, 2018.

Kangisser Cohen, Sharon. "A Child's View: Children's Depositions of the Central Jewish Historical Commission (Poland)." In *Children in the Holocaust and Its Aftermath: Historical and Psychological Studies of the Kestenberg Archive,* edited by Sharon Kangisser Cohen, Eva Fogelman, and Dalia Ofer, 43–61. New York: Berghahn Books, 2017.

———. *Testimony and Time: Holocaust Survivors Remember.* Jerusalem: Yad Vashem, 2014.

Kaplan, Suzanne. *Children in Genocide: Extreme Traumatization and Affect Regulation.* London: Karnac Books, 2008.

Kapralski, Sławomir, ed. *The Jews in Poland.* Vol. 2. Kraków: Judaica Foundation, 1999.

Karay, Felicja. *The Women of Ghetto Krakow.* Translated by Sara Kitai. Tel Aviv: n.p., 2001.

Kassow, Samuel D. *Who Will Write Our History? Rediscovering a Hidden Archive from the Warsaw Ghetto.* New York: Vintage Books, 2009.

Kestenberg, Judith S., and Charlotte Kahn, eds. *Children Surviving Persecution: An International Study of Trauma and Healing.* Westport, CT: Praeger, 1998.

Kicińska, Magdalena, and Monika Sznajderman. *Przecież ich nie zostawię: O żydowskich opiekunkach w czasie wojny.* Wołowiec, Poland: Wydawnictwo Czarne, 2018.

Kłoczowski, Jerzy. "The Religious Orders and the Jews in Nazi-Occupied Poland." In *Polin: Studies in Polish Jewry,* vol. 3, *Jews of Warsaw,* edited by Antony Polonsky, 238–243. Oxford: Littman Library of Jewish Civilization, 1988.

Kluczewski, Marian. *Bez zaciemnienia: Codzienność okupowanego Krakowa w materiałach Archiwum Państwowego w Krakowie / Without Blackout: Everyday Life of Occupied Krakow in Materials of the State Archive in Krakow.* Kraków: Archiwum Państwowe w Krakowie, 2009.

Knowles, Anne Kelly, Tim Cole, and Alberto Giordano, eds. *Geographies of the Holocaust.* Bloomington: Indiana University Press, 2014.

Kochanski, Halik. *The Eagle Unbowed: Poland and the Poles in the Second World War.* Cambridge, MA: Harvard University Press, 2012.

Kocik, Katarzyna. "Dokumentacja organizacji opiekuńczych jako źródło badań nad zagładą krakowskiej społeczności żydowskiej." In *Żydzi polscy w oczach historyków. Tom dedykowany pamięci Profesora Józefa A. Gierowskiego,* edited by Adam

Kaźmierczyk and Alicja Maślak-Maciejewska, 181–200. Kraków: Wydawnictwo Uniwersytetu Jagiellońskiego, 2018.

Kołacz, Grzegorz. *Czasami trudno się bronić: Uwarunkowania postaw Żydów podczas okupacji hitlerowskiej w Polsce*. Warsaw: Wydawnictwa Akademickie i Profesjonalne, 2008.

Kotarba, Ryszard. *Niemiecki obóz w Płaszowie 1942–1945*. Warsaw-Kraków: Instytut Pamięci Narodowej, 2009.

Kowalska-Leder, Justyna. *Doświadczenie Zagłady z perspektywy dziecka w polskiej literaturze dokumentu osobistego*. Wrocław, Poland: Wydawnictwo Uniwersytetu Wrocławskiego, 2009.

Kroll, Bogdan. *Rada Główna Opiekuńcza 1939–1945*. Warsaw: Książka i Wiedza, 1985.

Kurek, Ewa. *Dzieci żydowskie w klasztorach: Udział żeńskich zgromadzeń zakonnych w akcji ratowania dzieci żydowskich w Polsce w latach 1939–1945*. 1992. Zakrzewo, Poland: Replika, 2012.

Kurek-Lesik, Ewa. *Your Life Is Worth Mine: How Polish Nuns Saved Hundreds of Jewish Children in German-Occupied Poland, 1939–1945*. New York: Hippocrene Books, 1997.

Kuwałek, Robert. "Deportations of Kraków Jews to the Extermination Camp in Bełżec in 1942." In *The Eagle Pharmacy: History and Memory: A Collection of Essays Accompanying the Permanent Exhibition "Tadeusz Pankiewicz's Pharmacy in the Kraków Ghetto,"* edited by Jan Gryta, 13–51. Kraków: Muzeum Historyczne Miasta Krakowa, 2013.

Lagzi, István. *Uchodźcy polscy na Węgrzech w latach drugiej wojny światowej*. Warsaw: Wydawnictwo Ministerstwa Obrony Narodowej, 1980.

Langer, Lawrence. *Holocaust Testimonies: The Ruins of Memory*. New Haven, CT: Yale University Press, 1991.

———. *Versions of Survival: The Holocaust and the Human Spirit*. Albany: State University of New York Press, 1982.

Lenart, Maria Paschalisa. *Prowincja krakowska Niepokalanego Serca Najświętszej Maryi Panny Zgromadzenia Sióstr Felicjanek*. Vol. 2, pt. 2. Kraków: Instytut Teologiczny Księży Misjonarzy, 2000.

Leociak, Jacek. *Ratowanie: Opowieści Polaków i Żydów*. Warsaw: Wydawnictwo Literackie, 2010.

Lestschinsky, Jacob. *Crisis, Catastrophe and Survival*. New York: Institute of Jewish Affairs of the World Jewish Congress, 1948.

Libionka, Dariusz, ed. *Akcja Reinhard: Zagłada Żydów w Generalnym Gubernatorstwie*. Warsaw: Instytut Pamięci Narodowej, 2004.

Lilientalowa, Regina. *Dziecko żydowskie*. 1927. Warsaw: Biblioteka Midrasza, 2007.

Löw, Andrea, and Markus Roth. *Juden in Krakau unter deutscher Besatzung 1939–1945*. Göttingen, Germany: Wallstein, 2011.

Löw, Andrea, and Agnieszka Zajączkowska-Drożdż. "Leadership in the Jewish Council as a Social Process: The Example of Cracow." In *The Holocaust and European Societies: Social Processes and Social Dynamics*, edited by Frank Bajohr and Andrea Löw, 189–206. London: Palgrave Macmillan, 2016.

Lowenfeld, Margaret. *Play in Childhood*. Portland, OR: Sussex Academic, 2008.

Łubczyk, Grzegorz. *Polski Wallenberg: Rzecz o Henryku Sławiku*. Warsaw: Rytm, 2004.

Łubczyk, Krystyna, and Grzegorz Łubczyk. *Pamięć: Polscy uchodźcy na Węgrzech 1939–1945*. Warsaw: Rytm, 2009.

Lukas, Richard C. *Did the Children Cry? Hitler's War against Jewish and Polish Children, 1939–1945*. New York: Hippocrene Books, 1994.

Main Commission for the Investigation of Crimes against the Polish Nation, Institute of National Memory, and Polish Society for the Righteous among the Nations. *Those Who Helped: Polish Rescuers of Jews during the Holocaust*. Pt. 3. Warsaw: n.p., 1997.

Martin, Sean. *For the Good of the Nation: Institutions for Jewish Children in Interwar Poland*. Brighton, MA: Academic Studies Press, 2017.

———. *Jewish Life in Cracow, 1918–1939*. London: Vallentine Mitchell, 2004.

Mazur, Grzegorz. *Biuro Informacji i Propagandy SZP-ZWZ-AK 1939–1945*. Warsaw: PAX, 1987.

Melchior, Małgorzata. *Zagłada a tożsamość: Polscy Żydzi ocaleni na "aryjskich papierach": Analiza doświadczenia biograficznego*. Warsaw: Instytut Filozofii i Socjologii Polskiej Akademii Nauk, 2004.

Melezen, Abraham. *Przyczynek do znajomości stosunków demograficznych wśród ludności żydowskiej w Łodzi, Krakowie i Lublinie podczas okupacji niemieckiej*. Łódź, Poland: Wydawnictwa Centralnej Żydowskiej Komisji Historycznej przy CK Żydów Polskich, 1946.

Mendelsohn, Ezra. *The Jews of East Central Europe between the World Wars*. Bloomington: Indiana University Press, 1984.

Michlic, Joanna Beata. "Rebuilding Shattered Lives: Some Vignettes of Jewish Children's Lives in Early Postwar Poland." In *Holocaust Survivors: Resettlement, Memories, Identities*, edited by Dalia Ofer, Françoise S. Ouzan, and Judy Tydor Baumel-Schwartz, 46–87. New York: Berghahn Books, 2012.

Michman, Dan. *The Emergence of Jewish Ghettos during the Holocaust*. New York: Cambridge University Press, 2011.

Nachmany Gafny, Emunah. *Dividing Hearts: The Removal of Jewish Children from Gentile Families in Poland in the Immediate Post Holocaust Years*. Translated by Naftali Greenwood. Jerusalem: Yad Vashem, 2009.

Nalewajko-Kulikov, Joanna. *Strategie Przetrwania: Żydzi po aryjskiej stronie Warszawy*. Warsaw: Neriton, 2004.

Nicholas, Lynn H. *Cruel World: The Children of Europe in the Nazi Web*. New York: A. A. Knopf, 2005.

Noszczak, Bartłomiej. *W Matni: Kościół na ziemiach polskich w latach II wojny światowej*. Warsaw: Państwowe Wydawnictwo Naukowe, 2011.

Nuszkiewicz, Ryszard. *Uparci*. Warsaw: PAX, 1983.

Ofer, Dalia, and Lenore J. Weitzman, eds. *Women in the Holocaust*. New Haven, CT: Yale University Press, 1998.

Oliner, Pearl M. *Saving the Forsaken: Religious Culture and the Rescue of Jews in Nazi Europe*. New Haven, CT: Yale University Press, 2005.

Oliner, Samuel P., and Pearl M. Oliner. *The Altruistic Personality: Rescuers of Jews in Nazi Europe: What Led Ordinary Men and Women to Risk Their Lives on Behalf of Others?* New York: Free Press, 1988.

Orzeł, Olga, ed. *Dzieci żydowskie w czasach Zagłady: Wczesne świadectwa 1944–1948: Relacje dziecięce ze zbiorów Centralnej Żydowskiej Komisji Historycznej*. Warsaw: Żydowski Instytut Historyczny im. Emanuela Rinelbluma, 2014.

Pabis-Cisowska, Katarzyna. *Postęp kontra tradycja: Kwestia małżeństwa, dobroczynności i szkolnictwa w żydowskim Krakowie na przełomie XIX i XX w.* Kraków: Wydawnictwo Naukowe Uniwersytetu Pedagogicznego, 2019.

Patt, Avinoam J. *Finding Home and Homeland: Jewish Youth and Zionism in the Aftermath of the Holocaust.* Detroit: Wayne State University Press, 2009.

Peled Margolin, Yael. *Jewish Cracow, 1939–1943: Resistance, Underground, Struggle* [in Hebrew]. Tel Aviv: Ghetto Fighters' House, 1993.

Phil, Erwin. *Friendship in Childhood and Adolescence.* London: Routledge, 1998.

Piper, Franciszek, and Irena Strzelecka. *Księga pamięci: Transporty Polaków do KL Auschwitz z Krakowa i innych miejscowości Polski południowej 1940–1944.* Warsaw–Oświęcim: Towarzystwo Opieki nad Oświęcimiem, Państwowe Muzeum Auschwitz-Birkenau, 2002.

Pordes, Anis, and Irek Grin. *Ich miasto: Wspomnienia Izraelczyków, przedwojennych mieszkanców Krakowa.* Warsaw: Prószyński i S-ka, 2004.

Prag, Werner, and Wolfgang Jacobmeyer, eds. *Das Diensttagebuch des deutschen Generalgouverneur in Polen, 1939–1945.* Stuttgart: Deutsche Verlags-Anstalt, 1975.

Prekerowa, Teresa. *Konspiracyjna Rada Pomocy Żydom w Warszawie 1942–1945.* Warsaw: Państwowy Instytut Wydawniczy, 1982.

Rączy, Elżbieta, ed. *Sprawiedliwi wśród narodów Świata: Pomoc Polaków dla ludności żydowskiej w Małopolsce w latach 1939–1945 / Righteous among the Nations: Help of Polish People for the Jewish Population in Małopolska Province in the Years 1939–1945.* Kraków: Instytut Pamięci Narodowej Oddział w Rzeszowie and Gmina Miejska Kraków, 2008.

———. *Zagłada Żydów w dystrykcie krakowskim w latach 1939–1945.* Rzeszów, Poland: Instytut Pamięci Narodowej and Uniwersytet Rzeszowski, 2014.

Renwick Monroe, Kristen. *The Hand of Compassion: Portraits of Moral Choice during the Holocaust.* Princeton, NJ: Princeton University Press, 2004.

Ringelblum, Emmanuel. *Polish-Jewish Relations during the Second World War.* Edited by Joseph Kermish and Shmuel Krakowski. Translated by Dafna Allon, Danuta Dabrowska, and Dana Keren. Evanston, IL: Northwestern University Press, 1992.

Rosen, Alan. *The Wonder of Their Voices: The 1946 Holocaust Interviews of David Boder.* New York: Oxford University Press, 2010.

Sakowska, Ruta, ed. *Archiwum Ringelbluma.* Vol. 2, *Dzieci: Tajne Nauczanie w Getcie Warszawskim.* Warsaw: Państwowe Wydawnictwo Naukowe, Żydowski Instytut Historyczny, 2001.

Samsonowska, Krystyna. *Wyznaniowe Gminy Żydowskie i ich społeczności w województwie krakowskim.* Kraków: Societas Vistulana, 2005.

Shandler, Jeffery, ed. *Awakening Lives: Autobiographies of Jewish Youth in Poland before the Holocaust.* New Haven, CT: Yale University Press in cooperation with the YIVO Institute for Jewish Research, 2002.

———. *Holocaust Memory in the Digital Age: Survivors' Stories and New Media Practices.* Stanford, CA: Stanford University Press, 2017.

Sharif-Nassab, Arin. *Über-Lebensgeschichten: Der Holocaust in Krakau: Biographische Studien.* Innsbruck, Austria: Studienverlag, 2005.

Shenker, Noah. *Reframing Holocaust Testimony.* Bloomington: Indiana University Press, 2015.

Siwor, Grzegorz. *Enoszijut: Opowieść o Dawidzie Kurzmannie*. Kraków: Etiuda, 2014.

Skotnicki, Aleksander B., ed. *Kronika Szkolna uczennic żydowskich z lat 1933–1939 Miejskiej Szkoły Powszechnej nr 15 im. Klementyny Tańskiej-Hoffmanowej przy ul. Miodowej w Krakowie*. Kraków: Austeria, 2006.

———. *Szpital Gminy Wyznaniowej Żydowskiej w Krakowie 1866–1941*. Kraków: Stradomskie Centrum Dialogu, 2013.

Sliwa, Joanna. "Clandestine Activities and Concealed Presence: A Case Study of Children in the Kraków Ghetto." In *Jewish Families in Europe 1939–Present: History, Representation, and Memory*, edited by Joanna Beata Michlic, 26–45. Waltham, MA: Brandeis University Press, 2017.

———. "The Forced Relocation to the Krakow Ghetto as Remembered by Child Survivors." In *The Young Victims of the Nazi Regime: Migration, the Holocaust, and Postwar Displacement*, edited by Simone Gigliotti and Monica Tempian, 153–169. London: Bloomsbury Academic, 2016.

Śliwowska, Wiktoria, ed. *Czarny rok . . . Czarne lata . . .* Warsaw: Stowarzyszenie Dzieci Holocaustu w Polsce, 1996.

———. *The Last Eyewitnesses: Children of the Holocaust Speak*. Translated by Julian Bussgang and Fay Bussgang. Evanston, IL: Northwestern University Press, 1998.

Sofsky, Wolfgang. *The Order of Terror: The Concentration Camp*. Translated by William Templer. Princeton, NJ: Princeton University Press, 1997.

Sommer-Schneider, Anna. *Sze'erit hapleta: Ocaleni z Zagłady: Działalność American Jewish Joint Distribution Committee w Polsce w latach 1945–1989*. Kraków: Księgarnia Akademicka, 2014.

Stachów, Tomasz, and Anna Marszałek, eds. *Kościół krakowski 1939–1945 / The Church in Kraków, 1939–1945*. Kraków: Muzeum Historyczne Miasta Krakowa, 2014.

Stargardt, Nicholas. *Witnesses of War: Children's Lives under the Nazis*. New York: A. A. Knopf, 2006.

Steinert, Johannes-Dieter. *Holocaust und Zwangsarbeit. Erinnerungen jüdischer Kinder 1938–1945*. Essen, Germany: Klartext, 2018.

Sterling, Eric J., ed. *Life in the Ghettos during the Holocaust*. Syracuse, NY: Syracuse University Press, 2005.

Suwart, Adam. *Bp Albin Małysiak: Droga przez stulecie*. Poznań, Poland: Święty Wojciech, 2010.

Tec, Nechama. *When Light Pierced the Darkness: Christian Rescue of Jews in Nazi-Occupied Poland*. New York: Oxford University Press, 1986.

Tomaszewski, Irene, and Tecia Werbowski. *Code Name: Żegota—Rescuing Jews in Occupied Poland, 1942–1945: The Most Dangerous Conspiracy in Wartime Europe*. Santa Barbara, CA: Praeger, 2010.

Tomaszewski, Jerzy, ed. *Najnowsze dzieje Żydów w Polsce*. Warsaw: Państwowe Wydawnictwo Naukowe, 1993.

Trunk, Isaiah. *Jewish Responses to Nazi Persecution: Collective and Individual Behavior in Extremis*. New York: Stein and Day, 1979.

———. *Judenrat: The Jewish Councils in Eastern Europe under Nazi Occupation*. New York: Stein and Day, 1972.

Tych, Feliks, Alfons Kenkmann, Elisabeth Kohlhaas, and Andreas Eberhardt, eds. *Kinder über den Holocaust: Frühe Zeugnisse 1944–1948*. Berlin: Metropol Verlag, 2008.

Vishniac, Roman. *A Vanished World*. New York: Farrar, Straus and Giroux, 1983.

Vromen, Suzanne. *Hidden Children of the Holocaust: Belgian Nuns and Their Daring Rescue of Young Jews from the Nazis*. New York: Oxford University Press, 2008.

Wachsmann, Nikolaus. *KL: A History of the Nazi Concentration Camps*. New York: Farrar, Strauss and Giroux, 2015.

Waszkiewicz, Zofia. *Polityka Watykanu wobec Polski 1939–1945*. Warsaw: Państwowe Wydawnictwo Naukowe, 1980.

Werner, Emmy E. *Through the Eyes of Innocents: Children Witness World War II*. New York: Basic Books, 1999.

Wieviorka, Annette. *The Era of the Witness*. Ithaca, NY: Cornell University Press, 2006.

Winestone, Martin. *The Dark Heart of Hitler's Europe: Nazi Rule in Poland under the General Government*. New York: I. B. Tauris, 2015.

Wroński, Tadeusz, and Ewa Zachwieja, *Szkolnictwo podstawowe Miasta Krakowa w czasie okupacji hitlerowskiej 1939–1945 (Wybór dokumentów)*. Warsaw: Ministerstwo Sprawiedliwości Główna Komisja Badania Zbrodni Hitlerowskich w Polsce, 1977.

Zajączkowska-Drożdż, Agnieszka. *Od dyskryminacji do eksterminacji: Polityka Trzeciej Rzeszy wobec Żydów w Krakowie (1939–1943)*. Kraków: Wydawnictwo Uniwersytetu Jagiellońskiego, 2020.

Żbikowski, Andrzej, ed. *Polacy i Żydzi pod okupacją niemiecką 1939–1945: Studia i materiały*. Warsaw: Instytut Pamięci Narodowej, 2006.

———. *Żydzi krakowscy i ich gmina 1869–1919*. Warsaw: DiG, 1994.

Ziemian, Joseph. *The Cigarette Sellers of the Three Crosses Square*. Trowbridge, UK: Cromwell, 2005.

Zimmerer, Katarzyna. *Zamordowany świat: Losy Żydów w Krakowie 1939–1945*. Kraków: Wydawnictwo Literackie, 2004.

Zimmerman, Joshua. *The Polish Underground and the Jews, 1939–1945*. New York: Cambridge University Press, 2015.

PUBLISHED MEMOIRS AND DIARIES

Akavia, Miriam. *Jesień młodości*. Kraków: Wydawnictwo Literackie, 1989.

Avinun, Sara. *Rising from the Abyss: An Adult's Struggle with Her Trauma as a Child in the Holocaust*. Hod Hasharon, Israel: Astrolog, 2005.

Benisch, Pearl. *To Vanquish the Dragon*. Jerusalem: Feldheim, 1991.

Dąbrowa-Kostka, Stanisław. *W Okupowanym Krakowie, 6.IX.1939–18.I.1945*. Warsaw: Wydawnictwo Ministerstwa Obrony Narodowej, 1972.

Davidson Draenger, Gusta. *Justyna's Narrative*. Edited by David H. Hirsch and Eli Pfefferkorn. Translated by Roslyn Hirsch. Amherst: University of Massachusetts Press, 1996.

Dobrowolski, Stanisław Wincenty. *Memuary pacyfisty*. Kraków: Wydawnictwo Literackie, 1989.

Ferderber-Salz, Bertha. *And the Sun Kept Shining . . .* New York: Holocaust Library, 1980.

Fischler-Martinho, Janina. *Have You Seen My Little Sister?* London: Vallentine Mitchell, 1997.

Friedman, Ester. *Daleka droga do domu*. Kraków: Ambrozja, 1997.

Graf, Malvina. *The Kraków Ghetto and the Płaszów Camp Remembered*. Tallahassee: Florida State University Press, 1989.

Hescheles, Janina. *Oczyma dwunastoletniej dziewczyny*. Edited by Maria Hochberg-Mariańska. Kraków: Centralny Komitet Żydów Polskich, 1945.

Kamiński, Adam. *Diariusz Podręczny 1939–1945*. Edited by Anna Palarczykowa and Janina Stoksik. Warsaw: Instytut Pamięci Narodowej, 2001.

Keidar, Anat. *On the Road: The Story of Jeremy Keidar* [in Hebrew]. Kiryat Ono, Israel: Shanie Story, 2011.

Küchler-Silberman, Lena. *My Hundred Children*. Translated by David C. Gross. New York: Dell, 1987.

Ligocka, Roma. *The Girl in the Red Coat*. New York: St. Martin's, 2002.

Lobel, Anita. *No Pretty Pictures: A Child of War*. New York: HarperCollins, 1998.

Mariańscy, M. M. *Wśród przyjaciół i wrogów: Poza gettem w okupowanym Krakowie*. Kraków: Wydawnictwo Literackie, 1988.

Müller-Madej, Stella. *A Girl from Schindler's List*. Translated by William R. Brand. Kraków: DjaF, 2006.

———. *Oczami dziecka: Wspomnienia z dzieciństwa w getcie i obozach koncentracyjnych*. Kraków: Nakład Autora, 1991.

Nelken, Halina. *And Yet, I Am Here!* Amherst: University of Massachusetts Press, 1999.

Pankiewicz, Tadeusz. *The Cracow Ghetto Pharmacy*. Translated by Henry Tilles. Washington, DC: U.S. Holocaust Memorial Museum, 2000.

Perlberg-Shmuel, Miriam. *This Girl Is Jewish!* [in Hebrew]. Haifa, Israel: Shurot, 1997.

Polanski, Roman. *Roman*. New York: William Morrow, 1984.

Strzelichowski, Stanisław. *Dwa lata: Grudzien 1942–październik 1944*. Wrocław, Poland: Ossolineum, 1972.

Weichert, Michał. *Jewish Mutual Assistance, 1939–1945* [in Yiddish]. Tel Aviv: Menora, 1962.

Zimmerman, Henryk Zvi. *Przeżyłem, pamiętam, świadczę*. Kraków: Baran i Suszczyński, 1997.

DISSERTATIONS

Kaplan, Suzanne. "Children in the Holocaust: Dealing with Affects and Memory Images in Trauma and Generational Linking." PhD diss., Uppsala University, 2002.

Marlow, Jennifer Lynn. "Polish Catholic Maids and Nannies: Female Aid and the Domestic Realm in Nazi-Occupied Poland." PhD diss., Michigan State University, 2014.

Rothstein, Rachel. "'Small Numbers, Big Presence': Poland, the U.S., and the Power of Jewishness after 1968." PhD diss., University of Florida, 2015.

Schmidt Holländer, Hanna. "Ghetto Schools—Jewish Education in Nazi Occupied Poland." PhD diss., University of Hamburg, 2015.

ENCYCLOPEDIAS

Dean, Martin, and Mel Hecker, eds. *The United States Holocaust Memorial Museum Encyclopedia of Camps and Ghettos, 1933–1945*. Vol. 2, *Ghettos in German-Occupied Eastern Europe*. Bloomington: Indiana University Press in association with the U.S. Holocaust Memorial Museum, 2012.

Gutman, Israel, Sara Bender, and Shmuel Krakowski, eds. *The Encyclopedia of the Righteous among the Nations: Rescuers of Jews during the Holocaust: Poland*. Vols. 1 and 2. Jerusalem: Yad Vashem, 2004.

Megargee, Geoffrey P., ed. *The United States Holocaust Memorial Museum Encyclopedia of Camps and Ghettos, 1933–1945*. Vol. 1, *Early Camps, Youth Camps, and Concentration Camps and Subcamps under the SS-Business Administration Main Office (WVHA)*. Pt. B. Bloomington: Indiana University Press, 2009.

Miron, Guy, and Shlomit Shulhani, eds. *The Yad Vashem Encyclopedia of the Ghettos during the Holocaust*. Jerusalem: Yad Vashem, 2010.

ARTICLES

Agatstein-Dormontowa, Dora. "Żydzi w Krakowie w okresie okupacji niemieckiej." *Rocznik Krakowski* 31 (1949–1957): 183–223.

Aleksiun, Natalia. "Survivor Testimonies and Historical Objectivity: Polish Historiography since *Neighbors*." *Holocaust Studies: A Journal of Culture and History* 20, no. 1–2 (Summer/Autumn 2014): 157–178.

Aleksiun, Natalia, and Eliyana Adler. "Seeking Relative Safety. The Flight of Polish Jews to the East in the Autumn of 1939." *Yad Vashem Studies* 46, no. 1 (2018): 41–71.

Ansilewska, Marta. "Accepting Jewish Roots for a Pair of Shoes: Identity Dilemmas of Jewish Children in Poland during the Second World War and in the Early Post-war Years." In "Growing Up in the Shadow of the Second World War: European Perspectives," edited by Maren Röger and Machtfeld Venken. Special issue, *European Review of History* 22, no. 1 (2015): 348–367.

Bańkowska, Aleksandra. "Jewish Social Welfare Institutions and Facilities in the General Government from 1939 to 1944: A Preliminary Study." *Studia z Dziejów Rosji i Europy Środkowo-Wschodniej* 53, no. 3 (2018): 129–167.

Bartoszewski, Władysław. "Z Sądów Specjalnych: Prześladowcy Żydów podczas okupacji." *Gazeta Ludowa*, 4 January 1946.

Beorn, Waitman Wade. "Last Stop in Lwów: Janowska as a Hybrid Camp." *Holocaust and Genocide Studies* 32, no. 3 (Winter 2018): 445–471.

Berendt, Grzegorz. "Cena życia—ekonomiczne uwarunkowania egzystencji Żydów po 'aryjskiej stronie.'" *Zagłada Żydów: Studia i Materiały*, no. 4 (2008): 115–165.

Berenstein, Tatiana. "Ceny produktów żywnościowych w Warszawie i w getcie warszawskim w latach okupacji hitlerowskiej." *Biuletyn Żydowskiego Instytutu Historycznego*, no. 70 (April–June 1969): 3–19.

———. "O podłożu gospodarczym sporów między władzami administracyjnymi a policyjnymi w Generalnej Guberni (1939–1944)." *Biuletyn Żydowskiego Instytutu Historycznego*, no. 53 (January–March 1965): 33–79.

———. "Rada Pomocy Żydom w Polsce ('Żegota')" Wspomnienia centralnych i terenowych działaczy RPŻ." *Biuletyn Żydowskiego Instytutu Historycznego*, no. 65–66 (January–June 1968): 173–205.

Berenstein, Tatiana, and Adam Rutkowski. "O ratownictwie Żydów przez Polaków w okresie okupacji hitlerowskiej." *Biuletyn Żydowskiego Instytutu Historycznego*, no. 35 (July–September 1960): 15–46.

———. "Prześladowania ludności żydowskiej w okresie okupacji hitlerowskiej administracji wojskowej na okupowanych ziemiach polskich (1.IX.1939–25.X.1939)." *Biuletyn Żydowskiego Instytutu Historycznego*, no. 38 (April–June 1961): 3–38.

———. "Prześladowania ludności żydowskiej w okresie okupacji hitlerowskiej administracji wojskowej w Polsce (1.IX.1939–25.X.1939)." *Biuletyn Żydowskiego Instytutu Historycznego*, no. 39 (August–September 1961): 63–87.

Cohen, Boaz. "The Children's Voice: Postwar Collection of Testimonies from Child Survivors of the Holocaust." *Holocaust and Genocide Studies* 21, no. 1 (Spring 2007): 73–95.

Csorba, Helena. "Dzieci uratowane od Zagłady." *Biuletyn Żydowskiego Instytutu Historycznego*, no. 35 (July–September 1960): 100–105.

Darley, John, and Bibb Latane. "Bystander Intervention in Emergencies: Diffusion of Responsibility." *Journal of Personality and Social Psychology* 8 (April 1968): 377–383.

Datner, Szymon. "Zbrodnie hitlerowskie na Żydach zbiegłych z get: Groźby i zarządzenia 'prawne' w stosunku do Żydów oraz udzielających im pomocy Polaków." *Biuletyn Żydowskiego Instytutu Historycznego*, no. 75 (July–September 1970): 4–31.

Datner-Śpiewak, Helena. "Instytucje opieki nad dzieckiem i szkoły powszechne Centralnego Komitetu Żydów Polskich w latach 1945–1946." *Biuletyn Żydowskiego Instytutu Historycznego* 3 (1981): 37–40.

Dunin Wąsowiczowa, Janina. "Wspomnienia o akcji pomocy Żydom podczas okupacji hitlerowskiej w Polsce (1939–1945)." *Biuletyn Żydowskiego Instytutu Historycznego*, no. 45–46 (1963): 248–259.

Einwohner, Rachel. "Ethical Considerations on the Use of Archived Testimonies in Holocaust Research: Beyond the IRB Exemption." *Qualitative Sociology* 34, no. 3 (2011): 415–430.

Fatran, Gila, and Naftali Greenwood. "The 'Working Group.'" *Holocaust and Genocide Studies* 8, no. 2 (1994): 164–201.

Ferenc Piotrowska, Maria. "'Ma ono na twarzy grymas dojrzałego i gorycz pokrzywdzonego [. . .]—nie ma dzieciństwa.' Przemiany ról dzieci w rodzinie w getcie warszawskim." *Zagłada Żydów. Studia i Materiały* no. 11 (2015): 347–376.

Fuks, Marian. "Sytuacja w gettach Generalnej Guberni na tle 'Gazety Żydowskiej' 1940 r. (cz.III)." *Biuletyn Żydowskiego Instutytu Historycznego w Polsce*, no. 1 (January–March 1972): 41–70.

——. "Życie w gettach Generalnej Guberni na tle 'Gazety Żydowskiej' 1940–1942." *Biuletyn Żydowskiego Instytutu Historycznego w Polsce*, no. 3 (July–September 1971): 3–23.

——. "Życie w gettach Generalnej Guberni na tle 'Gazety Żydowskiej' (Publicystyka, lipiec-grudzień 1940)." *Biuletyn Żydowskiego Instytutu Historycznego w Polsce*, no. 4 (October–December 1971): 23–41.

Grabowski, Jan. "Rescue for Money: Paid Helpers in Poland, 1939–1945." *Search and Research: Lectures and Papers* 13 (2008).

Gross, Natan. "Days and Nights in the Aryan Quarters: The Daily Worries of a Jew Carrying 'Aryan Papers.'" *Yad Vashem Bulletin*, no. 5 (1959).

Heenan, Deirdre. "Art as Therapy: An Effective Way of Promoting Positive Mental Health." *Disability and Society* 21, no. 2 (2006): 179–191.

Hodara, Raquel. "The Polish Jewish Woman from the Beginning of the Occupation to the Deportation to the Ghettos." *Yad Vashem Studies* 32 (2004): 397–432.

Kamiński, Stefan, and Aleksandra Mianowska. "Wspomnienia: Żołnierze Żydzi w szpitalach jenieckich w Krakowie." *Przegląd Lekarski* 47, no. 1 (1990): 149–160.

Kangisser Cohen, Sharon. "The Silence of Hidden Child Survivors of the Holocaust." *Yad Vashem Studies* 33 (2005): 171–202.

Kowalska, Irena. "Kartoteka TOZ z lat 1946–1947 (Żydowskie dzieci uratowane z Holocaustu)." *Biuletyn Żydowskiego Instytutu Historycznego*, no. 3/95–2/96: 175–178 (July 1995–June 1996): 97–106.

"Krakowska 'Żegota.'" *Nasz Głos*, an addendum to *Fołks-Sztyme*, no. 7/8 (1963).

Kubiak, A. "Dzieciobójstwo podczas okupacji hitlerowskiej." *Biuletyn Żydowskiego Instytutu Historycznego*, no. 17–18 (January–June 1956): 60–105.

Mędykowski, Witold. "Przeciw swoim: Wzorce kolaboracji żydowskiej w Krakowie i okolicy." *Zagłada Żydów: Studia i Materiały* 2 (2006): 202–220.

Michlic, Joanna Beata. "Jewish Children in Nazi-Occupied Poland: Survival and Polish-Jewish Relations during the Holocaust as Reflected in Early Postwar Recollections." *Search and Research: Lectures and Papers* 14 (2008).

———. "'I Will Never Forget What You Did for Me during the War': Rescuer-Rescuee Relationships in the Light of Postwar Correspondence in Poland, 1945–1949." *Yad Vashem Studies* 39, no. 2 (2011): 169–207.

———. "The Raw Memory of War: Early Postwar Testimonies of Children in Dom Dziecka in Otwock." *Yad Vashem Studies* 37, no. 1 (2009): 11–52.

Nirensztein, A (Albert). "Ruch oporu Żydów w Krakowie pod okupacją niemiecką." *Biuletyn Żydowskiego Instytutu Historycznego*, no. 1 (January–June 1952): 126–186.

Paczkowski, Andrzej. "Kolaboracja—zimnym okiem." *Tygodnik Powszechny*, no. 21 (25 May 2003).

Paldiel, Mordechai. "Fear and Comfort: The Plight of Hidden Jewish Children in Wartime Poland." *Holocaust and Genocide Studies*, no. 4/6 (1991): 397–413.

Panz, Karolina. "Testimonies of Survivors of Post-War Anti-Jewish Violence: Deconstructing a Myth of Polish Collective Memory," *Societas/Communitas*, no. 25.1a (2018): 151–164.

Perlberger-Schmuel, Maria. "W chowanego ze śmiercią." *Więź*, no. 7–8 (July–August 1988): 185–224.

Podhorizer-Sandel, E. "O Zagładzie Żydów w dystrykcie krakowskim." *Biuletyn Żydowskiego Instytutu Historycznego*, no. 30 (April–June 1959): 87–109.

Prekerowa, Teresa. "Przewodniczący krakowskiej 'Żegoty' Stanisław Wincenty Dobrowolski 22 VI 1915–8 IX 1993." *Biuletyn Żydowskiego Instytutu Historycznego w Polsce*, no. 1–2, 65–66 (January–June 1993): 109–110.

Przybyszewski, Bolesław. "Dzieje kościelne Krakowa w czasie okupacji 1939–1945 (Część II)." *Chrześcijanin w świecie*, no. 83 (November 1979): 24–42.

Rafman, Sandra, Joyce Canfield, Jose Barbas, and Janusz Kaczorowski. "Children's Representations of Parental Loss due to War." *International Journal of Behavioral Development* 20, no. 1 (1997): 163–177.

Rozett, Robert. "From Poland to Hungary: Rescue Attempts 1943–1944." *Yad Vashem Studies* 24 (1994): 177–193.

Sakowska, Ruta. "O szkolnictwie i tajnym nauczaniu w getcie warszawskim." *Biuletyn Żydowskiego Instytutu Historycznego*, no. 55 (July–September 1965): 57–84.

Schmidt Holländer, Hanna. "Reinstating Normality: The Stabilizing Function of School in Jewish Ghettos in German-Occupied Poland." In Alltag im Ghetto: Strukturen, Ordnungen, Lebenswelt(en) im Blick neuer Forschung," edited by Stephan Lehnstaedt and Kristin Platt. Special issue, *Zeitschrift für Genozidforschung* 13, no. 1–2 (2012): 82–101.

Seweryn, Tadeusz. "Wielostronna pomoc Żydom w czasie okupacji hitlerowskiej." *Przegląd Lekarski*, no. 1 (1967): 163–173.

Sliwa, Joanna. "Coping with Distorted Reality: Children in the Kraków Ghetto." *Holocaust Studies* 16, no. 1–2 (Summer/Autumn 2010): 177–202.

———. "A Link between the Inside and the Outside Worlds: Jewish Child Smugglers in the Kraków Ghetto." In Alltag im Ghetto: Strukturen, Ordnungen, Lebenswelt(en) im Blick neuer Forschung," edited by Stephan Lehnstaedt and Kristin Platt. Special issue, *Zeitschrift für Genozidforschung* 13, no. 1–2 (2012): 53–81.

———. "Rescue and Parenting through Correspondence." In European Holocaust Research Infrastructure Document Blog, 2 November 2020.

Stańczyk, Ewa. "The Absent Jewish Child: Photography and Holocaust Representation in Poland." *Journal of Modern Jewish Studies* 13, no. 3 (2014): 360–380.

Stępień, Monika. "'Pamięci zamordowanych składamy hołd': Działalność Wojewódzkiej Żydowskiej Komisji Historycznej w powojennym Krakowie." *Kwartalnik Historii Żydów* 267, no. 3 (2018): 579–606.

"Sylwetka: Wiesław Korpal—lekarz artysta." *Gazeta Myślenicka*, no. 17/2015 (7 May 2015).

Szarota, Tomasz. "Niemcy w oczach Polaków podczas II wojny światowej." *Dzieje Najnowsze* 10, no. 2 (1978): 143–175.

Terr, L. C. "Forbidden Games: Post-traumatic Child's Play." *Journal of the American Academy of Child Psychiatry* 20, no. 4 (1981): 741–760.

Węgrzyn, Marek. "Julagi: Zapomniane obozy pracy dla Żydów na terenie Krakowa (1942–1943)." *Przegląd Archiwalny Instytutu Pamięci Narodowej* 11 (2018): 105–120.

Wroński, Tadeusz. "Ziemia krakowska pod okupacją hitlerowską." *Nauka dla Wszystkich*, no. 204 (1973).

Zajączkowska-Drożdż, Agnieszka. "Deportacje do obozów zagłady w Bełżcu i Auschwitz-Birkenau ludności żydowskiej z getta krakowskiego w relacjach ofiar." *Studia nad Faszyzmem i Zbrodniami Hitlerowskimi* 32 (2010): 397–407.

ARCHIVAL NEWSPAPERS

Gazeta Żydowska
Goniec Krakowski

WEBSITES

The Code of Canon Law: Latin-English Edition. Washington, DC: Canon Law Society of America, 1983. http://www.vatican.va/archive/ENG1104/_P2X.HTM.

Muzeum Armii Krajowej im. Generała Emila Fieldorfa. http://www.muzeum-ak.pl.

Parafia św. Antoniego. "Historia." http://antonibronowice.org/index.php?p=5.

Warsaw Rising Museum, Oral History Archive. http://ahm.1944.pl.

The YIVO Encyclopedia of Jews in Eastern Europe. http://www.yivoencyclopedia.org.

ARCHIVES

Israel

Ghetto Fighters' House, Western Galilee
Yad Vashem, Jerusalem

Poland

Archiwum Akt Nowych, Warsaw (Archive of New Records)
Archiwum Narodowe w Krakowie, Kraków (National Archive in Kraków)
Embassy of the State of Israel in Warsaw
Instytut Pamięci Narodowej, Oddział w Krakowie (Institute of National Remembrance, Kraków Branch)
Kuria Metropolitalna, Kraków (Metropolitan Curia)
Muzeum Historyczne Miasta Krakowa, Oddział Fabryka Schindlera, Kraków (Historical Museum of the City of Kraków, Schindler Factory Branch)
Zakon Braci Kapucynów, Kraków (Order of Friars Minor Capuchin)

Zgromadzenie Braci Albertynów, Kraków (Albertine Brothers of the Religious Brothers of the Third Order Regular of St. Francis)

Zgromadzenie Księży Misjonarzy, Kraków (Congregation of the Mission of St. Vincent De Paul)

Zgromadzenie Księży Zmartwychwstania Pana Naszego Jezusa Chrystusa, Kraków (Congregation of the Resurrection of Our Lord Jesus Christ)

Zgromadzenie Sióstr Kanoniczek Ducha Świętego de Saxia (Duchaczek), Kraków (Congregation of the Sisters of the Holy Spirit)

Zgromadzenie Sióstr Miłosierdzia św. Wincentego de Paulo (Szarytek), Kraków (Daughters of Charity of Saint Vincent De Paul)

Zgromadzenie Sióstr Najświętszej Rodziny z Nazaretu (Nazaretanek), Kraków (Sisters of the Holy Family of Nazareth)

Zgromadzenie Sióstr Urszulanek Serca Jezusa Konającego (Urszulanek), Kraków (Congregation of the Ursulines of the Agonizing Heart of Jesus)

Żydowski Instytut Historyczny, Warsaw (Jewish Historical Institute)

United States

American Jewish Joint Distribution Committee, New York

Fortunoff Video Archive for Holocaust Testimonies, Yale University

Museum of Jewish Heritage—A Living Memorial to the Holocaust, New York

United States Holocaust Memorial Museum, Washington, DC

Visual History Archive, Shoah Foundation, University of Southern California

YIVO Institute for Jewish Research, New York

Index

About the Author

JOANNA SLIWA is Historian at the Conference on Jewish Material Claims Against Germany (Claims Conference).

Printed in the United States
by Baker & Taylor Publisher Services